The **Politically Incorrect Guide**™ to

THE PRESIDENTS

from WILSON to OBAMA

The **Politically Incorrect Guide**™ to

THE PRESIDENTS

from WILSON to OBAMA

Steven F. Hayward

Since 1947
REGNERY
PUBLISHING, INC.

An Eagle Publishing Company • Washington, DC

Library of Congress Cataloging-in-Publication Data

Hayward, Steven F.
  The politically incorrect guide to the presidents / by Steven F. Hayward.
     p. cm.
  ISBN 978-1-59698-776-0
  1. Presidents--United States--Biography. 2. United States--Politics and government--20th century. 3. United States--Politics and government--21st century. I. Title.
  E743.H36 2012
  973.09'9--dc23
  [B]

                        2011051029

Published in the United States by
Regnery Publishing, Inc.
One Massachusetts Avenue NW
Washington, DC 20001
www.Regnery.com

Manufactured in the United States of America

10 9 8 7 6 5 4 3 2 1

Books are available in quantity for promotional or premium use. Write to Director of Special Sales, Regnery Publishing, Inc., One Massachusetts Avenue NW, Washington, DC 20001, for information on discounts and terms, or call (202) 216-0600.

Distributed to the trade by
Perseus Distribution
387 Park Avenue South
New York, NY 10016

To Natalie and Pete,
for the obvious reason

CONTENTS

Chapter 1

NOT WHAT THE FOUNDERS HAD IN MIND

"Before he enter on the Execution of his Office he shall take the following Oath or Affirmation: 'I do solemnly swear (or affirm) that I will faithfully execute the Office of President of the United States, and will to the best of my Ability preserve, protect, and defend the Constitution of the United States.'"
—U.S. Constitution, Article II, Section 1, Paragraph 8

The Founding Fathers would be appalled by the modern presidency. Of all the things that would horrify them about the scope and reach of government today, the one that might alarm them most is the character of the modern office of president. The scale of the presidential office and the conduct of modern presidents are very different from what the Founders envisioned. In fact, the modern presidency is the exact *opposite* of what the Founders intended. The behavior of most modern presidents—personally ambitious politicians (or demagogues, in the Founders' eighteenth-century vocabulary) making populist appeals, offering lavish promises, often impossible to fulfill, of what they will do for the people—is precisely what the Founders wanted to avoid when they created the institution. The modern presidency has become one of the chief ingredients in the recipe for endlessly expanding the government beyond the limits the Founders laid out for it in the Constitution.

But this is not what you will learn from the leading textbooks and histories of the presidency, or from biographies of modern presidents. Most of the leading academic textbooks and the prominent media figures who cover presidents implicitly teach that the greatest modern presidents are those who have made the government *bigger* and more powerful, and expanded the reach of the presidency. Thus Woodrow Wilson and Franklin Roosevelt are typically ranked very high by pundits and historians alike, despite those presidents' obvious political and policy failures, while presidents with a limited-government point of view, like Warren Harding, Calvin Coolidge, and Ronald Reagan, are ranked poorly and treated with dismissive scorn by historians and journalists.

Today the president stands at the apex of the American political system, and the presidency is the first thing most citizens think about when they turn their attention to politics. The president can truly be said to be the center of gravity in American politics today. But this is a wholly modern phenomenon. Before the twentieth century, Congress was considered the more important branch of government.

To be sure, we want great men—in the serious, classical sense of the phrase—to serve in the office of the president. We want men of high character and ability to preside over the operation of our government. But the president is the focal point of the chief paradox of the republican form of self-government. We choose our temporary rulers from amongst the ranks of our fellow citizens. We want to be able to look up to our government officials—the president most of all—but we do not want them to look back down upon us. We want to put the president up on a pedestal, but still gaze upon him at eye-level. The most successful and popular presidents were able to man-

★ ★ ★ ★ ★ ★ ★ ★ ★ ★ ★ ★ ★ ★

A Step Down?

Thomas Reed, the legendary Republican Speaker of the House between 1889 and 1899, dismissed suggestions that he run for president because he considered it a lesser office than Speaker of the House.

age this paradox, commanding the American people's respect and responding to the real needs of the moment (pre-eminently defending the nation from foreign threats and securing law and order) while still connecting with citizens as their equals. It is less clear that we are well-served, or the nation improved, by presidents with ambitious "visions" of how American society should be transformed.

A Book You're Not Supposed to Read

The Cult of the Presidency: America's Dangerous Devotion to Executive Power by Gene Healy (The Cato Institute, 2008).

Today too many Americans believe the president is or ought to be some kind of miracle worker. For those who seek solutions to all life's problems in politics, the "president as hero" makes perfect sense. Liberals swooned over the personality of Barack Obama, who reminded them of John F. Kennedy because of his "charisma."

In the early 1960s it was common to see photos of John F. Kennedy on the walls of Catholic homes alongside images of the Pope. In the 2008 election a local NBC affiliate in Denver broadcast the comments of Barack Obama supporter Peggy Joseph, who said that if Obama was elected, "I won't have to worry about putting gas in my car, I won't have to worry about paying my mortgage…. If I help him, he's going to help me." As the Cato Institute's Gene Healy put it, "We still expect the 'commander in chief' to heal the sick, save us from hurricanes, and provide balm for our itchy souls." Healy points to the presidents' "acquired situational narcissism," enabled by the American people, who have become "presidential romantics."

The expectation that a godlike president can or should solve all of our problems reinforces the central impulse of liberalism, which is to politicize more and more of private life, ever expanding the power of government. The inflation of the presidency and the expansion of government that goes with it have inflated status, power, and egos all the way down the food chain, with senators, representatives, and senior executive branch appointees

★ ★ ★ ★ ★ ★ ★ ★ ★ ★ ★ ★ ★ ★ ★ ★

Going Just a Bit Too Far?

"The presidency is the incarnation of the American people, in a sacrament resembling that in which the wafer and the wine are seen to be the body and blood of Christ."

Herman Finer, eminent University of Chicago political scientist in the Kennedy Era

coming to believe and act as though they are a separate, privileged elite ruling class. But the reach of the modern presidency, like the reach of government itself, exceeds its grasp: there is a huge gap today between the people's expectations and presidents' capacity to deliver. Our soaring expectations set our presidents up for failure—especially those like Barack Obama, who overpromise in vague, grandiose terms like "hope and change."

The cause of limited government requires that we return to the Founders' way of understanding self-government, and this involves recapturing their understanding of a limited presidency. Conservatives rightly celebrate the inspirational presidency of Ronald Reagan, who made good use of the "bully pulpit" and the other expanded powers of the modern office of president. But we should pause and consider that limiting government may require lowering the status of the president.

The Presidency Has Grown—and the Citizens Have Shrunk

Modern presidential politics is slowly degrading the self-reliant character of the American citizenry. When presidents and other leading political figures advocate doing something "for the children," their rhetoric betrays the tendency of modern government to make children out of all its citizens. (Sometimes liberals are quite forthright about their plans to infantilize the citizenry. In 1997, Gene Healy points out, "Vice President Al Gore said the federal government should act 'like grandparents in the sense that grandparents perform a nurturing role.'") Perhaps the worst example is the infamous moment in the final debate of the 1992 presidential campaign when a social worker named Denton Walthall asked Bill Clinton, George H. W. Bush, and Ross Perot the ultimate "what-will-you-do-for-me" question:

> And I ask the three of you, how can we, as symbolically the children of the future president, expect the two of you, the three of you, to meet our needs, the needs in housing and in crime and you name it…. [C]ould you make a commitment to the citizens of the United States to meet our needs, and we have many…?

The right answer to such a ridiculous question would have been, "Grow up, dude. I'm not your father. Get a grip on yourself." Or perhaps, "The job of the president is, as the Constitution says, to faithfully execute the laws of the nation. It is not the job of the president to meet every individual's needs or wants. If you're looking for help with your 'needs,' see a fellow social worker." That's the kind of answer Theodore Roosevelt might have given, or maybe even Harry Truman. But that's not how the candidates answered, because a candidate who did give that kind of answer would have been blasted as "insensitive" by the liberal news media. Instead, Governor Bill Clinton, who famously said that he could "feel your pain," reminded us that as governor of Arkansas he'd always worked hard "on the real problems of real people." The patrician President Bush stammered that "caring" goes into the conduct of the presidency.

What Makes a Truly Great President?

Inflating his own role at the expense of the citizenry is the wrong direction for a president to take. So what makes a truly great president? Both

★ ★ ★ ★ ★ ★ ★ ★ ★ ★ ★ ★ ★ ★

History or Hypocrisy?

Perhaps the worst example of liberal hypocrisy on the presidency was Arthur Schlesinger Jr.'s book, *The Imperial Presidency*, which appeared during the high tide of the Watergate scandal in 1973. The prolific Schlesinger had previously been giddy in his celebration of the strong use of presidential power under Franklin Roosevelt and John F. Kennedy, but deplored presidential power when it was used for purposes he disliked, especially by Lyndon Johnson and Richard Nixon.

citizens and scholars will give you lists of attributes that sound compelling—at least on the surface.

Leading political scientists will point to specific leadership and character traits, including administrative ability, communication skills, decision-making, interpersonal intuition, and worldview or "vision" ("the vision thing," as President George H. W. Bush memorably put it).

Historians will say presidential greatness depends on leadership "style," and particularly on how a president reacts to crises.

The regular citizen, whose views are the most important since in the end it is citizens and not expert elites who select the president, will tell pollsters that the most important traits are a president's "experience," that he "shares my values" and "cares about people like me," his understanding of the "needs of the country," and his charisma.

But neither experts' insights nor citizens' sentiments are a reliable blueprint for presidential greatness. It has proven impossible to develop a list of traits that will predict success in office. If a collection of character traits and check-boxes of experience could predict or explain presidential performance, George H. W. Bush should have been one of the nation's greatest presidents. Yet Americans tossed him out of office after one term. Likewise, Harry Truman should have been a colossal flop when he was in office, and indeed many Americans thought him a miserable failure at the time. Yet Truman was re-elected in 1948, and although he left office in 1953 with very low public approval ratings, his reputation subsequently rose with the passage of time and a lengthening historical perspective.

There is a large amount of subjective judgment involved in academic evaluations of presidents: liberals will always rate liberal presidents more highly than conservative presidents, and since liberals dominate academia it is no surprise that liberal Democratic presidents are usually more celebrated in the leading literature than conservative Republicans. Liberals howled that George W. Bush was abusing his power in the war on terror, yet have fallen strangely silent under President Barack Obama as he has continued and in some cases expanded the Bush administration's understanding of executive power.

Measuring Presidents—the Forgotten Yardstick

But bias is not the only reason that a "politically incorrect" perspective on modern presidents is needed. Even less ideologically skewed accounts of the presidency in modern times—both by journalists and in the leading historical literature—are inadequate. They overlook the single most important factor that should be considered in evaluating presidents and would-be presidents: *Does the president take seriously his oath of office to "preserve, protect, and defend the Constitution of the United States"?*

For most modern presidents, concern for "preserving, protecting, and defending" the Constitution ends with the recitation of that clause of the Oath of Office. They may take an interest in *interpreting* the brief and general language of the Constitution on close calls (especially involving national security). But are they concerned with *defending* the Constitution from explicit and implicit attempts to undermine it, or to change its meaning into something opposite to or beyond what the Founders intended? Some modern presidents (especially Woodrow Wilson and Franklin Roosevelt) have not merely failed to defend the Constitution, but have actively participated in undermining its limits on government power. Some presidents openly, and others implicitly, held the well-conceived boundaries of the Constitution in contempt, while others have simply failed to understand them in the first place.

In the nineteenth century, presidential candidates routinely talked about the Constitution in their campaigns, and most presidential inaugural addresses discussed the Constitution at some length.

In fact, the inaugural addresses of presidents from George Washington through William McKinley were typically focused on our revolutionary and constitutional heritage, and thus were strong rhetorical reinforcements of the duty of the president and all other federal officials to "preserve, protect, and defend" the Constitution. In other words, most of our presidents used their inaugural addresses to remind us of the first principles of our nation, as Founders such as John Adams said they should do.

In most inaugural addresses through the nineteenth century, the Constitution was held up as an object of veneration—its only rival as an object of reverence being God Himself. As George Washington put it memorably in his first inaugural address in 1789:

> No people can be bound to acknowledge and adore the Invisible Hand which conducts the affairs of men more than those of the United States. Every step by which they have advanced to the character of an independent nation seems to have been distinguished by some token of providential agency; and in the important revolution just accomplished in the system of their united government the tranquil deliberations and voluntary consent of so many distinct communities from which the event has resulted

can not be compared with the means by which most governments have been established without some return of pious gratitude, along with an humble anticipation of the future blessings which the past seem to presage.

Today the Constitution seldom comes up in presidential campaigns, with two partial and problematic exceptions. Sometimes individual items from the Bill of Rights do come up for discussion, for example when Senator Bob Dole mentioned the Tenth Amendment, without really explaining it, in his 1996 presidential campaign against Bill Clinton. But the Bill of Rights, as important as it is, is only a part of the Constitution.

The second way the Constitution sometimes comes up in presidential campaigns is in connection with the presidential power to appoint judges to the Supreme Court and lower federal courts. Conservative or Republican candidates starting with Richard Nixon have tended to promise to appoint "strict constructionists" or "originalists" who will interpret the Constitution as the Founders intended (and then have often failed to appoint such jurists), while liberal candidates disguise the fact that they prefer judicial activists who will legislate the liberal agenda from the bench. President Obama, for example, said that he wanted Supreme Court justices with "empathy," which was a code word for sympathy for the liberal welfare-state agenda, and for using the judiciary to "right wrongs," even if the written law has to be twisted or ignored in the process.

But the large role the issue of judicial appointments plays in presidential politics— especially as a proportion of the total attention

★ ★ ★ ★ ★ ★ ★ ★ ★ ★ ★ ★ ★ ★ ★

More Than Thirty Years Ago Now

The last president to refer to the Constitution in any substantive way in an inaugural address was Ronald Reagan in 1981; he was also the last president to make a sustained argument to the American people about how the Constitution should be interpreted.

paid to the Constitution—is a measure of how far the modern presidency has strayed from the Founders' intentions. Both liberal and conservative candidates do themselves and the American people a disservice in reinforcing the idea of judicial supremacy—the belief that the Constitution is what the Supreme Court says it is, rather than belonging to all three co-equal branches of government and, ultimately, to the people.

The Constitution Ignored

The constitutionality of presidential acts is often controversial. But students and citizens will learn little about key constitutional moments in presidential history from most of the leading textbooks, let alone from the news media. Amazingly, you can read through piles of college textbooks and historical surveys of the presidency without encountering a single mention of the president's relationship to the Constitution, or of how a president's arguments and actions changed the way our Constitution is understood and operates. Consider James David Barber's leading textbook, *The Presidential Character*, which has gone through four editions since it was first published in 1972. It is a worthy book in many ways, full of insight about presidents and the character traits that helped or hindered them in office. Yet the index to *The Presidential Character* does not contain a single entry for "Constitution" or its variants (such as "constitutional" or "constitutionalism"). Likewise, Richard E. Neustadt's widely used and widely acclaimed book, *Presidential Power and Modern Presidents*, which has gone through three editions since its first publication in 1960, also contains no index entry for the Constitution. And the same thing is true of another acclaimed book on the modern presidency, Princeton professor Fred I. Greenstein's *The Presidential Difference: Leadership Style from FDR to Clinton*.

The list of books omitting the Constitution in their treatment of the presidency could go on. Mentions of the Constitution in the text of these and other leading books are perfunctory and lacking in substance, as though the Constitution were irrelevant to the conduct of the office of president. This is a striking anomaly, as most books about Congress do not avoid discussing the Constitution, yet somehow the much larger literature about the presidency routinely ignores our founding document.

There are a few notable exceptions to this blindness, such as Marc Landy and Sidney Milkis's book *Presidential Greatness*, or Forrest McDonald's *The American Presidency: An Intellectual History*. (McDonald is one of the great conservative historians of our time.) And surprisingly even Arthur Schlesinger's *The Imperial Presidency* argues for reining in "presidential supremacy ... *within the Consti-*

> ## A Book You're Not Supposed to Read
>
> *The American Presidency: An Intellectual History* by Forrest McDonald (University Press of Kansas, 1994).

tution" [his emphasis], specifically by reviving the separation of powers between the president and Congress. But Schlesinger's argument is disingenuous. It was liberal thinkers like Schlesinger who had argued consistently for breaking down the separation of powers in favor of a stronger presidency—when Democrats held the that office. Liberal concern about presidential power seems to manifest itself chiefly when Republicans are in the White House.

But isn't historians' disregard for the constitutional dimension of the presidency simply a matter of realism about the conditions of our time, now that the office of the president has "evolved" over the last century to meet the changing conditions of the modern world? After all, President William McKinley conducted the presidency with a White House staff of twenty-seven people (President Ulysses S. Grant had just six), whereas today there are several hundred people on the White House staff, not to mention the nearly 3,000 executive branch appointments that the president must make upon taking office.

But the appeal to "realism" is a subtle dodge, as it tacitly accepts the premise of modern liberalism: that it is in the nature of government to grow without restraint to meet new "needs," regardless of any of the limits on government power stated explicitly or implicitly in the Constitution. The idea of the "living Constitution" (which in practice means the written Constitution is dead) is thoroughly embedded in most treatments of the modern presidency. Thus most leading books about the presidency ratify, without having to justify, the transformation of the modern presidency into an engine for the growth of government power, and for the broader liberal view that all human problems should come under the purview of politics.

To understand how much the modern presidency changed during the course of the twentieth century, we need to go back to the Founding and reacquaint ourselves with the original design the Founders had for our chief executive office.

Chapter 2

THE PRESIDENCY THE FOUNDERS CREATED

"The executive Power shall be vested in a President of the United States of America....

he shall take care that the laws be faithfully executed...."

U.S. Constitution, Article II, Section 1, Paragraph 1 and Section 3

A stonishing as it may seem today, America's Founding Fathers doubted whether our new republic should have a chief executive officer at all. It was only with great difficulty and long debate that they settled on creating the office of the president. In fact, in the nation's first constitution, the Articles of Confederation, under which the nation was governed from 1781 to 1788, there was no chief executive. Under the Articles all matters, including national defense, foreign relations, and government spending (such as it was), were to be decided by a supermajority of nine votes in a Congress of all thirteen states. Each state had one vote. If Congress was out of session—as it was most of the time—an executive committee of nine states could convene to exercise the powers of the national government, but only by a unanimous vote of all.

As the new nation made its way through the first few years of peaceful independence after the final victory over the British in Yorktown in 1781, almost everyone came to agree that the national government was too feeble and needed to be reformed. The new nation nearly failed in the 1780s under the Articles of Confederation. The economy plunged into a depression, and state legislatures were illustrating exactly the kind of "tyranny of the majority" that the Founders feared even more than a strong executive. In fact, the Founders thought many of the runaway state legislatures were behaving as lawlessly and arbitrarily as King George III had done. Thomas Jefferson observed that "173 despots would surely be as oppressive as one." And Elbridge Gerry wrote, "The evils we experience arise from an excess of democracy." Forrest McDonald explains the situation in his *Constitutional History of the United States*:

> If Congress had inadequate power, the states had an excess—and sorely abused it. During the war the unbridled state legislatures recklessly suppressed the legal rights of hordes of people suspected, or accused, of being loyal to Britain; they passed bills of attainder, declaring long lists of people guilty of treason without trial; they confiscated private property wantonly. Nor did lawless government end with the coming of peace. The legislatures overturned private contracts, reneged on public debts, openly violated treaty obligations, enacted fraudulent systems of public finance, and censured courts when they dared interfere to protect private rights. On top of that, they levied taxes twenty to a hundred times as high as in the colonial period. On the whole, Americans were less secure in their lives, liberty, and property than they had been under royal authority.

It was for these reasons that the Philadelphia Convention of 1787 was convened. That famous convention—an "assembly of demigods" as it has often been called—had a number of serious problems to work through to remedy the weaknesses of the Articles of Confederation, but perhaps none was more difficult than the question of how to design the executive office. It was necessary to create a presidency as a check on runaway legislators, but it was equally important to make sure that the president himself did not become a tyrant. Keep in mind that the chief object of criticism in the Declaration of Independence was King George III. All the political history that the Founders had studied reinforced the lesson that tyranny was a constant threat to liberty, even in a well-constructed republic. Many among the Founders did not simply doubt whether a chief executive was necessary, but feared that it might be *dangerous* to have one.

The Founders' belief that the powers of the presidency must be limited is best understood in light of their debates about how the office should be designed: whether the president should be a single wholly independent executive or should be a plural council of several individuals, and whether he should be selected from and answerable to Congress directly or chosen by the people. The Philadelphia Convention decided that the office of the president needed to be independent of the legislative branch.

Alexander Hamilton thought the president should serve for life, but a president-for-life looked to the Founders too much like an elected king, and the idea was swiftly rejected. The Framers debated proposals for a single six-year term, but settled on four years. There was vigorous debate about whether the president should be eligible for re-election, or limited to a single term. Skeptics of executive power feared that a president would trade on personal popularity to be re-elected indefinitely, becoming essentially an elected monarch. (Here they anticipated Franklin

A Parliamentary System for the United States?

In the 1780s, some state governors were chosen by state legislatures and answerable to them in much the same fashion as European prime ministers are answerable to parliaments. But the governors who were creatures of state legislatures were considered weak figures, and most states abandoned this method of selecting their chief executives early on.

Roosevelt's presidency.) Hamilton's argument that eligibility for re-election would be an instrument of accountability and an inducement to better presidential performance carried the day.

The Electoral College and the Creation of "Deliberative Majorities"

The Electoral College has become an extremely unpopular feature of our Constitution in recent decades, especially after the 2000 election, when Democrat Al Gore won the largest number of popular votes (though still less than 50 percent), but George W. Bush won the presidency because he won more electoral votes. The modern liberal complains that the Electoral College method of choosing the president is *anti-democratic*. The Founders would have answered: *Precisely*.

A Book You're Not Supposed to Read

Enlightened Democracy: The Case for the Electoral College by Tara Ross (World Ahead, 2004).

The logic of the Electoral College needs to be understood within the broader logic of the Founders' main concern with avoiding the tyranny of the majority—the historic downfall of most democracies. While the president was conceived as a counterweight to the majoritarian tendencies of Congress, the Founders also worried that the president himself could be the focus of populist majoritarianism if he were a directly and popularly elected figure. The Founders believed that presidents who were concerned with popularity—as all modern presidents are—would be more prone to demagoguery. There was little debate at the Philadelphia Convention on this question: the Founders most emphatically did not want the president chosen by direct popular election.

The Electoral College system, in which each state gets one vote for each representative in the House and one vote for each of its senators, should be seen as one more of the many subtle checks to tyranny of the majority in the Constitution—like the separation of powers and the indirect election of senators. (Remember that at the time of the Founding and up until the early twentieth century, the Senate was chosen by state legislatures rather than by popular election. It is no accident that the move to direct election of U.S. senators coincided with the transformation of the presidency during the Progressive Era.)

Just as it was thought—correctly, for the most part—that state legislatures would choose eminent men for the Senate, the Founders believed that an electoral college would prove a "filtering" mechanism by which eminent men of sound disposition and broad appeal would be chosen for president.

Modern critics of the Electoral College fail to understand that the Founders wanted to create a certain type of democratic republic, one that did not run by simple majority rule, but rather one whose institutions would create a certain type of majority—a *deliberative* majority—a majority less prone to the unsound populist passions of the moment, and to self-interest. In simple language, the Founders wanted to generate majorities that think. This is one reason for the many constitutional limits on government power, the deliberate procedural and institutional roadblocks to hasty lawmaking, our independent judiciary, and American federalism.

The Electoral College is entirely consistent with the Founders' aim of creating what might be called, in contrast to a simple majority, a *constitutional* majority. The electoral college assists in generating a deliberative majority by compelling candidates to get votes distributed among *all* the states—large and small; north, south, east, and west; industrial and agricultural; urban and rural—and not just in big cities or a handful of populous states. A presidential candidate has to keep the diverse interests of different states and populations in mind to win a truly national majority. Candidates with only regional appeal, such as Strom Thurmond in 1948 or George Wallace in 1968, cannot succeed in winning the constitutional majority required by the Electoral College.

The controversial 2000 election actually shows the logic of the Electoral College playing out as the Founders intended. While Al Gore won about 500,000 more popular votes than George W. Bush, Bush won majorities in thirty states, while Gore only won majorities in twenty. In fact, the entire margin of Gore's popular majority came from just a single large state—California—meaning that he actually received fewer votes than Bush in the other forty-nine states. Bush's votes were more evenly distributed throughout the nation than Gore's—which is exactly the logic of a *constitutional* majority, as opposed to a mere popular majority. In other words, Bush was more widely acceptable to the nation than Gore was. The 2000 election showed the Electoral College system at its best, ensuring that the interests of small states could make a difference—something the delegates from small states worried about in 1787.

Al Gore lost the traditionally Democratic state of West Virginia in part because of his well-known hostility to the coal industry, one of the state's major economic sectors. Had Gore won West Virginia as Democratic presidential candidates typically have, he would have won the Electoral College, and the fracas in Florida would not have mattered. (Gore also lost his home state of Tennessee, in part because of his hostility to coal and also because of his ambivalence about gun control.)

The Magic of the Electoral College

Both Richard Nixon in 1968 and Bill Clinton in 1992 received only about 43 percent of the popular vote in a three-way election, but both had large majorities in the Electoral College—bolstering the legitimacy of election results, and therefore the stability of the country.

The Constitution did not specify how the individual states were to select their electors for the Electoral College, but most adopted some scheme of popular election, and the winner-take-all format that we know today. This method of choosing electors has the advantage of transforming a small majority or even a mere plurality in the popular vote into a large *constitutional* majority in the Electoral College vote.

Political parties, which developed rapidly in the early years of the American republic, came to perform some of the same "filtering" function as the Electoral College, especially in the long-time practice of party bosses meeting and compromising on what candidate a party should put forward for the presidency. Although the Electoral College has survived, the rise of primary elections and the decline of parties has moved our presidential selection closer to the kind of populist demagogic system the Founders feared.

The Founders on the Character of the Executive Office

Today we take for granted the cliché that the president of the United States is "the most powerful man in the world." But consider that for the Founders the term "president" had a much more modest and restrained meaning. "President" derives from "preside"—as in an officer who presides over a meeting the way a chairman sits at the head of a committee. The Latin root from which it derives, *praesidere*, means "to sit in front or at the head of." Consider George Washington's practice as the president of the Constitutional Convention in Philadelphia in 1787. He barely spoke on the substance of the issues, in part because he thought it would be improper to do so.

In contrast to Article I of the Constitution, which sets out the specific "enumerated powers" of Congress, Article II, establishing the presidency, is shorter and much less specific about the powers of the presidency. Many scholars have noted an ambiguity between the language of Article I, which speaks of the powers "herein granted" to Congress, and Article II, which speaks of "the executive power" without defining "executive power" in any detail. It is clear that the president has some specific responsibilities and unitary powers, such as conducting foreign relations and defending the nation as "commander in chief." And the president has the power to veto

★ ★

What's in a Name?

It is significant that the Founders chose the term "president" for the new nation's chief executive officer rather than the more familiar term "governor." In fact, the Philadelphia Convention considered calling the new chief executive "governor of the united People and States of America," but the term was rejected precisely because the Framers disliked the memory of strong colonial governors. "President" was little used as a political term prior to the Constitution's adoption of the title.

congressional legislation. But many of his powers are deliberately mixed or tempered—such as his executive branch and judicial appointments and treaty-making powers, all of which require the "advice and consent" of the Senate. And even the "commander in chief" power is mitigated by the fact that Congress, not the president, is given the power to declare war, as well as to determine the size and nature of our armed forces. The structure of the president's powers makes clear that the Founders intended the president to stand guard over a whole system that is designed to keep *him* in check at the same time.

George Washington's Republican Modesty

There is nothing in Article II that specifies how a president should behave in office, or even what his most important duties actually are. America was fortunate to have as its first president a man of extraordinary character who set a precedent for presidential conduct that most of his successors have followed. In fact, the Philadelphia Convention might not have finally approved the office of the president if it had not been known by everyone that the trusted George Washington would be its first occupant. Washington is by far the most important man ever to hold the office.

The reason Washington had the near-universal respect of leading Americans at the time had more to do with his authentic republican character than his generalship in the Revolutionary War. And a single moment in Washington's pre-presidential career tells why. In 1783, a group of army officers, angered by the lack of pay and disgusted with the feebleness of the national government under the Articles of Confederation, met in Newburgh, New York, to contemplate what amounted to a military coup. Forrest McDonald's narrative of the climactic meeting, which Washington decided to attend, cannot be improved upon:

> To the surprise of everyone, [Washington] attended the meeting in person, and by virtue of rank he presided over it. By the score, officers came in, tempers blazing, only to sit in embarrassed silence as Washington rose. He had written a short speech, and as he took it from his coat pocket he reached with his other hand and extracted a pair of eyeglasses, which only a few intimates knew he needed. "Gentlemen," he began, "you will permit me to put on my spectacles, for I have not only grown gray, but almost blind, in the service of my country.... This dread alternative, of either deserting our Country in the extremist hour of her distress, or turning our arms against it ... has something so shocking in it, that humanity revolts at the idea.... I spurn it," he added, as must every man "who regards that liberty, and reveres that justice for which we contend." The officers wept tears of shame, and the mutiny dissolved. As Thomas Jefferson said later, "The moderation and virtue of one man probably prevented this Revolution from being closed by a subversion of liberty it was intended to establish."

What a rare moment this is in the long history of politics. Washington could easily have led a military coup and installed himself as king or ruler of the new American nation. Seldom is it that a person of Washington's presence and force of character passes up the opportunity to take power for himself, let alone gives it up willingly and easily.

A Book You're Not Supposed to Read

Founding Father: Rediscovering George Washington by Richard Brookhiser (Free Press, 1997).

Shortly after the Newburgh meeting, the final peace treaty with Britain was signed, and Washington resigned as head of the Continental army, returning to his farm at Mt. Vernon and saying he would never again enter public life, like Cincinnatus returning to the plow. As McDonald puts it, "This was an awesome display of disinterested love of country."

Americans in 1787 knew they could count on the "moderation and virtue" of this one man enough to entrust him with the brand new and undefined office of the presidency. And Washington knew his decisions and actions would be crucial to whether the office—and the Constitution—would succeed for the ages. "Few who are not philosophical spectators," he wrote, "can realize the difficult and delicate part which a man in my situation has to act.... In our progress toward political happiness my station is new; and, if I may use the expression, I walk on untrodden ground. There is scarcely any part of my conduct which may not hereafter be drawn into precedent."

Right away Washington's republican modesty showed itself in setting important early precedents. One of the first was the seemingly simple matter of how the president should be formally addressed. Vice President John Adams thought the dignity of the office required that the president be treated with an august salutation; he wanted "His High Highness the President of the United States and protector of their Liberties." But this sounded to many people too much like a European-style "title of nobility" such as is expressly forbidden in the Constitution, and Washington preferred to be addressed simply as "the President of the United States."

Article II mentions that the president may "recommend to [Congress] such Measures he shall judge necessary and expedient," but Washington did not send a steady stream of legislative proposals to Congress, as is the common practice of modern presidents, instead leaving many important matters of policy up to Congress. Washington used the veto power only twice, believing, along with most early presidents, that he should block only laws he believed were unconstitutional, rather than any legislation he thought unwise. He declined to veto a tariff bill, for example, that did not contain features he desired, nor did he veto a congressional pay act that he disagreed with. He did cast one veto on national security grounds, of a bill that would have reduced the size of the frontier army, but his only other veto was of a bill apportioning congressional seats in a way that he thought violated a clause in Article I.

Perhaps the most important precedent Washington set was his decision to relinquish the office after two terms, even though he could have remained president as long as he wished to. All of his successors followed his example until Franklin Roosevelt, whose election to a fourth term led Congress to pass the Twenty-second Amendment to the Constitution limiting presidents to two terms.

Washington was completely unique. Unlike any other president, he filled the role of a head of state "above party politics or partisanship." Washington is the only president we've ever had who did not belong to a political party, and his famously quarrelsome Cabinet reflected both sides of the American political divide at that time. It was always inevitable that American politics—and therefore presidential contests—would divide into parties. But many of the precedents for presidential conduct in office that Washington set are still with us.

★ ★ ★ ★ ★ ★ ★ ★ ★ ★ ★ ★ ★ ★ ★

A Disturbing Thought

Is there any doubt that in the absence of the Twenty-second Amendment, Bill Clinton would have run for re-election as many times as he possibly could?

Many of the arguments we have today about presidential power, such as on executive privilege, the commitment of military forces to hostilities, and other national security matters, arose in Washington's presidency in almost exactly the same terms as today. The checks and balances in the Constitution are hard to work out rigidly or precisely, and the virtue and character of leaders are important—a fact we shall return to in some of the portraits of particular modern presidents in this book.

Our Early Presidents: Defenders of the Constitution

Partly inspired by Washington's example, and partly because of Americans' deep attachment to the principles behind the Constitution, presidents for our first century followed Washington's example in considering themselves responsible for measuring legislation and policy by the standard of the Constitution. During Washington's presidency there was a ferocious argument about whether the Constitution authorized the federal government to charter a national bank. Jefferson and James Madison thought a bank was unconstitutional, but Alexander Hamilton persuaded Washington that it was permitted by the Constitution.

Both sides in the bank dispute had strong arguments, and it is not self-evident which side was right. The point is, all the political leaders at that time thought it necessary to argue for or against any proposed government action on constitutional grounds—a practice that fell into desuetude in the twentieth century. (In the twenty-first, though, Obamacare's individual mandate to purchase health insurance has revived constitutional debate in a way probably never intended or desired by President Obama.)

Even if the "General Welfare" and "necessary and proper" clauses of Article I of the Constitution allow for a wide latitude of interpretation, resorting to the Constitution for legislative and executive authority had a salutary effect on our political deliberations, and limited the growth of government. The culture of budgetary "earmarks" that has become so pervasive in Congress today would have been unthinkable in the nineteenth century, when many presidents simply vetoed special interest spending bills that Congress passed. As James Madison had argued in Federalist No. 45, "The powers delegated by the proposed Constitution to the federal government are few and defined ... to be exercised principally on external objects, as war, peace, negotiation, and foreign commerce."

So when Congress in 1794 appropriated $15,000 for relief of French refugees who had fled from insurrection in San Domingo to the U.S., Madison, still in the House at that time, objected. "I cannot undertake to lay my finger on that article of the Constitution which granted a right to Congress of expending, on objects of benevolence, the money of their constituents. If once they broke the line laid down before them for the direction of their conduct, it was impossible to say to what lengths they might go." It was not surprising, then, that when he was president a few years later, Madison vetoed spending bills that he thought were unconstitutional, such as John C. Calhoun's "internal improvement" bill to have the federal government build interstate roads. Madison took a strict view of congressional power, arguing that there was no clause in the Constitution that gave Congress power over internal improvements:

> I am constrained by the insuperable difficulty I feel in reconciling the bill with the Constitution of the United States.... The legislative powers vested in Congress are specified and enumerated in the eighth section of the first article of the Constitution, and it does not appear that the power proposed to be exercised by the bill is among the enumerated powers, or that it falls by any just interpretation within the power to make laws necessary

and proper for carrying into execution those or other powers vested by the Constitution in the Government of the United States.

In the 1840s and 1850s it became popular in Congress to give away land instead of money to favored special interests. Several presidents resisted this congressional profligacy on constitutional grounds. In 1854, for example, Congress passed an act granting 10 million acres of public land to be used on behalf of the mentally ill. President Franklin Pierce vetoed the act, noting that while he sympathized with the cause of aiding the mentally ill,

I can not find any authority in the Constitution for making the Federal Government the great almoner of public charity throughout the United States. To do so would, in my judgment, be contrary to the letter and spirit of the Constitution and subversive of the whole theory upon which the Union of these States is founded. And if it were admissible to contemplate the exercise of this power for any object whatever, I can not avoid the belief that it would in the end be prejudicial rather than beneficial in the noble offices of charity to have the charge of them transferred from the States to the Federal Government.

In 1859, Congress passed a land grant act, which would have given 6 million acres of federal land to the states to establish agricultural colleges. President James Buchanan's long veto message discussed at length how the bill exceeded constitutional limits:

The Constitution is a grant to Congress of a few enumerated but most important powers, relating chiefly to war, peace, foreign and domestic commerce, negotiation, and other subjects which can be best or alone exercised beneficially by the common Government. All other powers are reserved to the States and to the people. For the efficient and harmonious working of both, it is necessary that their several spheres of action should be kept distinct from each other. This alone can prevent conflict and mutual injury. Should the time ever arrive when the State governments shall look to the Federal Treasury for the means of supporting themselves and maintaining their systems of education and internal policy, the character of both Governments will be greatly deteriorated. The representatives of the States and of the people, finding a more immediate interest in obtaining money to lighten the burdens of their constituents than for the promotion of the more distant objects intrusted to the Federal Government, will naturally incline to obtain means from the Federal Government for State purposes.... This would confer on Congress a vast and irresponsible authority.

President "No"

Grover Cleveland vetoed three hundred bills in all, many of them private pension bills that made appropriations of tax money to single individuals, usually Civil War veterans Congress wished to reward. Cleveland called all such bills "raids on the public treasury."

This was not the only instance in which Buchanan defended the Constitution from congressional attempts to slip its bonds and give away money or land to favored interests. In 1860, Congress passed a similar land grant bill, this time the first Homestead Act that proposed to give away or sell western lands for settlers. This Buchanan vetoed as well, referring to the logic and argument of his previous veto:

This state of the facts raises the question whether Congress, under the Constitution, has the power to give away the public lands either to States or individuals....

The advocates of this bill attempt to sustain their position upon the language of the second clause of the third section of the fourth article of the Constitution, which declares that "the Congress shall have power to dispose of and make all needful rules and regulations respecting the territory or other property belonging to the United States." They contend that by a fair interpretation of the words "dispose of" in this clause Congress possesses the power to make this gift of public lands to the States for purposes of education.

It would require clear and strong evidence to induce the belief that the framers of the Constitution, after having limited the powers of Congress to certain precise and specific objects, intended by employing the words "dispose of" to give that body unlimited power over the vast public domain. It would be a strange anomaly indeed to have created two funds—the one by taxation, confined to the execution of the enumerated powers delegated to Congress, and the other from the public lands.... This would be to confer upon Congress a vast and irresponsible authority utterly at war with the well-known jealousy of Federal power which prevailed at the formation of the Constitution.

The third kind of legislation that drew presidential opposition on constitutional ground was disaster relief. In 1887, Congress passed a bill granting federal funds for drought relief in Texas. President Grover Cleveland, a Democrat, vetoed the bill, writing,

I can find no warrant for such an appropriation in the Constitution, and I do not believe that the power and duty of the General Government ought to be extended to the relief of individual suffering which is in no manner properly related to the public service or benefit. A prevalent tendency to disregard the limited mission of this power and duty should, I think, be steadfastly resisted, to the end that the lesson should be constantly enforced that though the people support the Government, the Government should not support the people.

These examples, and the reasoning these presidents gave for their vetoes, are discussed here at length because they stand in stark contrast to the constitutional discourse, or lack of it, that we hear from our politicians today, aside from a few throwbacks like Ron Paul and some Tea Party-influenced members of Congress who are attempting to revive this older style of constitutional reasoning. The principled constitutional objections of the eighteenth- and nineteenth-century presidents (and many eminent members of Congress, too) have been swept aside, so that land grants, disaster relief, and appropriations for favored individuals and special interests are now commonplace, and few are the instances where modern presidents attempt to interpose themselves to defend the Founders' intended limits on central government power. The gradual desuetude of constitutionalism is why we seldom hear the Constitution discussed in presidential campaigns, or mentioned even in inaugural addresses any more.

The Birth of the Modern Presidency

Why did the president cease to be the defender of the Constitution against populist enthusiasms and congressional mischief? How did this tectonic shift in American politics happen, and when?

There are two main reasons for the development of the presidency as we know it today. The first is that the theorists of

A Book You're Not Supposed to Read

The Rhetorical Presidency by Jeffery K. Tulis (Princeton University Press, 1987).

the Progressive Era, especially Woodrow Wilson, sought deliberately to eliminate the Constitution's limits on government power, and especially to inflate the power and status of the president. But also, presidents simply started *talking too much*.

Today it is forgotten that presidents before the twentieth century spoke publicly very seldom, and then usually in the most general terms, such as greetings or "information about the state of the union." Our first twenty-five presidents gave an average of just twelve speeches a year. And even this low average is skewed upward by late-nineteenth-century presidents, who began giving more speeches around the country after the spread of the railroads made presidential travel more feasible. George Washington averaged three public speeches a year; John Adams only one; Thomas Jefferson five; and James Madison—zero. Even President Andrew Jackson, thought with good reason to have introduced a measure of populism into presidential politics, was reticent about making too many speeches. He averaged only one public speech a year as president.

Two of the nineteenth-century exceptions to this pattern of rhetorical modesty are exceptions that prove the rule. It is nearly forgotten today that one of the charges of impeachment brought against President Andrew Johnson in 1868 was that he simply *talked too much*, and in a manner that we would today call "divisive." In contrast to all of his predecessors, President Johnson toured the nation giving campaign-style speeches to drum up support for his policy proposals and to attack the Republican Congress. One of the articles of impeachment read, in part:

That said Andrew Johnson, President of the United States, unmindful of the high duties of his office and the dignity and

---

★ ★ ★ ★ ★ ★ ★ ★ ★ ★ ★ ★ ★ ★

The Strong, Silent Type

"Madison took the country into war, the British burned down his house, and he still didn't give a speech."

George Will

---

propriety thereof ... did ... make and deliver *with a loud voice* certain intemperate, inflammatory, and scandalous harangues, and did therein utter loud threats and bitter menaces as well against Congress as the laws of the United States.... Which said utterances, declarations, threats, and harangues, highly censurable in any, are *peculiarly indecent and unbecoming of the Chief Magistrate of the United States*, by means whereof ... Andrew Johnson has brought the high office of the President of the United States into contempt, ridicule, and disgrace, to the great scandal of all good citizens. [emphasis added]

Johnson's predecessor, Abraham Lincoln, is the other exception that proves the rule. But it should be noted that the subject of Lincoln's many speeches—the division of the nation, North from South—was a *constitutional* issue, and that most of his speeches (as well as those of his opponents) were centered on resolving constitutional problems.

Prior to the twentieth century, most presidents communicated with Congress and the public through written messages rather than speeches and seldom spoke on behalf of specific policy proposals. According to presidential scholar Jeffrey Tulis, author of the seminal study of the history of presidential rhetoric, only four presidents before Theodore Roosevelt attempted to defend or attack specific proposed legislation in speeches. At one appearance on tour in New York, President Benjamin Harrison begged off commenting on current issues before Congress, saying, "You ask for a speech. It is not very easy to know what one can talk about on such an occasion as this. Those topics which are most familiar to me, because I am brought in daily contact with them, namely public affairs, *are in some measure forbidden to me...*" [emphasis added].

The presidency of Theodore Roosevelt is the clear dividing line between what Tulis calls "the common law of presidential rhetoric" before the twentieth century and the modern practice. It is not coincidence that we remember Roosevelt for referring to the presidency as "the bully pulpit." Roosevelt's highly combative public campaign starting in 1905 on behalf of the Hepburn Act—a proposal to extend federal government regulation of railroad rates—set a new precedent for public presidential advocacy for a specific policy idea. While presidents had long recommended measures to Congress in their written reports, Roosevelt was the first to go beyond this, to go "over the heads" of Congress directly to the American people, in the manner of an election campaign, to whip up public pressure on Congress to enact a specific measure. Presidents of both parties ever since have followed this mode of conduct, which is very different from what the Founders had in mind. Far from being a brake on public opinion as the Founders intended, the modern presidency has thrown out its braking function and has pushed the political accelerator through the floor.

Most conventional analyses of the presidency ascribe the beginning of the modern expanded conception of presidential power to Franklin Roosevelt and the New Deal, but in fact Woodrow Wilson and his fellow Progressives were really responsible for the most radical break in the understanding of the nature of the office and the conduct appropriate to it. Wilson went far beyond Theodore Roosevelt not only in his practice but also his theory of the presidency. He completed the revolution that Roosevelt started.

Among other things, Wilson started the now-familiar spectacle of the in-person state of the union speech before a joint session of Congress. Article II of the Constitution says that the president "shall from time to time give to the Congress Information of the State of the Union ... he may, on extraordinary Occasions, convene both Houses, or either of them...." Notice that the Constitution does not specify that state of the union messages must be annual events, but only that they be made "from time to time," and that the president can convene Congress on "extraordinary" occasions, not every year in January, for a speech. Every president prior to Wilson had transmitted his state of the union message in the form of a long letter to Congress rather than appearing in person. Nearly every president since Wilson has followed his practice, and the state of the union speech has evolved into a media ritual akin to the Queen's speech that opens new Parliaments in Britain. The Queen's speech, though, is understood as purely ceremonial and without major political significance. The annual state of the union speeches are now major events on every president's calendar, regarded as premier occasions for presidents to gain some political momentum on behalf of their agenda. Rather than providing "information" on the state of the union, today's state of the union speeches are typically long laundry lists of proposals the president wishes to see enacted.

Four eminent conservative political scientists summarize what this profound change in presidential rhetoric means for us today:

> Popular or mass rhetoric, which Presidents once employed only rarely, now serves as one of their principal tools in attempting to govern the nation. Whatever doubts Americans may now entertain about the limits of presidential leadership, they do not consider it unfitting or inappropriate for presidents to attempt to "move" the public by programmatic speeches that exhort and set forth grand and ennobling views. It was not always so. Prior to this century, popular leadership through rhetoric was suspect.

Grading the Presidents

The modern presidency has become exactly what the Founders most feared and opposed. Skeptics of the new institution, such as the Anti-federalist author who wrote under the pen name of "Cato," predicted that the office would come to be characterized by "ambition with idleness—baseness with pride—aversion to truth—flattery—treason—perfidy—violation of engagements—contempt of civil duties—hope from the magistrate's weakness; but above all, the perpetual ridicule of virtue." (Sounds like a pretty good description of the Clinton presidency in particular.)

The Founders would have regarded Barack Obama's promises of "hope and change" with abhorrence. In fact, reining in public expectations of the president would be an important step in re-establishing the primacy of the Founders' view of America. It may be unrealistic to expect that any president in a mass media age will revive the nineteenth-century practice of rhetorical restraint, or go from taking an active role in advocating policy changes to leaving the leading role to Congress, as the Founders envisioned. Even conservatives judge Ronald Reagan a successful president because he was "the great communicator" who used the modern mass media effectively to achieve important policy changes and to revive the nation's flagging spirits in the early 1980s. But the inflation of the presidential office has undermined our ability to be a self-governing people.

★ ★ ★ ★ ★ ★ ★ ★ ★ ★ ★ ★ ★ ★ ★

More Prominent Presidents, Less Liberty?

The image of Liberty was used prominently on coins issued by the United States throughout the nineteenth century—on dollars, half dollars, quarters, dimes, and at different periods even on the nickel and the penny. Only in 1909, with the Lincoln penny, did a president first appear on our coinage. Today Liberty has been replaced by images of presidents (often after a transitional period involving an Indian Head, an Eagle, or some other prominent person) on all these denominations of coins.

There is one important yardstick from the Founding that ought still to be applied to every president: whether he defends the Constitution. This presupposes that a president understands and agrees with the founding document. Many modern presidents have seldom discussed the Constitution in any substantive way. Apart from their statements on the Constitution—and their record of abiding by its limits, or not—presidents' constitutionalism can also be judged by their judicial appointments, especially to the Supreme Court. Some presidents have approached this duty casually or—in the case of some Republican presidents—with extraordinary incompetence. This book will assign a letter grade to each president according to his understanding and defense of the Constitution, or lack thereof, and the character of his Supreme Court appointments—evaluating the modern presidency, and the men who have held the office, according to the constitutional perspective of the men who designed it in 1787.

Chapter 3

WOODROW WILSON, 1913–1921

"The President is at liberty, both in law and in conscience, to be as big a man as he can be."
—*Woodrow Wilson*

President Wilson's Constitutional Grade: F

Woodrow Wilson is usually counted among America's greatest or near-greatest presidents, but he should be regarded as one of America's worst.

Wilson's conventional reputation chiefly reflects the "opportunity" for "greatness" afforded to presidents who happen to preside in times of large events (especially wars), and the prevailing bias of historians who prefer presidents of "vision" who expand the size of the presidency and the scope of government. In the absence of World War I, Wilson would likely be remembered as a domestic reformer who brought us the federal income tax and the direct election of senators through the Sixteenth and Seventeenth Amendments (though both constitutional amendments had been proposed before Wilson took office), the Federal Reserve Bank, and the ill-conceived Federal Trade Commission—hardly a legacy many Americans admire. He might not have won re-election in 1916; as it was, Wilson barely won re-election on the slogan "he kept us out of war."

Even that accomplishment didn't last long. America entered World War I in 1917, and although Wilson did preside over a war effort that helped end the fighting on the European battlefield, he bequeathed to American political

Did you know?

★ Wilson was the last president to grow up in a household with slaves

★ Wilson was the first and only Ph.D. to serve as president, and was, until Barack Obama, our only president who had been a college professor

★ Wilson openly criticized the Constitution and disdained the American founding

thought a doctrine—"Wilsonian idealism," sometimes just called "Wilsoniansm"—that has inspired the interventionist wings of both political parties. But Wilson's reputation for big-hearted "idealism" is at odds with many of his actions in office, which can support the judgment that he comes closer to deserving the title of "dictator" than any other president. His political ideology continues to inform the so-called "Progressives" of today, though most contemporary "Progressives" do not even know it.

It is hard to count Wilson as a successful president, let alone a great one. His chief aim coming out of World War I, American participation in the League of Nations, utterly failed to win political support in the United States and was ultimately voted down by the U.S. Senate—largely through Wilson's own fault. He dealt with Congress in a contemptuous and high-handed manner and refused reasonable compromises that might have secured his object. A president who had treated Congress with more respect or had more political skill, like Ronald Reagan or Bill Clinton, would have been able to accommodate the nation's well-founded reservations about foreign entanglements. But instead of trying to persuade, Wilson attempted to bully the Senate into submitting to his will. He refused to budge when his closest advisers urged him to accommodate Senate sentiment in favor of modifying the League of Nations treaty, despite the fact that our European allies declared themselves willing to permit U.S. participation in the League with the reservations and conditions Republicans

> ★ ★ ★ ★ ★ ★ ★ ★ ★ ★ ★ ★ ★ ★
>
> ## Even an Ivy League Historian Notes Wilson's Nasty Personality
>
> "Wilson's private model for political behavior suffered first of all from his lack of joy, his protective diffidence that built a wall between him and other men…. He never knew the kind of fellowship that eased the burden of both Roosevelts' days; he never had their saving sense of humor…. Without a sense of playfulness in men, the President denied a place to playfulness in politics, insulated himself from the lessons taught by fun, choked off that flood of fondness Americans display for leaders who evoke it."
>
> Morton Blum of Yale University

were demanding. Wilson broke off one of his closest friendships with his top aide, Edward House, and forced the resignation of his unsympathetic secretary of state, Robert Lansing. John Morton Blum observed, "Even Wilson's intimates were shocked by his display of peevishness. After the episode [of Lansing's firing], as his secretary sorrowfully told him, he had very few friends left."

Felled by a serious stroke during a speaking tour in 1919, Wilson barely presided over the nation at all for a year and a half of his administration. If the Twenty-fifth Amendment, adopted in 1967 in the aftermath of John F. Kennedy's assassination to deal with vice presidential succession and presidential disability, had been in place in 1919, it would likely have been invoked to declare Wilson "unable to discharge the powers and duties of his office," and Vice President Thomas Marshall would have become president. Instead, Wilson's second wife, Edith Wilson, essentially functioned as the nation's un-elected president for an astonishing eighteen months. Today this would be intolerable, and probably grounds for impeachment.

> ★ ★ ★ ★ ★ ★ ★ ★ ★ ★ ★ ★ ★
>
> ## Wilson's Matrimonial Constitution
>
> Wilson is the only president, and maybe the only human being in history, who contemplated writing up a formal "constitution" for his first marriage, setting out the rights and duties, and separation of powers, between husband and wife: "I'll draw up a Constitution in true legal form, and then we can make by-laws at our leisure as they become necessary."
>
> Must've been a fun guy.

Wilson the Conservative?

Some historians make out Wilson to be a conservative of sorts, in part because of his Presbyterian faith and Christian rhetoric, but also because he was a vicious racist and segregationist who supported states' rights and opposed child labor laws. Wilson screened the infamous movie *Birth of a Nation*, glorifying the Ku Klux Klan, in the White House, and recommended

Woodrow Wilson: The First Supply-Side President?

Wilson's voluminous record offers something for everyone if you look long enough. For example, in his annual message to Congress in 1919, Wilson wrote something that today's liberals surely ignore when they look back to Wilson: "The Congress might well consider whether the higher rates of income and profits tax can in peacetimes be effectively productive of revenue, and whether they may not, on the contrary, be destructive of business activity and productive of waste and inefficiency. There is a point at which in peace times high rates of income and profits taxes destroy energy, remove the incentive to new enterprise, encourage extravagant expenditures and produce industrial stagnation with consequent unemployment and other attendant evils."

that it be widely viewed. He supported legislation Southern Democrats sponsored to make interracial marriage illegal in the District of Columbia, and he reintroduced segregation into many parts of the federal government, including the Post Office and the military. When blacks objected, Wilson said, "Segregation is not a humiliation but a benefit, and ought to be so regarded by you gentlemen." But Wilson's racial views were based on *liberal* ground—Darwinian evolution—and his attachment to states' rights did not arise from any constitutional scruples about federalism, but out of convenience: states' rights were a bulwark against national legislation that Republicans were sponsoring to break down Southern discrimination against blacks.

And more than any other single figure, Wilson is responsible for turning the Democratic Party into a big-government party bent on centralizing power in Washington, D.C., and hostile to a free market economy. In addition, he was the most interventionist president in history: besides taking the country into World War I, he also employed American troops in Mexico, the Dominican Republic, Haiti, Cuba, and Panama—though often with little to show for it.

Although Wilson often cloaked his views in conservative or traditional-sounding rhetoric, underneath he was an adherent of a distinctly untraditional, not to say un-American, political philosophy. Historians who are incompetent, lazy, or uninterested in political ideas have ignored Wilson's political philosophy and thus misunderstood and misrepresented Wilson to generations of American students and citizens. They do have the excuse that Wilson's thought often appears contradictory or paradoxical. Wilson is certainly confusing and hard to follow on many key points—mainly because he uses traditional American political ideas in an idiosyncratic way (often opposite to the way they were originally meant and still are understood by most Americans). He also appears to have changed his mind on some issues as time passed. Thus Wilson can be understood as America's first "modern" president, and even as America's first "post-modern" president. He is certainly the chosen model for the presidency of Barack Obama and for today's "Progressives."

The Revolutionary President

If not "great" in the older and more meaningful sense of the term, Wilson was among the most consequential presidents in our history, though not in a good way. He was the principal architect of the modern "heroic" presidency—even more so than his great rival Theodore Roosevelt. Wilson's ambition transcended Theodore Roosevelt's merely personal egotism, and ironically prepared the way for the second Roosevelt—Franklin. Wilson is more responsible than any other political figure for changing how many Americans came to think about the Constitution, in large part because he was the first American president to repudiate the American founding and to hold the Constitution in disdain. Wilson compared the American people's reverence for the Constitution to the old doctrine of the divine right of kings: "The divine right of kings never ran a more preposterous course than did this unquestioned prerogative of the Constitution to receive universal homage." Madison had written in the Federalist Papers that the people's "reverence" for the Constitution was one of the chief objects of the Philadelphia

Convention of 1787, because "without [reverence] the wisest and freest governments would not possess the requisite stability." But Wilson criticized the American people's "blind worship" of the Constitution, and doubted whether the nation could survive shackled by the limits imposed upon government power by the Founders. In 1876, on the occasion of the nation's centennial, Wilson wrote, "The American Republic will in my opinion never celebrate another Centennial. At least under the present Constitution and laws."

Wilson thought the political philosophy of the American founding, especially Thomas Jefferson's language about individual rights in the Declaration of Independence, derived from John Locke and other English sources, was obsolete and should be discarded. He believed the logic of the Constitution, the thought of its Framers including James Madison and Alexander Hamilton, was equally defective and should be replaced. While Wilson was originally enamored of the British constitutional tradition, and especially the thought of Edmund Burke and the great British constitutional historian Walter Bagehot, in time he turned to German philosophy. For the Anglo-American tradition of the Founders, Wilson wanted to substitute the state-worshipping ideas of the German philosopher Georg Wilhelm Friedrich Hegel—and the evolutionary doctrines of Charles Darwin.

A Book You're Not Supposed to Read

Woodrow Wilson and the Roots of Modern Liberalism by Ronald J. Pestritto (Rowman & Littlefield, 2005).

As the only academic ever to become president (he was a professor and then president of Princeton University before becoming governor of New Jersey in 1910), Wilson is the only president to have written a series of comprehensive books about American government. His complete writings comprise sixty-nine volumes, but his four principal books are *Congressional Government*, published in 1885; *The State*, in 1889; *Constitutional*

Government, in 1908; and *The New Freedom,* in 1913. These books are not always consistent, and, like Karl Marx's voluminous writings, they lend themselves to conflicting interpretations. But, while Wilson's views evolved over time, certain central themes emerge to explain his view of the presidency and his stubborn conduct in office.

Four key ideas underlie Wilson's subversion of America's Constitution. They are his philosophy of Progress; his novel understanding of individual liberty; his then-idiosyncratic view of the role of the president; and his views on the nature of modern bureaucratic government. All four have become cornerstones of modern American liberalism.

Wilsonian "Progress," on a Collision Course with the Constitution

Wilson's general philosophy of history colored his views of human nature, individual freedom, and the role of government. Wilson believed in Progress with a capital "P," that is, the idea that human history was unfolding in a specific direction. This was not a brand new concept, but the Progressive political philosophy of Wilson was very different from the traditional Christian understanding of the redemptive course of human history culminating in the next world, rather than this one. For Wilson and the Progressives, "Progress" replaced Divine Providence in the American story. Before Wilson, most presidents had made reference to Divine Providence in their inaugural addresses and other major speeches. In Wilson's view, government—or the State, with a capital "S"—would be the agent of Progress; indeed, for Progressives, the State not only takes the place of God in human affairs; it is godlike in its attributes.

Wilson took his cues on this subject from Georg W. F. Hegel, the German philosopher perhaps more responsible than any other for modern state-worship and moral relativism. (Hegel was the main inspiration for Karl Marx, as well as Wilson.) Hegel, who was often obscure and hard to understand, put this aspect of his teaching very plainly: "The State is the Divine Idea as it exists on Earth. We have in it, therefore, the object of History in a more definite shape than before...." The Holy Roman Emperor would hardly have made such a claim. After Hegel, modern liberalism can be said to have gone from overthrowing the Divine Right of Kings to embracing the Divine Right of the State. Wilson admitted that he "wore out a German dictionary while writing" *The State.* It is ironic that Wilson would end up taking the United States to war against Germany when he was doing his best to reshape the American political scene in the image of German philosophy of history and politics.

Darwinism was the other great influence on Wilson's mature thought, and it explains his racism (or at least it gave it scientific justification; Wilson was the last president to grow up in a house with slaves). Wilson believed that there were superior and inferior races. The superior races are those with the modern spirit: "Other races have developed so much more slowly, and accomplished so much less."

Wilson's combination of Hegelian ideas of "Progress" and Darwinian ideas of the mutability of human nature explain why he came to regard the Constitution with contempt, especially the principle of the separation of powers between the branches that deliberately limited government power and speed of action. In his first major book, *Congressional Government*, Wilson called the separation of powers a "grievous mistake" and "folly." He repeatedly criticized separation of powers, and the Constitution, for not conforming to Darwinian realities:

★ ★ ★ ★ ★ ★ ★ ★ ★ ★ ★ ★ ★ ★

Bet You Didn't Know

Woodrow Wilson was the father of "the living Constitution."

The government of the United States was constructed upon the Whig theory of political dynamics, which was a sort of unconscious copy of the Newtonian theory of the universe. In our own day, whenever we discuss the structure or development of anything, whether in nature or in society, we consciously or unconsciously follow Mr. Darwin.... The trouble with the [Newtonian] theory is that government is not a machine, but a living thing.... Living political constitutions must be Darwinian in structure and in practice.

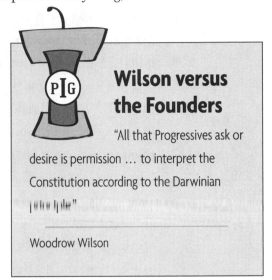

Wilson versus the Founders

"All that Progressives ask or desire is permission ... to interpret the Constitution according to the Darwinian principle."

Woodrow Wilson

Wilson went on to add: "No living thing can have its organs offset against each other as checks, and survive.... You cannot compound a successful government out of antagonisms."

Wilson went as far as to argue that if the Founders were somehow brought back to life in his time, they would readily see the defects of their handiwork—a thoroughly condescending view of great men who believed, with good reason, that they had built a permanent foundation for America's future. So complete was Wilson's rejection of the American Founding that he even argued that Thomas Jefferson's thought was "thoroughly ... un-American." He said the same thing about James Madison and Alexander Hamilton.

Wilson wanted radical changes to the Constitution, but he knew that, as a practical matter, it was difficult to amend. So with the exception of an early proposal for an amendment to allow members of Congress to serve in the president's Cabinet (a prohibition he called "the most obvious error" of the Constitution), Wilson never proposed rewriting the Constitution by amendments. Instead, he found in his Hegelian-Darwinian philosophy a perfect answer: simply reinterpret the Constitution as an organic, evolving document. Wilson openly called for "wresting the Constitution to strange and as yet unimagined uses." He explicitly scorned the original intent of the Founders and rejected the original meaning of the Constitution as the standard for how we should understand and interpret it: "As the life of the nation changes so must the interpretation of the document which contains it change, by a nice adjustment, determined, *not by the original intent of those who drew the paper*, but by the exigencies and the new aspects of life itself" [emphasis added]. Who would make this "nice adjustment"? The Supreme Court. Wilson legitimized the Supreme Court in its now familiar role as interpreter of "the living Constitution." Thanks to Wilson, the Supreme Court now acts as a roving constitutional convention, revising the Constitution for the convenience of government power: "The explicitly granted powers of the Constitution are what they always were; but the powers drawn from it by implication have grown and multiplied beyond all expectation, and each generation of statesmen *looks to the Supreme Court to supply the interpretation which will serve the needs of the day*" [emphasis added].

Wilson's Progressivism explains his contempt for the Constitution as written. The political philosophy of America's Founders was based the idea that human nature has permanent characteristics; they saw limited government as the only means of harmonizing the good and bad aspects of human nature. On the one hand, the Founders recognized the natural desire and capacity for liberty and self-government. On the other hand, they also recognized the equally natural attributes of human selfishness and self-interest. They knew that the accumulation of too much political power had all too often led to tyranny or oppressive government. Hence the Constitution's emphasis on limited and enumerated powers, and the separation of powers—all to prevent the government from threatening the liberty and well-being of the people.

But under the influence of Darwin, Wilson and other Progressives no longer believed in a fixed human nature. They thought that evolution and

"Progress" would deliver constant improvement in human affairs and even in human nature. So they saw no reason that political institutions should be bound any longer by the Founders' idea that flawed human nature prescribed limits to government power. Although Wilson and the Progressives did not share the same outlook as Marxist socialists and other revolutionary utopians, they did believe that human nature was susceptible to improvement—perhaps even infinite improvement and ultimately perfection—under the guidance of the modern State and enlightened leaders such as Wilson. Government power—the State—was no longer something to be feared; it should rather be expanded and celebrated.

Wilson's "Mature Freedom" versus the Founders' "Liberty"

Wilson utterly rejected the concept of liberty that was central to America's founding. For the Founders, preserving individual freedom required limiting the power of government. Wilson had the exact opposite view. He embraced a novel understanding of freedom that required government to have a larger scope of action to promote it. This is why Wilson made the title of his 1912 campaign book *The New Freedom*. He wrote of "mature freedom"—by which he meant the positive fulfillment of individuals rather than just the absence of outside restraint. Wilson even used some very contemporary-sounding language to describe his new understanding of freedom, such as "self-liberation" and "man's ability to make more of himself and to make more out of nature" (which really means escaping from nature). Here can be found the beginning of the distinction between "freedom from" and "freedom to." Wilson contrasted the two in *The New Freedom*, decades

Wilson versus the Founders

"Synthesis, not antagonism, is the whole art of power, the whole art of government. I cannot imagine power as a thing negative and not positive."

Woodrow Wilson

before the British philosopher Isaiah Berlin popularized the distinction: "Freedom today is something more than being left alone. The program of freedom must in these days be positive, not negative merely."

While this understanding of freedom may be opaque, it has a clear political implication: for individuals to realize their "mature" freedom, the government needs to be *more* powerful to help them find that positive fulfillment. In practice, "mature freedom" means that the government will exercise more power to regulate private activities, and command more private resources. It will exercise power in a way that necessarily brings it into conflict with the "inalienable rights" of the Declaration of Independence. So Wilson's Progressivism rejects the philosophy of natural rights that underlies Jefferson's Declaration.

Wilson wrote that "a great deal of nonsense has been talked about the inalienable rights of the individual," and said, "If you want to understand the real Declaration of Independence, do not repeat the preface," by which Wilson meant exactly that portion that speaks of man's "inalienable rights" descending from "the laws of nature and nature's God." The Founders believed that individual rights were universal rights, self-evident and sure to be acknowledged by "a candid world." Wilson argued, in contrast, *"There is no universal law, but for each nation a law of its own which bears evident marks of having been developed along with its national character, which mirrors the special life of the particular people whose political and social judgments it embodies"* [emphasis added]. This is moral relativism in a remarkably pure form.

Wilson versus the Founders

"Some citizens of this country have never got beyond the Declaration of Independence."

Woodrow Wilson

The object of Wilson and other Progressives was to justify their intervention into and control of more and more spheres of private life and private enterprise. Wilson's attack on Jefferson's ideas of liberty included this revealing formula: "You know that it was Jefferson who said that the best government is that which does as little governing as possible.... But that time is passed. America is not now and cannot in the future be a place for unrestricted individual enterprise."

Wilson turned the idea of individual freedom inside-out, and in the process introduced a vast confusion into American politics. Franklin Roosevelt's "freedom from want" and "freedom from fear" and the entitlement culture that was fostered by Lyndon Johnson would have been impossible without Woodrow Wilson. There is a straight line from Wilson's way of looking at freedom to today's common impulse to regard any need or demand as a fundamental "human right." Thus many Americans believe that they have the right to health care, to housing, or to a job—"rights" that require that the government force one citizen to give resources to another. The Founders' "liberty" was freedom from just the kind of government tyranny that would be necessary to enforce this novel kind of "right."

Wilson on the President: Visionary Leader, Voice of the People, and Crusher of the Opposition

The Founders intended the president to be the chief magistrate whose main function was to administer the laws and run the government, but Wilson thought the president should be an active visionary. In Wilson's view, the president should become the active Leader—with a capital "L"— in our political life, guiding the Progress of the people according to his farsighted ideas of where we should be going. The modern president, Wilson wrote, should be "a man who understands his own day and the needs of the country, and who has the personality and the initiative to enforce his views both upon the people and upon Congress." Wilson makes it crystal clear here that his view of the balance of power between legislative and executive branches is the exact reverse of that of the Founders, who thought Congress would play the leading role in expressing American popular opinion and shaping the direction of the nation. But it is important to recognize that here Wilson is going beyond merely reversing the places of the executive and legislative branches in our government. More than just *responding* to public opinion, Wilson wanted the president to *shape* it: "A president whom [the country] trusts cannot only lead it, but shape it to his own views."

These and other passages from Wilson's theoretical writings prefigured the arrogant stubbornness that marked his presidency and his poor relations with Congress. In "Leaders of Men," the essay that most fully laid out his theory of leadership, Wilson wrote, "Leadership does not always wear the harness of compromise.... Resistance is left to the minority, and such as will not be convinced are crushed." This sounds awfully close to what liberals today, such as Paul Krugman, decry as "eliminationist rhetoric." (It turns out that this passage in Wilson's essay is taken almost verbatim from Hegel's *Philosophy of History*, where Hegel celebrates the leader "so mighty in form" that he will "crush to pieces many an object in his path.") Throughout "Leaders of Men" and other writings, Wilson envisions the modern president as a leader who not only sees the future, but sees it as his duty to force the pace toward that future. The president should use his "persuasion and conviction—the control of other minds by a strange personal influence and power."

Some of Wilson's writings about political leadership ought to send chills down the spine of anyone who reflects on the bitter history of such "leaders" ("führer" is German for "leader") in the twentieth century: "Men are as clay

Wilson Articulates His Respect for Congress

"A little group of willful men reflecting no opinion but their own have rendered the great Government of the United States helpless and contemptible [by voting down his proposed legislation]."

in the hands of the consummate leader.... A [true leader] uses the masses like [tools]. He must inflame their passions with little heed for the facts. Men are as clay in the hands of the consummate leader."

Or this:

> A nation is led by a man who ... speaks, not the rumors of the street, but a new principle for a new age; a man in whose ears the voices of the nation do not sound like the accidental and discordant notes that come from the voice of a mob, but concurrent and concordant like the united voices of a chorus, whose many meanings, spoken by melodious tongues, unite in his understanding in a single meaning and reveal to him a single vision, so that he can speak what no man else knows, the common meaning of the common voice.

In his first inaugural address in 1913, Wilson made it clear that he intended to put his leadership theory into practice, declaring that with his election, "At last a vision has been vouchsafed us of our life as a whole.... We know our task is to be no mere task of politics, but a task which shall search us through and through, whether we be able to understand our time and the need of our people, *whether we be indeed their spokesmen and interpreters*, whether we have the pure heart to comprehend and the rectified will to choose our high course of action" [emphasis added].

Wilson, Enthusiast for Bureaucracy

Woodrow Wilson was an early proponent of what we now call "the modern administrative state." In Progressive ideology, political questions could be considered "solved," and most or all issues facing government were administrative in character, best consigned to expert elites not subject to direct political pressure—or accountability to the public. That administrative bureaucracies would be insulated from elections and unaccountable to the American public was a feature, rather than a bug, in Wilson's view.

Wilson was utterly unconcerned with the possibility that concentrated, centralized administrative power could be abused. He dismissed the possibility "of a domineering, illiberal officialdom" because he believed in the superior wisdom and virtue of the elites that would be selected for administrative government as he conceived it. One of the most chilling, menacing, and ultimately preposterous passages in all of Wilson's writings explains, "If I see a murderous fellow sharpening a knife cleverly, I can borrow his way of sharpening the knife without borrowing his probable intent to commit murder with it; and so, if I see a monarchist dyed in the wool managing a public bureau well, I can learn his business methods without changing one of my republican spots." It is only a short step from this moral blindness to admiring Mussolini because "he made the trains run on time."

Wilson and his Progressive heirs are unconcerned with the concentration of centralized power in Washington. They are willing to take on a paternal role, seeing themselves as superior to the American people. Wilson went so far as to say, "If I saw my way to it as a practical politician, I should be willing to go farther and superintend every man's use of his chance."

For these reasons columnist Jonah Goldberg calls Wilson the American inventor of "statolatry"—that is, idolatry of the State. Goldberg goes so far as to name Wilson America's first (and so far only) fascist dictator; if this label seems extreme, it is worth noting the discomfort Wilson causes even to moderate liberal historians who have been willing to assess Wilson's actions and policies honestly. In his short biography of Wilson, historian John

A Book You're Not Supposed to Read

Liberal Fascism: The Secret History of the American Left, from Mussolini to the Politics of Meaning by Jonah Goldberg (Doubleday, 2008).

Morton Blum casts a jaundiced eye on the World War I "campaign of propaganda without precedent in American history," conducted by Wilson's Committee on Public Information under George Creel. The Committee not only disseminated pro-war propaganda but imposed censorship on American media. At Wilson's urging, Congress passed a Sedition Act that allowed him to punish dissenting opinion about the war on the grounds that dissent amounted to direct "sabotage" of the war effort. Of the more than 1,500 arrests under this act, only ten were for actual sabotage. "Perhaps more than any other factor," Blum writes, "this shocking record stimulated among men of good will an incipient disenchantment with Wilson.... The President turned his back on civil liberties not because he loved them less but because he loved his vision of eventual peace much more.... Did the conduct of government override the privacy and decency democracy demanded? No matter—there was coming a great day." In other words, the end justifies the means.

Arrogance in Office

Wilson's political philosophy goes a long way toward explaining why he was the most arrogant president ever, and it also explains much about the ideas of so-called "Progressives" today, especially their view that they are on "the side of history." Progressives are necessarily hostile to any person or idea (such as the Tea Party today) that does not submit to their "enlightened" will. Unfortunately, Wilson's ideas have inspired modern presidents of both parties, but especially left-liberal presidents such as FDR and Obama.

In keeping with his view of the president as the larger-than-life "Leader" of the nation, superseding Congress as the motive force in American public life, Wilson introduced the practice of delivering the annual state of the union message in person to a joint session of Congress (rather than by letter)—a practice that has by now grown into a high-profile televised ritual in which presidents are expected to produce a laundry list of new things for government to do (and spend money on). Beyond this bit of political theater, Wilson held Congress in contempt, especially insofar as it behaved as the Founders intended, as a co-equal branch of government rather than supinely following Wilson's lead.

Wilson's Progress-with-capital-P "idealism" influenced his understanding of foreign policy and colored his view of the use of American military force. Wilson was the first president to describe himself as the "leader of the free world," a description that made sense during the Cold War, but which was highly presumptuous at the time of World War I. Wilson upended the view, taken by every prior president, that America goes to war to defend its self-interest. As President John Quincy Adams famously put it in 1821, America "goes not abroad in search of monsters to destroy. She is the well-wisher to the freedom and independence of all. She is the champion and vindicator only of her own." But when Wilson sent troops into Mexico with the aim of deposing the revolutionary government, he explained that he wanted to "teach the South American republics to elect good men!" to advance the world toward "those great heights where there shines unobstructed the light of the justice of God." And most famously Wilson described American participation in World War I in Europe as a crusade "to end all wars" and "to make the world safe for democracy." Neither purpose, of course, comprised any of the aims of the principal European belligerents, and the Allied victory achieved with American help not surprisingly failed to accomplish either goal. In fact, it has often been argued that the redrawing of the map of Europe in line with Wilson's "Fourteen Points" and the Treaty of Versailles made a Second World War all but inevitable.

Wilson's Progressive idealism and his contempt for Congress contributed to the greatest failure of his presidency, on the League of Nations, which was rejected by the Senate. Wilson's party went down to disaster in the 1920 election chiefly because of his arrogance. Despite the bitter ending to his presidency, Wilson changed the nature of the office and the course of the nation. He provided the model that many modern presidents, of both parties, have followed, especially the president who matches him mostly closely in philosophy and ill-temper—our current professor-president, Barack Obama.

For someone of Wilson's extremely radical views about the Constitution, his Supreme Court appointments were an odd mix. His first appointment was James C. McReynolds, a conservative Democrat who had served in Theodore Roosevelt's Justice Department before Wilson picked him for attorney general. McReynolds surprised no one when he settled in as one of the most conservative justices on the Court for his twenty-seven years on the bench. The *Oxford Companion to the Supreme Court* expresses the conventional liberal wisdom that McReynolds "was a staunch conservative … opposed to the growing social and economic regulatory power of government and believed that the Constitution fairly committed the nation to a policy of laissez faire capitalism." McReynolds was one of the justices who voted to strike down many of Franklin Roosevelt's early New Deal measures including the National Recovery Act and the Agricultural Adjustment Act, and he dissented in the 1937 decision that upheld the constitutionality of Social Security, agreeing with the nineteenth-century President Pierce that "I can not find any authority in the Constitution for making the Federal Government the great almoner of public charity throughout the United States." The high point of McReynolds' resistance to the tide of the New Deal came when the Court upheld the repudiation of gold contracts in a series of cases in

★ ★ ★ ★ ★ ★ ★ ★ ★ ★ ★ ★ ★ ★

Wilson "Ruined the 20th Century"

"The most important decision undertaken by anyone anywhere in the 20th century was where to locate the Princeton graduate school. Woodrow Wilson wanted it down on the main campus, about which he was probably right…. Dean West, his rival, wanted it up where it is. Wilson lost, and had one of his not uncharacteristic tantrums, quit Princeton, went into politics, and ruined the 20th century."

Columnist (and Princeton alumnus) George F. Will

1935, which amounted to a de facto default on sovereign obligations. McReynolds, in dissent, was so incensed that he proclaimed from the bench, "This is Nero at his worst. The Constitution is gone!"

McReynolds was probably the last consistently conservative Supreme Court justice a Democratic president ever nominated. Certainly Louis Brandeis, Wilson's other major appointment to the Court, was more in tune with his constitutional philosophy. Brandeis was a practitioner of liberal result-oriented jurisprudence, having been a pioneer of what was then called "sociological jurisprudence." He was known for what came to be called the "Brandeis brief," that is, arguments to the Court that emphasize social conditions rather than precedents and principles of law. In other words, Brandeis pulled on the heartstrings of judges, often with success. But this "success" comes at the cost of turning judges into legislators.

Wilson's third appointment to the Court, John H. Clarke, was a liberal in the Brandeis mode, but Clarke only served a short time and left no lasting legacy in legal thought or in the Court's history.

The McReynolds appointment notwithstanding, between Wilson's direct attack on the constitutional philosophy of the Framers and his appointment of Brandeis and Clarke, he deserves an F grade.

Chapter 4

WARREN G. HARDING, 1921–1923

"Standing in this presence, mindful of the solemnity of this occasion, feeling the emotions which no one may know until he senses the great weight of responsibility for himself, I must utter my belief in the divine inspiration of the founding fathers. Surely there must have been God's intent in the making of this new-world Republic."

—*President Harding, Inaugural Address, 1921*

President Harding's Constitutional Grade: B+

Warren Harding is routinely judged America's worst modern president, and maybe the worst in the nation's entire history. He is portrayed as negligent, corrupt or tolerant of corruption, and ill-equipped for the modern presidency. Journalist Nathan Miller, author of a book on the ten worst presidents, expresses the conventional wisdom: "Harding is a prime example of incompetence, sloth, and feeble good nature in the White House." Alice Roosevelt Longworth pronounced him "a slob." Harding has been widely ridiculed, from his own day into the twenty-first century, for having called for a return to "normalcy"—which amateur linguists wrongly believe is an incorrect word like George W. Bush's "strategery."

Yet at the time of Harding's death in 1923, he was beloved by the American public. In fact, the most recent revisionist look at Harding says that "he was kind, decent, handsome, a man of eminent reason. He also had a rare political attribute: courage." James David Robenhalt, the author of this account, goes on to point out an obvious contrast before posing the key question:

Did you know?

★ Harding chewed tobacco, and served whiskey in the White House during Prohibition at his twice-a-week poker games

★ We get our image of party bosses making secret decisions in a "smoke-filled room" from the brokered Republican convention that nominated Harding for president

★ He literally "saved the Constitution." The deteriorating document had been improperly stored at the State Department. Harding ordered it restored and placed in a protective glass case.

John Kennedy (the only other senator until President Obama to ascend directly from the Senate to the White House) was president for almost the same length of time as Warren Harding, but his record was decidedly mixed: Disasters such as the Bay of Pigs and involvement in Vietnam weigh against successes such as the handling of the Cuban missile crisis and the nuclear test ban treaty. Yet history could not have treated these two men more differently. Kennedy became an icon; Harding was deemed a failure.

What happened?

This question is not difficult to answer. The harsh summary judgment of Harding reflects the massive ideological and historical bias of the mid-twentieth century, when this image of Harding took root as a result of a relentless onslaught of partisan and sensational criticism. The course of Harding's reputation is an object lesson in the contingency of historical reflection. Contemporary research has cast a more favorable light on Harding, but his poor reputation lingers—a lesson in how images, positive or negative, are hard to shake once they are lodged in the public mind. A dispassionate review of Harding's record in office will support the conclusion that he was the kind of president the Founders would have approved.

The Most Underrated Modern President

Paul Johnson, one of the first modern historians to stick up for Harding, has written, "The deconstruction of the real Harding and his reconstruction as a crook, philanderer, and sleazy no-good was an exemplary exercise in false historiography." And according to Jeremy Rabkin of George Mason Law School, who compares him favorably to Andrew Johnson, Harry Truman, and Bill Clinton, "Harding must be considered the most successful postwar president in American history." Johnson and Rabkin are both conservatives who might be expected to swim against the prevailing liberal current. But Harding has started to get better treatment even from some liberals.

Harding's most recent biographer is John Dean, made infamous by Richard Nixon's Watergate scandal. Dean has moved sharply to the left in recent years, even suggesting that George W. Bush should be impeached. Yet his judgment on Harding is surprisingly fair and balanced. "Warren Harding is best known as America's worst president," Dean writes in the first sentence of his biography. But then he adds, "A compelling case can be made, however, that to reach such a judgment one must ignore much of the relevant information about Harding and his presidency.... [W]hen assembling my narrative, I found myself often addressing, and flagging, the distorted and false Harding history...." Elsewhere Dean has written, "There was much to be revealed that showed what a fine man, and able president, Harding had been, a far better president than history has ranked him." James Robenhalt, author of another recent book on our twenty-ninth president, agrees: "Harding was a breath of fresh air to a war-weary nation, a pillar of steadiness in a world staggering from economic and political instability."

Books You're Not Supposed to Read

The best-known and most complete biography of Harding is Francis Russell's *The Shadow of Blooming Grove: Warren G. Harding in His Times* (McGraw-Hill, 1968), and although it exonerates Harding from many of the most familiar criticisms, it amplifies others that are poorly founded.

A more surprising positive evaluation of Harding comes from an unlikely contemporary author, John Dean, who wrote a positive assessment of Harding for a book series conceived by liberals and intended to reinforce the liberal narrative about the evolution of the presidency: *Warren G. Harding* (The American Presidents Series) (Times Books, 2004).

Ronald Radosh, author of *The Rosenberg File*, is currently writing a revisionist biography of Harding that will surely become the definitive corrective to a century of misinformation and distortion.

An Unlikely Nomination, a Landslide Election

Harding won the election of 1920 with a then-record landslide vote of 60.2 percent of the popular vote, taking every state outside the solidly Democratic South. Critics then and since have portrayed Harding as ill-prepared for the presidency, though he had considerably more experience than our current president—or the president he succeeded, for that matter. By 1920, Harding had been in politics for twenty-one years, having begun as an Ohio state senator in 1899, served as Ohio's lieutenant governor from 1904 to 1905, and been a U.S. senator starting in 1915. During the ten-year gap in his political resume, Harding was a newspaper proprietor in Marion, Ohio (one of his paperboys was Norman Thomas, later the perennial Socialist Party presidential candidate), and took an active role in Republican Party affairs in the Buckeye state.

To be sure, the Republican Party's nomination of Harding in 1920 was an unlikely one; it came about only because of the political vacuum created by the untimely death of Theodore Roosevelt in 1919. Following Roosevelt's death, the party leadership fragmented, supporting several different candidates, with the front-runners being Army General Leonard Wood (TR's personal favorite) and Illinois Governor Frank Lowden. Harding was occasionally mentioned as a potential candidate, partly because he was from the electorally crucial state of Ohio; but he was regarded as strictly second-tier. Harding did poorly in the Midwestern states that held popular primaries, losing not only Indiana but even his own home state of Ohio. His prospects for the nomination seemed very poor heading into the GOP's national convention in Chicago in mid-June. Harding biographer Francis Russell quotes a reporter writing on the eve of the convention, "Nobody is talking Harding, not even considered as among the promising dark horses."

But the convention was badly deadlocked, with Wood and Lowden jockeying for the lead in the early ballots. When neither man could prove himself acceptable to a majority of delegates, it became clear to party leaders that the nominee would have to come from the ranks of the second-tier candidates. The subsequent process of brokering the nomination gave to American politics the famous image of the "smoke-filled room," as the party bosses, amidst thick clouds of cigar smoke, worked through the night to settle on a compromise candidate from among the crowded field. "However many times the political cards were shuffled and dealt and discarded," Russell writes, "somehow the Harding card always remained." Gradually opinion began to gel that Harding would be the strongest candidate the party could field, and the next day the tenth ballot of the convention awarded Harding the nomination. Harding, a little bit stunned himself, described his nomination in terms of a weak hand bluff in poker: "We drew to a pair of aces and filled."

Harding, the Anti-Wilson

Harding was in every respect the anti-Wilsonian president. One of the traits that recommends Harding in our hyper-politicized age of self-selecting and relentlessly self-aggrandizing politicians is his becoming modesty about his own political abilities and his bounded view of the political world. Paul Johnson observed of Harding that "he did not believe that politics were very important or that people should get excited about them or allow them to penetrate too far into their everyday lives." In marked contrast to Woodrow Wilson, Harding had a modest view of the presidency, much closer to the intentions of the Founders. He told his chief campaign strategist that "greatness in the presidential chair is largely an illusion of the people." In his inaugural address Harding sensibly warned, "Our most dangerous tendency is to expect too much of government."

To this healthy attitude Harding added a sense of his own limitations. In the summer of his first year in the White House, Harding wrote a friend: "Frankly, being President is rather an unattractive business unless one relishes the exercise of power. That is a thing which has never greatly appealed to me." On another occasion he told a golf partner, "I don't think

★ ★ ★ ★ ★ ★ ★ ★ ★ ★ ★ ★ ★ ★

Could a President Be Any More Different from Woodrow Wilson?

"Harding will not try to be an autocrat but will do his best to carry on the government in the old and accepted Constitutional ways."

Senator Henry Cabot Lodge

I'm big enough for the Presidency." But like Ronald Reagan, Harding understood that there was value in being underestimated by opponents and rivals. In a letter to a friend in 1921, Harding wrote, "I think perhaps it has been of some advantage to start into office so poorly appraised, because one does not need to accomplish very much to find himself somewhat marked up in value."

But Harding lacked neither confidence nor the ability to lead. He appointed a distinguished Cabinet that included a future president (Herbert Hoover), a future chief justice of the Supreme Court who had also been a presidential candidate (Charles Evans Hughes), and the only Treasury secretary to serve three consecutive presidents (Andrew Mellon). The *Atlantic Monthly* opined, "No presidential cabinet during the last half-century has been better balanced, or has included within its membership a wider range of political experience." (Other Cabinet appointments were less successful, about which more in a moment.) In addition, Harding included Vice President Calvin Coolidge in Cabinet meetings, which was unprecedented. The inclusion of Coolidge made for a smooth and easy transition following Harding's death in 1923. To promote candor in Cabinet meetings, Harding prohibited staff and sub-cabinet officers from attending, and purposely omitted having a secretary make notes. A lesser man would not have chosen so many leading figures for his inner circle, nor charged the Cabinet to give him their candid advice and counsel on all matters. Harding eventually settled into the presidency, remarking once to a friend that "being president is an easy job"—though this remark obscures the fact that Harding had consistent work habits, with distinct periods of the day for reviewing correspondence and documents and taking phone calls. He typically worked up to fifteen hours a day, yet somehow was later called a "lazy" president. White House usher Ike Hoover, who served under ten presidents, later said he could not recall a president who spent more time at his desk than Harding.

Harding reinstituted weekly meetings with reporters (Wilson had called off all personal meetings with the press), and journalists liked Harding, praising his openness and transparency. John Dean observes, "With the exception of the early years of FDR, no president has ever had the open and comfortable relationship with reporters that Harding did.... Reporters liked his frankness in confessing his limitations and his refreshing candor about presidential problems. The press was taken behind the scenes and shown the inner workings of the presidency to an extent never allowed before." After Woodrow Wilson's starchy and aloof demeanor, Harding brought a "folksy" style back to the White House, even opening the White House once a week to casual visitors, with whom the president would converse and shake hands.

On policy matters, Harding's legacy is substantial. Harding inherited an economic situation that should rightly be described as a depression. Between 1914 and 1920 the national debt had grown from $1 billion to $24 billion. Runaway wartime inflation had more than doubled industrial wages, and retail prices continued to skyrocket after the war. There were no official government inflation gauges as there are today, but the value of the dollar depreciated by at least 50 percent. As the United States was still on the gold standard in 1920, a deep recession was inevitable. By the end of 1920, as Harding was preparing to take office, GDP had contracted by one-quarter, wages had fallen 20 percent or more, and 100,000 businesses had gone bankrupt.

Several leading figures, including Herbert Hoover, Harding's choice to serve as his secretary of commerce, were urging aggressive government

Communism and Liberalism— Seeing the Parallels

"Abroad, particularly in Russia, there has grown up the idea that by some impossible magic a government can give out a bounty by the mere fact of having liberty and equality written over its door, and that citizenship need make no deposit in the bank of the common weal in order to write checks upon the bank. Here at home we have had too much encouragement given to the idea that a government is a something for nothing institution."

Harding in a 1920 campaign speech

programs to stimulate the economy. Harding had different ideas. His inaugural address is remarkable for its forthright recognition that the nation had to take its medicine if it was to recover. The war, he observed, had caught up the United States "in the delirium of expenditure, in expanded currency and credits, in unbalanced industry, in unspeakable waste, and disturbed relationships."

Harding didn't sugarcoat the rough adjustment that was necessary to get the country back on a sound economic footing, or invoke liberal bromides about "fairness" or "shared sacrifice." Instead he warned,

Perhaps we never shall know the old levels of wages again, because war invariably readjusts compensations, and the necessaries of life will show their inseparable relationship, but we must strive for normalcy to reach stability. All the penalties will not be light, nor evenly distributed. There is no way of making them so. There is no instant step from disorder to order. We must face a condition of grim reality, charge off our losses and start afresh. It is the oldest lesson of civilization. I would like government to do all it can to mitigate; then, in understanding, in mutuality of interest, in concern for the common good, our tasks will be solved. No altered system will work a miracle. Any wild experiment will only add to the confusion....

Yet Harding was no stand-pat, do-nothing president. Upon taking office he called Congress into special session to move quickly on his agenda of budget cuts, tax cuts, and tariff reform—this last issue being one of the most intractable political issues of the time. One of the first modern revisionist biographies of Harding, Robert K. Murray's 1969 *The Harding Era*, notes that Harding's 1921 special message to Congress "showed that he possessed an awareness of every major problem confronting the nation even though he did not have a solution for each one." Harding signed tariff reform legislation and instituted a special commission to review and adjust tariff rates. In retrospect Harding may be said to be the person who began the long, slow transition of the Republican Party from protectionism to free trade.

His most important reform, however, was his modernizing the government's budget process, without which no president could hope to control spending. Harding's most significant achievement in this area was his advocacy, in the teeth of considerable congressional resistance, of the Budget and Accounting Act of 1921, which established a Bureau of the Budget, and a unitary budget process, for the first time in American history. (The Bureau of the Budget is today the Office of Management and Budget.) If ever there was a reform that expert administrative-minded "Progressives" should have enacted, it was this. Prior to Harding the nation's budget was a chaotic mess, made worse by the run-up in government spending in World War I under Wilson. Harding knew that achieving a reduction in federal spending—one of his main objectives—required better managerial tools for the president. John Dean points out, "No presidential action by

What Would He Say about Our Deficits Today?

"There is not a menace in the world today like that of growing public indebtedness and mounting public expenditure."

Harding on runaway government spending

Harding was more discerning nor longer-lasting than his imposition of business practices on government."

Between 1920 and 1922, federal spending fell almost by half, from $6.3 billion in 1920 to $3.2 billion in 1922. Harding cut top income tax rates from 73 percent in 1920 to 46 percent by 1924 (Coolidge would lower them further). The $24 billion national debt started falling. Harding blocked or vetoed several attempts to enact politically popular bonus pensions for World War I veterans, which would have cost billions. Passing such benevolent measures, Harding said in casting a veto only a few weeks before the mid-term election of 1922, would "establish a precedent of distributing public funds whenever the proposal and numbers affected made it seem politically appealing to do so."

Harding's traditional approach to the country's economic problems prevented the depression of 1920–21 from becoming a Great Depression, and in fact set the stage for the roaring twenties. Harding's administration, Paul Johnson observed, "was the last time a major industrial power treated a recession by classic *laissez-faire* methods, allowing wages to fall to their natural level.... By July 1921 it was all over and the economy was booming again."

While Harding was popular with the public, he was no slave to public opinion and conformed to no ideological stereotype, as is perhaps best seen in his pardons of political dissenters Woodrow Wilson had jailed during World War I, especially the socialist firebrand Eugene Debs. Harding also proposed civil rights protection for blacks in a speech in Birmingham, Alabama, that John Dean has called "the most daring and controversial speech of Harding's political career": "I want to see the time come when black men will regard themselves as full participants in the benefits and duties of American citizens," Harding said in the speech. "We cannot go on, as we have gone on for more than half a century, with one great section of our population ... set off from real contribution to solving national issues, because of a division on race lines." Harding also urged Congress "to wipe out the stain of barbaric lynching from the banners of a free and orderly, representative democracy," but Southern Democrats made sure this suggestion died swiftly in Congress. Harding's support for advancing the interests of black Americans went beyond mere words. He appointed blacks to senior positions in the Departments of Labor and Interior, and over 100 blacks to lower-ranked administration posts—a high number for the time, especially after Wilson had purged blacks from government jobs and bestowed permanent civil service status on their white replacements a few years before—and also lobbied his entire Cabinet for more appointments of blacks. Harding also proposed federal child labor legislation and attempted, with less success, to mediate labor disputes as an honest and neutral broker between business and labor unions.

Solid Achievements in Foreign Affairs

In the U.S. Senate, where Harding served on the Foreign Relations Committee, he had been among the critics of Wilson's internationalism and the League of Nations. Harding was most skeptical about Wilson's crusade to spread democracy around the world, saying that it was "none of our business what type of government any nation on this earth may choose to have.... I have not thought it helpful to magnify the American purpose to force democracy upon the world." In his inaugural address, Harding sounded a distinct echo of George Washington's Farewell Address:

> The recorded progress of our Republic, materially and spiritually, in itself proves the wisdom of the inherited policy of noninvolvement in Old World affairs. Confident of our ability to work out our own destiny, and jealously guarding our right to do so, we seek no part in directing the destinies of the Old World. We do not mean to be entangled.

But Harding was no narrow or inward-looking isolationist. He went on to say,

> We are ready to associate ourselves with the nations of the world,
> great and small, for conference, for counsel; to seek the expressed
> views of world opinion; to recommend a way to approximate
> disarmament and relieve the crushing burdens of military and
> naval establishments. We elect to participate in suggesting plans
> for mediation, conciliation, and arbitration, and would gladly
> join in that expressed conscience of progress, which seeks to
> clarify and write the laws of international relationship, and
> establish a world court for the disposition of such justiciable
> questions as nations are agreed to submit thereto.

Noting that the American public had decisively rejected Wilson's League of Nations and the Versailles Treaty, Harding quickly signed a separate peace treaty with Germany and Austria—setting the stage for Harding's most significant foreign policy achievement, the Washington Naval Conference of 1921. This was the conference at which the U.S., Great Britain, Japan, France, and Italy agreed to limit the future growth of their navies—the first successful arms control agreement of modern times. Harding worked assiduously behind the scenes both to negotiate the treaty and to get a reluctant Senate to ratify it, succeeding where Wilson had failed. But Harding also tried to rescue what he considered the reasonable parts of Wilson's agenda by having the United States participate in the League of Nations' Permanent Court of International Justice (like today's World Court), but the League would not agree to Harding's proposed reservations.

In sum, as Jeremy Rabkin argues, "The Harding [foreign] policy was not one of isolation, but of independence." And Rabkin adds: "Those who fault Harding for boycotting the League of Nations imagine that the League would have been more successful if only the United States had added its prestige to it—forgetting that even with American participation, the United Nations has not been much help to the world or much of an asset to American policy."

Harding on the Constitution

Harding, who lacked a college degree, did not have a deeply developed constitutional philosophy like either Woodrow Wilson, Ph.D., or the self-taught Abraham Lincoln. As he prepared his second message to Congress at the end of 1921, Harding considered recommending a constitutional amendment calling for a single six-year term for presidents, an idea that has recurred periodically in American politics, usually at times when the president seems to be in distress. The idea appealed to Harding because he disliked the rough and tumble of partisan politics and dreaded the 1924 re-election campaign ahead of him. Harding withdrew the idea only after the strenuous objections of his wife, though he told an aide he planned to revive the proposal before the end of his first term.

★ ★ ★ ★ ★ ★ ★ ★ ★ ★ ★ ★ ★ ★

Father of the Famous Phrase

Harding is the person most responsible for popularizing the now commonplace phrase "Founding Fathers." He is thought to have used the phrase first in a speech in 1918.

While Harding was no deep theorist of the Constitution like his predecessor (and his successor, as we shall see), he revered the Constitution. In his inaugural address Harding fully embraced the presidential theme typical of nineteenth-century presidents' speeches but increasingly rarely touched on by twentieth-century presidents: "I must utter my belief in the divine inspiration of the founding fathers. Surely there must have been God's intent in the making of this new-world Republic."

Harding's good constitutional judgment can be seen in his four appointments to the Supreme Court: William Howard Taft (the former president), George Sutherland, Pierce Butler, and Edward T. Sanford. John Dean says, "By any historical criteria, Harding's selections to the U.S. Supreme Court were quite strong." While Taft is the best known of Harding's appointments, Sutherland was arguably the best, as he was a stalwart champion of the Founders' constitutional philosophy and defender of individual economic rights against arbitrary government regulation. Sutherland together with Butler were two of the four consistent votes (the "Four Horsemen," as their critics called them) against Franklin Roosevelt's most egregious New Deal measures a decade later. Sanford was the author of the Court's important majority opinion in *Gitlow v. New York* (1926), which articulated the doctrine that the Fourteenth Amendment "incorporated" the Bill of Rights into state law. Harding also disliked Oliver Wendell Holmes—a sign of good judgment—and expressed hopes that Holmes would retire from the Court. "The bench would be well rid of him," Harding said.

★★★★★★★★★★★★★★★

Good Looks Will Get You Pretty Far

The reason Harry Daugherty claimed he began boosting Harding for the Republican nomination? "He looked like a president."

Harding's Posthumous Reputation

Harding died in San Francisco in August 1923, at the age of fifty-eight, of an undiagnosed heart condition. Harding was extremely popular at the time of his death, and the nation mourned. His secretary of state, the former and future Supreme Court Justice Charles Evans Hughes, offered the best one-sentence summary of Harding's virtue: "He belonged to the aristocracy of the plain people of this country."

Why was Harding so popular? He was ruggedly handsome, and he spoke well, though his rhetoric harkened back to the classic nineteenth-century style rather than the conversational tone we are used to now. Harding's rhetoric, and especially his call for a "return to normalcy"—a supposed neologism—has long been an object of criticism. Critics read "normalcy" as a mistake for "normality." A comment by British historian G. N. Clark is typical of the condescension directed at Harding: "If 'normalcy' is ever to become an accepted word, it will presumably be because the late President Harding did not know any better." But, as Harding pointed out, he got the word from the dictionary: "normalcy" had appeared in three editions of the Merriam-Webster Unabridged Dictionary between 1864 and 1909.

Beyond the linguistic argument is a more serious political issue: what, normally, is wrong with either "normalcy" or "normality"? Clearly writers

> And if either Harding or his successor ever found themselves transfixed by "great visions" that set their souls afire, they had the good sense to keep quiet about it and rest until it passed. Perhaps there's a lesson here: where there is no vision, the people ... do just fine, actually.

So why did Harding's reputation suffer so grievously in the years and decades that followed his presidency? There was, to borrow the overused cliché, a perfect storm of misinformation and ancillary scandal that became attached to Harding's name and legacy—much of it inaccurate, completely untrue, or in dispute.

The Scandals

There were two major scandals associated with members of Harding's Cabinet. Secretary of the Interior Albert Fall was thought to have accepted bribes (in the infamous "Teapot Dome scandal"), and Attorney General Harry Daugherty, who had been Harding's chief political aide in Ohio, was believed to be complicit in bribery and in self-dealing transactions by friends. Fall had been a senator from New Mexico, and regarded so highly that he was the first Cabinet officer the Senate ever confirmed by acclamation—which belies the canard that Harding chose second-rate "cronies" for his administration.

The Justice Department investigated both Fall and Daugherty, and both men eventually faced criminal prosecution several years after Harding's death. While neither man behaved well in office, the full circumstances—especially in Fall's case—remain unclear. Fall was belatedly convicted of wrongdoing in 1931 and became the first former Cabinet official to be sent to prison. Daugherty was acquitted, but didn't help his public reputation by invoking the Fifth Amendment right against self-incrimination at his trial. And the suicides of several collateral figures add to the cloud of suspicion over the motives and actions of these two figures.

But there was never any evidence that Harding was complicit in their dubious decisions. To the contrary, Harding expressed dismay when the first rumors of wrongdoing reached his ears, saying to one friend, "My God, this is a hell of a job. I have no trouble with my enemies. I can take care of them, all right. But my damn friends.... They're the ones that keep me walking the floors nights." There is also a famous story of Harding slamming Charles Forbes, a corrupt head of the Veterans Administration, against a wall at the White House, grabbing Forbes by the throat "as a dog would a rat," and yelling, "You double-crossing bastard."

Harding might have escaped some of the reputational damage from the corruption of his appointees if not for a cascade of rumors—about his death, about his love life, about his ancestry. Rumors that Harding's death stemmed from a suspicious cause, even that his wife might have poisoned him, began to spread and eventually became a book. His political enemies in Ohio had long stoked rumors that one of Harding's ancestors was black, and this, too, became the centerpiece of an anti-Harding book. (Neither of these claims has any factual foundation.)

The picture of Harding's personal life is murkier. There is no doubt that the ruggedly handsome Harding was something of a "chick magnet" in his day. Frederick Lewis Allen—a doubtful witness of overblown reputation—helped fix Harding's reputation as "one of cheap sex episodes." It is well established that as a rising Ohio politician and during his Senate term he carried on an affair with Carrie Phillips, the wife of a merchant in Harding's home town of Marion, Ohio. Although the affair ended during Harding's Senate term, at which time her pro-German sympathies aroused suspicions in Washington of possible communications between Germany, Phillips blackmailed Harding into his presidency. The extensive correspondence between Harding and Phillips was hidden away for decades and subject to protracted litigation and intrigue, but finally was made public in 2009, confirming the depth of their relationship but dispelling some of the tawdry rumors about what their letters contained.

More dubious is Harding's alleged relationship with Nan Britton, a woman thirty-one years younger than he, who claimed in a sensational book four years after Harding's death that they had carried on a long-running affair that involved trysts in a White House closet and culminated in Harding fathering a child with Britton. Britton's tale is rich with detail, but there is reason to doubt that it is true. A number of modern researchers have reviewed the Britton story carefully and concluded that, in the words of John Dean, "There is much evidence that Britton's claims are not possible." Yet the image of Harding's escapades in the White House closet has persisted, acquiring a second life during the Clinton scandals in the 1990s.

Then, too, there was the supposed fact that Harding's widow, Florence, had destroyed all of Harding's papers shortly after his death—which seemed circumstantial evidence of his complicity in wrongdoing, and which also

Revisionist History Smiles on Harding

"Revisionist" histories typically downgrade the person being discussed. The opposite is starting to happen with Harding. Historian Ron Radosh, author of a forthcoming revisionist biography of Harding, writes: "Warren G. Harding has come to be thought of as one of the worst presidents America has ever had. Yet the truth about his presidency is quite the opposite. He achieved a good deal more in the two and a half years he served before his sudden death than many presidents accomplish in a full term.... He succeeded in healing a divided country by combining fiscal conservatism with some socially progressive attitudes. His efforts to end lynching and his belief in racial equality showed him to be more enlightened than many of his countrymen. They entitle him to be regarded as one of the first modern civil-rights presidents."

had the effect of dampening interest in Harding among professional historians. "Believing no records existed," John Dean writes, "writers felt free to write the Harding history as they wished, and they did." Most historians simply ignored Harding, or lumped him in with Coolidge and Hoover when they made sweeping denunciations of the Republican "mismanagement" of the 1920s that purportedly culminated in the Great Depression. By the time the Harding papers were opened up in the 1960s, after decades of languishing in the basement of the Harding home in Marion, Ohio, the Harding myth had taken firm hold in the American mind.

An unbiased assessment of Harding would conclude that, all in all, he was the kind of president the Founders had in mind—unassuming, not out to remake the nation or the world according to some fanciful "vision," working hard at administering the laws while showing Congress the proper deference when he recommended measures for their attention. The nation should be so lucky as to have another steady man such as Harding in the White House.

For the excellence of his Supreme Court nominations and the respect for the Constitution demonstrated by his conduct in office, Harding deserves a high grade as president. Countervailing factors—his lack of a deep constitutional philosophy, his proposal to amend the Constitution to create a six-year presidential term, the boost he gave Herbert Hoover's career—knock his overall grade down to a B+.

The newspaper Harding founded and ran, the *Marion Star*, carried on its masthead the motto: "Remember there are two sides to every question. Get them both. Be truthful. Get the facts. Be decent, be fair, be generous." It is long past time that American historical memory lives up to this admonition and judges the man who wrote it more fairly.

Chapter 5

CALVIN COOLIDGE, 1923–1929

"Great men are the ambassadors of Providence sent to reveal to their fellow men their unknown selves.... When the reverence of this nation for great men dies, the glory of the nation will die with it."

—*Calvin Coolidge*

"It is a great advantage to a President, and a major source of safety to the country, for him to know that he is not a great man. When a man begins to feel that he is the only one who can lead in this republic, he is guilty of treason to the spirit of our institutions."

—*Calvin Coolidge*

President Coolidge's Constitutional Grade: A+

Liberal historians have reviled and belittled Calvin Coolidge even more than Warren Harding and Herbert Hoover, chiefly because Coolidge is a more formidable figure who presents the most serious challenge to the pretentions of Progressivism. Coolidge was the anti-Wilson in every way—except that he was just as interested as Wilson in theoretical questions about the applicability of the Constitution to modern America. To Harding's reverence for our Founding documents and restrained conduct in the presidential office, Coolidge added a principled and intellectually sophisticated defense of constitutional government against the Progressives' attack on it. He was personally modest, he harbored no grand aspirations for transforming America in accordance with his own self-generated "vision," and he conducted himself in office more like the presidents of the nineteenth century. But Coolidge ably defended America's founding documents against the Progressive assault on the founding, as no nineteenth-century president had to do. And he has been punished for taking up arms against the Progressive revolution by historians who share its principles and cheer its victories.

Memorable Words from "Silent Cal"

"One with the law is a majority."

"I want the people of America to be able to work less for the government and more for themselves."

"Ultimately property rights and personal rights are the same thing."

"Don't expect to build up the weak by pulling down the strong."

"Perhaps one of the most important accomplishments of my administration has been minding my own business."

"Prosperity is only an instrument to be used, not a deity to be worshipped."

"To live under the American Constitution is the greatest political privilege that was ever accorded to the human race."

Historian Thomas B. Silver summarizes the conventional wisdom: "Coolidge has been subjected to more ridicule perhaps than any other president in American history. His policies are regarded by most historians as beneath contempt." Liberals dismiss Coolidge as "Silent Cal," an appellation meant to suggest that he said little and achieved no deeds or thoughts worthy of recollection. Allan Nevins and Henry Steele Commager criticize Coolidge as "thrifty with words and ideas … a thoroughly limited politician, dour and unimaginative"— as though having a president who declined to speak at us on an almost daily basis about his grand "vision" for transforming the nation was a bad thing.

In fact Coolidge said a lot, and displayed a dry, terse wit. When someone once walked up to him and said, "I didn't vote for you," Coolidge replied: "Someone did." But much of what he said drew deeply on his reverence for and attachment to the principles of the American Founding—which led him to reject the premises of the Progressive Era. Rather than take up the challenge Coolidge presents, liberal historians choose to distort or ignore his thoughts and actions. A close and unbiased look at Coolidge will reveal him to have been one of the most thoughtful and substantive presidents of any century.

A close look at the second most common charge made against Coolidge—after the "Silent Cal" epithet—reveals the bad faith and distortions of liberal historians and journalists. Coolidge is said to have been a simple-minded, pro-business president; the supposed evidence for this canard has become his most famous statement: "The business of America is business." Mark Shields calls the quotation "Cal's most-repeated epigram." Long-time *Washington Post* reporter Haynes Johnson chimes in, "It was Coolidge who gave Americans such memorable examples of presidential wisdom as: 'The business of America is business.'" A thousand quotation books have passed along this familiar chestnut, and two generations of history students have been taught it. John Hicks's *Republican Ascendancy* reads, 'The business of America is business,' [Coolidge] later proclaimed; and the business of government, he might have added, was to help business in every possible way."

There's only one problem. This is a misquotation.

Not only is it a misquotation, but it ignores the context of Coolidge's actual remark, a context that shows Coolidge to have been much more thoughtful than his critics. This is what Coolidge really said:

> After all, the *chief* business of the American people is business. They are profoundly concerned with producing, buying, selling, investing and prospering in the world. I am strongly of the opinion that the great majority of our people will always find these are moving impulses of our life.... Wealth is the product of industry, ambition, character and untiring effort. In all experience, the accumulation of wealth means the multiplication of schools, the increase of knowledge, and dissemination of intelligence, the

encouragement of science, the broadening of outlook, the expansion of liberties, the widening of culture. *Of course, the accumulation of wealth cannot be justified as the chief end of existence.* But we are compelled to recognize it as a means to well-nigh every desirable achievement. *So long as wealth is made the means and not the end, we need not greatly fear it.* [emphasis added]

Saying that the *chief* business of the American people is business is simply acknowledging the uncontroversial fact that America is a commercial republic. Coolidge, far from being a pro-business simpleton, was warning against exactly the worship of commerce and wealth that he is accused of recommending. Haynes Johnson's judgment that Coolidge was "the patron saint of business" is as incorrect as it is crude.

Coolidge subordinated wealth and commerce to the political principles of liberal democracy consistently throughout his life. In 1925, Coolidge wrote,

> ★ ★ ★ ★ ★ ★ ★ ★ ★ ★ ★ ★ ★ ★
>
> ## Coolidge Wasn't All Business
>
> In the very same speech in which Coolidge said the chief business of the American people was business, he also claimed, "The chief ideal of the American people is idealism."

Great captains of industry who have aroused the wonder of the world by their financial success would not have been captains at all had it not been for the generations of liberal culture in the past and the existence all about them of a society permeated, inspired, and led by the liberal culture of the present. If it were possible to strike out that factor from present existence, he would find all the value of his great possessions diminish to the vanishing point, and he himself would be but a barbarian among barbarians.

Clearly there is more to this man than meets the liberal eye.

A Classical American Education

Coincidence though it may be, the twentieth-century president who understood and loved the Constitution best was the only American president born on the Fourth of July. Coolidge acquired his insight into, and reverence for, the principles of the American founding the old-fashioned way—he had the benefit of a classical education, the kind it would be nearly impossible to acquire in an elite American university today. There are few better arguments for the connection between a sound moral education and magnanimous statesmanship than Coolidge's charming memoir, *The Autobiography of Calvin Coolidge*, written shortly after he left the presidency in 1929. At 247 pages, this short work is utterly unlike nearly all other memoirs of former presidents; it is not the least concerned with providing either a narrative account of his tenure or justification for his acts in office. In fact, the book stops recounting Coolidge's political career at 1924, with his election to his first full term as president. Like Winston Churchill's reflections on his self-education in *My Early Life*, Coolidge's autobiography is an eloquent affirmation of the crucial value of a traditional and moral education, and it is well worth reading today. Coolidge relates that he first encountered the Constitution in school at the age of thirteen, and that "the subject interested me exceedingly. The study of it which I then began has never ceased, and the more I study it the more I have come to admire it, realizing that no other document devised by the hand of man ever brought so much progress and happiness to humanity. The good it has wrought can never be measured."

Coolidge studied Greek and Latin classics in grade school and read the speeches of Cicero and Demosthenes, the poetry of Homer, and works by giants of American literature. He also excelled at mathematics, proceeding through calculus. He was an extremely hard worker, noting, "I joined the French class in mid year and made up the work by starting my study at about three o'clock in the morning."

At Amherst College Coolidge especially enjoyed his studies in history. In the hands of Anson Morse, his favorite professor, "Washington was treated with the greatest reverence, and a high estimate was placed on the statesmanlike qualities and financial capacity of Hamilton, but Jefferson was not neglected.... The whole course was a thesis on good citizenship and good government. Those who took it came to a clearer comprehension not only of their rights and liberties but of their duties and responsibilities." His coursework in philosophy "revealed that man is endowed with reason, that the human mind has the power to weigh evidence, to distinguish between right and wrong and to know the truth." Armed with this classical and reverential education, Coolidge won the Sons of the American Revolution's national contest for the best essay by a college senior. Coolidge's topic was "The Principles Fought for in the American Revolution."

His education enabled Coolidge to recognize how "Progressivism" was undermining the constitutional foundations of American government—and to dig down to the root of the error, in the Progressive's denial of the natural rights philosophy in the Declaration of Independence. Liberals reacted with outrage when Ronald Reagan replaced Thomas Jefferson's portrait in the White House cabinet room with a portrait of Coolidge. Columnist (and former Democratic speechwriter) Mark Shields was incredulous: "Don't try and tell me that Calvin Coolidge could ever substitute for Thomas Jefferson," Shields wrote; "That's almost a national sacrilege." The irony is that Coolidge was the most fervent presidential defender of Jefferson's Declaration of Independence in the twentieth century—indeed, the most fervent defender of the Declaration since Lincoln.

A Book You're Not Supposed to Read

The Autobiography of Calvin Coolidge by Calvin Coolidge.

As the example of Woodrow Wilson shows, it is liberal presidents who would have removed Jefferson's portrait from the White House, if their decorating choices had followed their political philosophy. By 1922, liberals were starting to agree with the prominent historian Carl Becker, whose book on the Declaration of Independence asserted, "To ask whether the natural rights philosophy of the Declaration of Independence is true or false is essentially a meaningless question." Coolidge took Jefferson's side and argued otherwise, against the Progressive intellectuals who were the guiding lights, then and now, of the Democratic Party. "About the Declaration," Coolidge said in a speech in Independence Hall in Philadelphia in 1926,

> there is a finality that is exceedingly restful. It is often asserted that the world has made a great deal of progress since 1776, that we have had new thoughts and new experiences which have given us a great advance over the people of that day, and that we may therefore very well discard their conclusions for something more modern. But that reasoning cannot be applied to this great charter. If all men are created equal, that is final. If they are endowed with inalienable rights, that is final. If governments derive their just powers from the consent of the governed, that is final. No advance, no progress can be made beyond these propositions. If anyone wishes to deny their truth or their soundness, the only direction in which he can proceed historically is not forward, but backward toward the time when there was no equality, no rights of the individual, no rule of the people. Those who wish to proceed in that direction can not lay claim to progress. They are reactionary. Their ideas are not more modern, but more ancient, than those of the Revolutionary fathers.

Even a superficial reader of this passage will see that Coolidge is explicitly rejecting the premises of his Progressive predecessors. This is the real reason for the liberal contempt for Coolidge.

Coolidge also understood how Progressive ideology and the administrative state, with its ever-growing independent bureaucracy, threatened to undermine both the rule of law and the character of the American citizenry. In a wide-ranging 1922 speech to the American Bar Association on "The Limitations of the Law," Coolidge took dead aim at Progressivism, noting that a government that tries to do too much will govern badly:

> So long as the National Government confined itself to providing those fundamentals of liberty, order, and justice for which it was primarily established, its course was reasonably clear and plain. No large amount of revenue was required. No great swarms of public employees were necessary. There was little clash of special interests or different sections, and what there was of this nature consisted not of petty details but of broad principles. There was time for the consideration of great questions of policy. There was an opportunity for mature deliberation. What the government undertook to do it could perform with a fair degree of accuracy and precision.

A Book You're Not Supposed to Read

Coolidge and the Historians by Thomas B. Silver (Carolina Academic Press, 1984).

But now, Coolidge observed, the federal government was taking on more and more responsibilities, acquiring more and more power, and becoming less and less limited. This, Coolidge made clear, represented not merely a small change in the scale and focus of government, but a fundamental transformation in the nature and character of government. He viewed this development with foreboding, both for the nation and for the presidency. In one passage he almost anticipates the mass appeal of Barack Obama:

> This is not the government which was put into form by Washington and Hamilton and popularized by Jefferson.... Behind very many of these enlarging activities lies the untenable theory that there is some short cut to perfection. It is conceived that there can be a horizontal elevation of the standards of the nation, immediate and perceptible, by the simple device of new laws. This has never been the case in human experience....
>
> Under the attempt to perform the impossible there sets in a general disintegration. When legislation fails, those who look upon it as a sovereign remedy simply cry out for more legislation. *A sound and wise statesmanship which recognizes and attempts to abide by its limitations will undoubtedly find itself displaced by that type of public official who promises much, talks much, legislates much, expends much, but accomplishes little.* [emphasis added]

No wonder liberals acquired an abiding hatred of Coolidge and embarked on a project to denigrate him.

Rising Political Star

Following a brief apprenticeship as a lawyer after graduating from college, Coolidge entered politics. It is often said that every person elected to the town council dreams of some day becoming president, but Coolidge is the only president who in fact began his path to the presidency on that very lowest rung of the political ladder, winning election to the city council of Northampton, Massachusetts, in 1898. Coolidge's political career proceeded rapidly through the state Senate, to lieutenant governor, to governor in 1918. In contrast to his later reputation among liberals as a rigid conservative reactionary, Coolidge was known throughout his time in Massachusetts politics as a moderate "progressive," supporting women's suffrage, more generous workers' compensation benefits, maximum hours labor laws for women and children, veterans' bonuses, and the direct election of U.S. senators. About pro-labor legislation, Coolidge said, "We must humanize industry, or the system will break down."

Coolidge won national fame—and the subsequent disdain of liberals—for his handling of the Boston police strike in 1919. In what looks like a foreshadowing of current controversies over public employee unions, Boston police proposed to form a union with the encouragement of the American Federation of Labor (AFL). The city's police commissioner, Edwin Curtis, threatened to suspend or fire the union organizers in the police force. Matters spun out of control when three-quarters of the police force walked out in a wildcat strike. The city, left unpatrolled, quickly saw a wave of rioting and looting. Up to this point Governor Coolidge had watched events from the sidelines, leaving the matter to local government to resolve. But when Boston's panicked mayor Andrew Peters fired Curtis and called up Massachusetts National Guard troops to patrol Boston's streets without Coolidge's authorization, Governor Coolidge stepped in to gain control of the situation. He restored Curtis as police commissioner and backed Curtis's decision to fire the striking policemen and hire replacements. The climax of the episode came when Coolidge replied sternly to a pleading telegram from the AFL's legendary leader Sam Gompers, "There is no right to strike against the public safety by anyone, anywhere, any time.... I am equally determined to defend the sovereignty of Massachusetts and to maintain the authority and jurisdiction over her public officers where it has been placed by the Constitution and laws of her people." Coolidge's widely publicized answer to Gompers made him a national figure and propelled him to the national Republican ticket; he was Warren Harding's running mate in the 1920 election. President Reagan recalled Coolidge's firm handling of the Boston police strike when he confronted the similar air traffic controllers' strike in 1981.

Coolidge in the White House

Another reason liberals hate Coolidge is that he was a tax cutter, and a model for Ronald Reagan's "supply-side" economics. Coolidge understood that his tax cuts would work in the very way that the Laffer Curve explained fifty years later. In his 1924 state of the union message to Congress, Coolidge argued that "the larger incomes of the country would actually yield more revenue to the Government if the basis of taxation were scientifically revised downward.... There is no escaping the fact that when the taxation of large incomes is excessive they tend to disappear." And earlier in the year, at a Lincoln Day dinner, he had argued,

> **A Book You're Not Supposed to Read**
>
> *Coolidge: An American Enigma* by Robert Sobel (Regnery, 1998).

> I agree perfectly with those who wish to relieve the small taxpayer by getting the largest possible contribution from the people with large incomes. But if the rates on large incomes are so high that they disappear, the small taxpayer will be left to bear the entire burden. If, on the other hand, the rates are placed where they will produce the most revenue from large incomes, then the small taxpayer will be relieved.

Coolidge—and the Laffer Curve—turned out to be right in the 1920s.

Arthur Schlesinger Jr.'s *The Age of Roosevelt* says Coolidge "concentrated on cutting taxes for millionaires." The facts of the Coolidge-era tax cuts are as follows: Coolidge cut income taxes three times. His chief target each time was the emergency income surtax rates that had been enacted during World War I, but which had not been lowered after the war ended, as is typical of "temporary" or "emergency" government measures. The surtax kicked in at an income of $6,000, and the top rate was originally 73 percent. A household with a $1 million income in 1924 paid a net tax of $550,000. Harding and Coolidge between them lowered the top surtax rate from 73 percent to 25 percent, and finally to 20 percent. Coolidge also cut the lowest tax bracket from 4 percent to 1.5 percent. He raised the income threshold at which the surtax took effect from $6,000 to $10,000, removing thousands of households from the income tax rolls entirely. While Coolidge's tax cut is pejoratively described as a giveaway to the rich, 70 percent of the tax reduction went to households with income under $10,000. This is one reason the Coolidge tax cuts were broadly popular with Americans. Ironically, the Coolidge tax cuts were highly progressive in their effects: the proportion of the total income tax burden paid by those earning $100,000 and above increased from 28 percent in 1921 to 61 percent in 1928.

In 1922, the surtax yielded only $77 million from taxpayers with incomes over $300,000, down from $243 million in 1919 and $220 million in 1918. In 1927, by which time the top surtax rate had been reduced to 20 percent, the Treasury netted $230 million from taxpayers with incomes over $300,000. In the first year after Coolidge's 1924 tax cut there was a decline of $127 million in total income tax revenues, though, as economist Lawrence Lindsey discovered upon sifting the data, tax receipts from taxpayers with incomes over $100,000 *increased*. In other words, *all* of the lost revenue came from lower and middle incomes. Coolidge's tax cuts shifted more of the tax burden onto upper-income taxpayers—exactly the opposite of what critics of tax cuts claimed, both then and now. And by 1928 income tax revenues had risen $310 million above where they had been before the first tax cut, and 61 percent of total tax revenues came from taxpayers with incomes over $100,000. Only 4 percent of income tax receipts came from taxpayers with incomes under $10,000.

Coolidge also hewed to conservative principle on farm relief. The farm economy had been devastated by the roller-coaster economy of the years during and immediately after World War I, and the farm belt recovered from the near depression of 1920–1921 much more slowly than the rest of the economy. By 1924 farm income had only recovered about half way to its pre-recessionary level. There was sentiment in Congress for various farm relief measures, including subsidies and tariff protection against food imports. Coolidge vetoed or threatened to veto several proposed measures, such as the two McNary-Haugen farm relief bills, that would have required the federal government to buy surplus farm products to prop up prices and therefore incomes (the exact policy Roosevelt would embrace in the Great Depression a decade later). In his veto message Coolidge noted,

> ★★★★★★★★★★★★★
>
> ## Praise for Coolidge from an Unlikely Source
>
> "A whole generation of historians has assailed Coolidge for the superficial optimism which kept him from seeing that a great storm was brewing at home and also more distantly abroad. This is grossly unfair.... There was much that was good about the world of which Coolidge spoke.... the twenties in America were a very good time."
>
> John Kenneth Galbraith, *The Great Crash 1929*

> Nothing is more certain than that such price fixing would upset the normal exchange relationships existing in the open market and that it would finally have to be extended to cover a multitude of other goods and services. Government price fixing, once started, has alike no justice and no end. It is an economic folly from which this country has every right to be spared.

Demonstrating his economic literacy, Coolidge observed that offering subsidies would cause farmers to grow *more* crops, thereby putting additional downward pressure on prices, and increasing the demand on Washington to offer still more subsidies. Coolidge added that there were several other reasons to disapprove the bill, but that "the most decisive one is that it is not constitutional." Far from being indifferent to the difficulties of the farm belt, Coolidge proposed alternative remedies that would rely on private sector agricultural cooperative arrangements to stabilize farm prices and incomes without government support.

Coolidge's similar attitude on the question of flood relief for the Mississippi River basin, which suffered record flooding in 1927 that was not equaled until the 1990s, has also attracted liberal criticism. While Coolidge did place Commerce Secretary Herbert Hoover, known for his food relief efforts in Europe after World War I, in charge of relief efforts, he resisted calls for large federal spending on flood relief and flood control projects. Coolidge thought that these problems should be the responsibility of state governments, and that interstate flood control projects should be paid for by property owners who benefitted from them rather than by the U.S. taxpayer. Under pressure, Coolidge ultimately relented on a $500 million flood control bill in 1928 (Congress had wanted $1.4 billion), which, Coolidge biographer Robert Sobel has noted, "marked an important step in the expansion of government responsibilities and obligations."

In both cases—farm price supports and disaster relief—Coolidge's principles have been fully vindicated in subsequent decades, as farm subsidies have swollen into the hundreds of billions of dollars, and Washington has become the indemnifier of first resort for every natural calamity, with disaster relief managed by one of the more egregious federal bureaucracies, the Federal Emergency Management Agency (FEMA).

Liberals attack Coolidge for his supposed "isolationism," but ignore his one major foreign policy initiative, the distinctly *un*-conservative Kellogg-Briand Pact of 1928, in which sixty-two nations promised to renounce war forever as an instrument of national policy and to resolve all international disputes peacefully. Coolidge did not subscribe to the sentimental and utopian premises behind the Pact, but he embraced it nonetheless, likely because Kellogg-Briand aided the cause of spending restraint, as Coolidge was resisting calls for a naval arms race with Britain and France. Coolidge's Secretary of State, Frank Kellogg, won the Nobel Peace Prize for negotiating the Pact, which has justly gone down in history as a laughable misadventure of liberal internationalism.

Coolidge decided not to run for a second full term in 1928, issuing a typically terse and enigmatic statement: "I do not choose to run for president in 1928." He was not enthusiastic about his prospective replacement, Herbert Hoover, remarking to an associate that "for six years that man has given me unsolicited advice—all of it bad."

There are apocryphal accounts that Coolidge said he expected a depression was on its way, but it is more likely that his sense of modesty, closely associated with his constitutional scruples, guided his decision not to run for re-election. As he explained it afterward,

> It is difficult for men in high office to avoid the malady of self-delusion. They are always surrounded by worshipers. They are constantly, and for the most part sincerely, assured of their greatness. They live in an artificial

★ ★ ★ ★ ★ ★ ★ ★ ★ ★ ★ ★ ★ ★

Coolidge on the Death of His Son

Coolidge's teenage son Calvin Jr. died of sepsis after developing a blister playing tennis at the White House. Coolidge wrote of the death's effect on him in his *Autobiography*, "We do not know what would have happened to him under other circumstances, but if I had not been President he would not have raised a blister on his toe, which resulted in blood poisoning, playing lawn tennis in the South Grounds.

"In his suffering he was asking me to make him well. I could not.

"When he went the power and the glory of the Presidency went with him.

"The ways of Providence are often beyond our understanding. It seemed to me that the world had need of the work that it was probable he could do.

"I do not know why such a price was exacted for occupying the White House.... It costs a great deal to be President."

atmosphere of adulation and exaltation which sooner or later impairs their judgment. They are in grave danger of becoming careless and arrogant.

Would that more of our presidents had this firm a grasp on reality.

Coolidge's One Supreme Court (Dis)Appointment

Coolidge's sole appointment to the Supreme Court was Harlan Fiske Stone in 1925, and the disappointing nature of this appointment can be summed up in a single fact: Franklin Roosevelt elevated Stone to Chief Justice in 1941. Stone had been dean of Columbia University Law School and then served as Coolidge's attorney general. His appointment to the Court was controversial, with some senators concerned about his Wall Street connections; and Stone proposed the step of answering questions before the Senate Judiciary Committee—thereby establishing a practice that has continued ever since.

But on the Court Stone generally sided with liberals such as Brandeis and Holmes in upholding government regulation. Indeed, in the 1930s he voted most of the time in favor of FDR's New Deal legislation when it came before the Court. Stone is most notorious as the author of one of the worst Supreme Court decisions of all time, the 1938 *U.S. v. Carolene Products* case, in which he invented an entirely extra-constitutional distinction between individual economic rights, which the Court would allow wide deference to Congress to regulate, and other civil rights, to which the Court would apply "strict scrutiny."

Stone's appointment has to be ranked as the only significant disappointment of Coolidge's record in respect to his constitutional duties. But Coolidge did not anticipate that the Supreme Court would increasingly fail in its duty to uphold the Constitution over the coming decades; he could not have foreseen the damage that a Supreme Court cut loose from its constitutional moorings might do. In his speech on the limitations of the law, Coolidge expressed the still common view that Hamilton had been right in supposing the judiciary to be the "least dangerous branch": "This court is human," Coolidge had said in 1922, "and therefore not infallible; but in the more than one hundred and thirty years of its existence its decisions which have not withstood the questioning of criticism could almost be counted upon one hand."

Despite this one disappointment, Coolidge still deserves an A+ grade for his principled constitutionalism.

Chapter 6

HERBERT HOOVER, 1929–1933

"He is certainly a wonder, and I wish we could make him President of the United States.
There could not be a better one."
—Franklin Delano Roosevelt on Herbert Hoover, 1920

"No one better illustrated Tacitus's verdict on Galba, omnium consensus capax imperii nisi
imperasset (by general consent fit to rule, had he not ruled)."
—Paul Johnson on Hoover, Modern Times

President Hoover's Constitutional Grade: C-

Herbert Hoover is the great tragic figure among modern American
presidents. Universally acknowledged for his ability, and acclaimed
for his great humanitarian accomplishment in organizing food
relief for a Europe in desperate conditions after World War I (ironically, the
anti-Communist Hoover may have saved Soviet Communism by ameliorating
the Communist-caused famine in Russia), Hoover had the misfortune to
preside over the worst economic calamity of the twentieth century. On paper
he seemed to be the ideal president to respond to the crisis. In addition to his
humanitarian record, Hoover had been secretary of commerce under the
previous two presidents, and he was well known and respected in the business community. He seemed to blend the best of Progressivism with a belief
in enterprise and individual initiative—having made his own personal
fortune as a mining engineer in his youth. Yet because of how he actually
handled the crisis when he was called into action, Hoover is not loved by
anyone.

Did you know?

★ Hoover was
orphaned at age
ten and worked his
way through the
brand new Stanford
University, where
he was in the first
graduating class

★ Hoover, a strong
anti-Communist,
may have inad-
vertently assured
the success of the
Bolshevik revolution
in Russia

★ Hoover was the first
president to have a
telephone installed
on his desk in the
Oval Office

It was his double misfortune that the crisis of the Great Depression coincided with the arrival of the media presidency. No one knew it at the time, but as FDR showed upon succeeding Hoover in 1932, Americans were now ready for presidents who "emoted." Hoover, in sharp contrast to his successors, was seemingly incapable of conveying empathy. He did not, like Bill Clinton, "feel your pain," or, like FDR, say to Americans, "Tell me your troubles." While he intervened extensively in the economy—in all the wrong ways—in a vain effort to ameliorate the Depression, his inability to "connect" with the American people was his political undoing. Later he would become a strong critic of FDR and the New Deal, implicitly repudiating many of his own policies. Partisan liberal historians have unfairly attacked Hoover along with Harding and Coolidge for decades—enabling Democrats to blame the Republican Party generally and conservative economics in particular for the legacy of his failure.

Hoover's most authoritative biographer, conservative historian George H. Nash, calls Hoover "the Rodney Dangerfield of American politics—he gets no respect." And for good reason. It was understandable that liberals would criticize the Republican Hoover. But conservatives eventually came to abandon him too, even though he was a vehement anti-Communist, a friend of Joseph McCarthy and Richard Nixon, and a financial supporter of some important initiatives of the modern conservative movement. In the 1950s Hoover was a favorite, if not a hero, of many leading libertarians such as Rose Wilder Lane and John Chamberlain.

And ironically, at one time—shortly after the end of World War I—*both* parties wanted Hoover and hoped he might become their presidential can-

A Harbinger of Unhappy Times?

Hoover was sworn in at noon on March 4, 1929, and delivered his inaugural address in a heavy downpour of rain, a gloomy portent, perhaps, of his unhappy single term. "By the time we arrived at the White House," Hoover recorded in his memoirs, "both Mrs. Hoover and I were thoroughly soaked."

didate. Today, however, Hoover has become a complete political orphan, embraced by neither political party. (In a way Hoover has come full circle, since he was literally orphaned at the age of ten.) Nowadays Hoover is just as likely to be attacked by conservatives and libertarians as by liberals. And while Calvin Coolidge, Dwight Eisenhower, and Richard Nixon have received belated revisionist praise from some liberals, Hoover continues to languish in the reputational basement. Pretty much his only recent champion was Oregon's late Senator Mark Hatfield, a liberal Republican with a limited following.

The problem with Hoover is that the closer you look, the more elusive and contradictory he becomes. If you read Hoover's spoken and written words (and he wrote a lot—a bibliography of his published writings and speeches contains over 1,200 entries), you can find many examples of fervently expressed conservative principles. He published a book in 1922 entitled *American Individualism* that embraced free enterprise and attacked collectivism. This phrase from one of his 1928 campaign speeches is typical of Hoover's rhetoric: "You cannot extend the mastery of the government over the daily working life of a people without at the same time making it the master of the people's souls and thoughts."

But despite many statements in favor of free enterprise, Hoover was no devotee of free markets, and he failed to perceive that free enterprise depends upon them. At times he could be a vocal critic of "laissez faire,"

★ ★ ★ ★ ★ ★ ★ ★ ★ ★ ★ ★ ★ ★

Mister, We Could Use a Man like Herbert Hoover Again

Hoover was a backer of *Human Events*, *The Freeman*, and *National Review*. Before he entered politics in the 1920s, he founded one of the most important conservative intellectual institutions, the Hoover Institution for the Study of War, Revolution, and Peace at Stanford University—decades before such independent research organizations became commonplace. Hoover's early initiative to gather records of the Russian revolution at the close of World War I provided the main repository of evidence for scholars and investigators of the Soviet Union for several decades.

and he supported lots of government regulations. Back in 1912 Hoover considered himself an "independent progressive," supported Theodore Roosevelt and his Progressive "Bull Moose" Party—and then he went on to serve in the Wilson administration. In fact he boasted in his memoirs, "Those who contended that during the period of my administration our economic system was one of *laissez faire* have little knowledge of the extent of government regulation." As secretary of commerce under both Harding and Coolidge, Hoover distinguished himself as a busybody, causing Coolidge at one point to refer to Hoover as a "meddlesome liberal." As Paul Johnson described him, "Hoover showed himself a corporatist, an activist and an interventionist, running counter to the general thrust, or rather non-thrust, of the Harding-Coolidge administrations.... There was no aspect of public policy in which Hoover was not intensely active, usually personally: child health, Indian policy, oil, conservation, public education, housing, social waste, agriculture—as President, he was his own Agriculture Secretary, and the 1929 Agricultural Marketing Act was entirely his work." Indeed, Hoover's memoirs are quite unlike any other president's; they are organized more topically than chronologically, with sequential chapters on "water," "conservation," and "public buildings." The book reads more like a policy manual than an autobiography.

A Book You're Not Supposed to Read

The Life of Herbert Hoover by George H. Nash, 3 vols. (W. W. Norton, 1983, 1988, and 1996).

As George Nash put it, Hoover was "too progressive for the conservatives, and too conservative for the radicals." But this does not mean he was either a moderate or an unprincipled compromiser. A closer look at Hoover yields some important lessons about modern politics and the requirements for success in the presidency.

Politics Is Not Engineering

The source of Hoover's difficulties may have been mostly intellectual, and only partly temperamental. Trained as an engineer, he brought an engineer's mentality to politics, a domain that resists the orderly, mechanistic approach of engineers. (The *Philadelphia Record* newspaper hailed Hoover as the model of "engineering statesmanship.") It is not a coincidence that the president to whom Hoover bears the closest resemblance in terms of being aloof from the nitty-gritty of politics was also an engineer—Jimmy Carter. It was precisely Hoover's reputation as a supreme administrator, along with his humanitarian record, that raised expectations for the thirty-first president. Americans expected that they were electing a "miracle worker," a fact which worried Hoover himself. As he wrote to a friend, "They have a conviction that I am a sort of superman, that no problem is beyond my capacity."

One passage in Hoover's memoirs reveals precisely what Hoover didn't understand about the changing nature of presidential politics in the twentieth century: "I was convinced that efficient, honest administration of the vast machine of the Federal government would appeal to all citizens. *I have since learned that efficient government does not interest the people so much as dramatics*" [emphasis added]. While Hoover was busy with the machinery of government—as he conceived it—his opportunistic and partisan critics were able to create a morality play that gripped the public, capitalizing on the president's seeming indifference to the plight of the "bonus army" of World War I veterans who marched on Washington in 1932 hoping to pressure Washington to release their war pensions early as a relief measure. This was unfair, as no one was more aggressive in using government to try to ameliorate the nation's suffering economy. But that was a large part of Hoover's problem.

Hoover Tries to Fix the Depression, Inadvertently Makes It Great

The great British historian Paul Johnson ably summarizes the standard liberal narrative of Hoover that stood for more than two generations:

> The received view is that Hoover, because of his ideological attachment to *laissez-faire*, refused to use government money to reflate the economy and so prolonged and deepened the Depression until the election of Roosevelt, who then promptly reversed official policy, introducing the New Deal, a form of Keynesianism, and pulled America out of the trough. Hoover is presented as the symbol of the dead, discredited past, Roosevelt as the harbinger of the future, and 1932–3 the watershed between old-style free market economics and the benevolent new managed economics and social welfare of Keynes.

Over the last couple decades the true picture has come into focus: far from being a contrast to FDR, Hoover paved the way for the New Deal by setting in motion most of its central elements. Moreover, had he followed the example of President Harding—and the advice of his treasury secretary, Andrew Mellon—and let the economy take its natural self-correcting course, the sharp recession set off by the stock market crash of 1929 might not have turned into a deep depression that lasted for a decade.

George Mason University historian Steven Horwitz reflects the recent scholarship, writing, "Herbert Hoover deserves a good deal of the blame for turning what would have most likely been a steep but short recession into a much deeper and eventually much longer Great Depression." First, far from being a frugal fiscal manager like Harding and Coolidge, Hoover increased federal spending by 48 percent, from $3.1 billion in 1929 to

$4.7 billion in his last budget for 1933. (Under Coolidge federal spending had been nearly flat.) Under Hoover government spending was skyrocketing during a time of deflation—meaning that the real, inflation-adjusted increase in spending was much higher than 48 percent. Hoover's budget deficits were actually larger as a proportion of total spending than any of FDR's New Deal budget deficits, and even larger than President Obama's huge deficit is today. That he was reluctant to spend money is one charge against Hoover that is simply false.

But huge deficit spending was only the beginning of Hoover's mistakes.

Instead of letting markets adjust to new conditions, Hoover intervened across the board in an attempt to manipulate prices and wages. He established agricultural cartels to prop up farm prices, in a precursor to the policies FDR adopted. He "jawboned" business into not cutting wages (even though prices were falling), thinking high wages would preserve consumer spending and aggregate demand. Many industries complied, but compensated by laying off more workers, making the problem of unemployment worse. Hoover stepped up anti-trust lawsuits against "destructive competition." He promoted public works projects, just like President Obama's 2009 "stimulus," but with an added twist: Hoover signed into law the Davis-Bacon Act, a pro-union law that requires that all government-funded construction projects pay the "prevailing wage," which means a union wage. Davis-Bacon, which is still in force today, not only raised the price of public works to taxpayers, but for decades had the effect of excluding

> ## Quick: Who Created These New Deal-Era Programs, Hoover or FDR?
>
> 1. The Reconstruction Finance Corporation, which lent tax dollars to banks and other firms?
> 2. The Home Loan Board, to give money to the construction sector?
> 3. The Public Works Administration, to coordinate and expand federal construction projects?
>
> Answers: 1. Hoover. 2. Hoover. 3. Hoover.

immigrants and minorities from public works projects (which was part of the intention of the sponsors of Davis-Bacon in the first place).

★★★★★★★★★★★★★★★★

A Liberal Columnist Reveals the Real President Hoover

"It was Mr. Hoover who abandoned the principles of laissez-faire in relation to the business cycle, established the conviction that prosperity and depression can be publicly controlled by political action, and drove out of the public consciousness the old idea that depressions must be overcome by private adjustment."

Walter Lippmann, 1935

Perhaps the most disastrous move Hoover made was agreeing to the Smoot-Hawley tariff bill in 1930. Smoot-Hawley was old-fashioned trade protectionism; it raised tariffs on a wide range of imports. It had the desired effect: imports to the U.S. fell by 40 percent over the next two years. But Smoot-Hawley set off a wave of retaliatory tariffs enacted by our trading partners—devastating U.S. exports and worsening the already severe depression; unemployment, which had eased a bit before Smoot-Hawley, began rising again. The stock market fell sharply the day Hoover signed the bill.

The final insult to the American economy was a massive tax increase passed in 1932, which raised personal income taxes and revived a number of World War I-era excise taxes, on top of which Hoover supported a higher inheritance tax. Hoover favored higher taxes out of concern for the budget deficit, but the middle of a depression is the worst time to raise taxes. This is the main reason why decades later, after the Republican Party embraced supply-side economics under Ronald Reagan, Hoover's reputation among conservatives collapsed on account of what Jack Kemp called "Hoover's root-canal school of economics." Steven Horwitz's judgment is harsh but dead-on: "Hoover preferred the visible fist of government to the invisible hand of the market." Hoover himself would later boast that the Republican Party had "created seven out of the ten great Federal regulating agencies of today."

In the 1932 campaign Franklin Roosevelt actually attacked Hoover from the right for his free-spending ways. FDR charged Hoover with "reckless and extravagant" spending, calling Hoover's "the greatest spending administration in peacetime in all of history." FDR also charged that Hoover thought "that we ought to center control of everything in Washington as rapidly as possible." Roosevelt's running mate, John Nance Garner, went so far as to say Hoover was "leading the country down the path of socialism."

Many of FDR's top advisers later came to admit that Hoover paved the way for the New Deal. Raymond Moley, one of FDR's political aides and speechwriters, wrote years later, "When we all burst into Washington, we found every essential idea enacted in the 100-day Congress in the Hoover administration itself."

Hoover and Roosevelt have always been understood as great political rivals—which is obviously true from one point of view, since they ran against each other in 1932. But as political scientist Gordon Lloyd points out, it is more accurate to understand them not as ideological rivals, but as "The two faces of liberalism."

> ★ ★ ★ ★ ★ ★ ★ ★ ★ ★ ★ ★ ★ ★
>
> ## FDR = Hoover Redux
>
> "I once made a list of New Deal ventures begun during Hoover's years as Secretary of Commerce and then as President…. Practically the whole New Deal was extrapolated from programs that Hoover started."
>
> Rexford Tugwell, one of FDR's more radical advisers

Out of Office, Hoover Moves Right

One reason Hoover is a lasting enigma is that after his defeat at the hands of FDR in 1932, he moved sharply to the right and became a strong critic of the very policies he had embraced as president. If you didn't know about Hoover's record and went only by his post-presidential speeches and writings, you would acclaim him a great conservative figure. As of Richard

Nixon decades later, it can be said of Hoover that he was much better out of office than in it. This is one reason why Hoover's reputation in the public mind is at odds with his record. The final irony, therefore, is that Hoover was himself responsible for the misperception—which has been so useful in the liberal mythology about the Depression and the New Deal—that Hoover was a conservative, even a reactionary, president.

Throughout the 1930s Hoover attacked what he called the New Deal's "assaults on the spirit of American liberty" and "the gigantic shift of government from the function of umpire to the function of directing, dictating, and competing in our economic life." In particular, in 1937 Hoover attacked FDR's "court packing" plan to take over the Supreme Court. In a speech entitled "Hands Off the Supreme Court," Hoover blasted FDR for seeking "a quick and revolutionary change in the Constitution" that would hand FDR's administration "a blank check upon which they can write future undisclosed purposes."

Herein lies the clue to unraveling the enigma of Hoover. It is usually said that Hoover's technocratic and almost machine-like persona was ill-suited to the political shock of the Depression, especially in contrast to Franklin Roosevelt's large personality. Hoover might have been more politically successful if he had had a warmer personality and had foreseen, as FDR did, how retail politics was changing fast with the rise of modern mass media such as radio (and later television). This is true as far as it goes, but it glosses over how Hoover's

Do As I Say, Not As I Do

"Self-government never dies from direct attack. No matter what his real intentions may be, no man will arise and say that he intends to suspend one atom of the rights guaranteed by the Constitution. Liberty dies from the encroachments and disregard of the safeguards of those rights. And unfortunately it is those whose purposes have often been good who have broken the levees of liberty to find a short cut to their ends."

Hoover in 1937, by which time he was a critic of the New Deal engineering mentality led him to embrace the very kind of social engineering that is anathema to a free economy and to the founding principles of a self-governing people. Hoover's attack on FDR's "court packing" scheme was one of Hoover's very few expressions of concern for the Constitution. His memoirs barely mention the Constitution; and unlike other inaugural addresses up to that time that dwelt at length on the Constitution and the nation's Founding principles, Hoover's barely mentioned either. For all of Hoover's decency and ability, his lack of appreciation for, and understanding of, limited government explain many of his inconsistencies and failures in office, and his lack of a coherent view of the limits of state power or the limits of his own reach. Indeed, it is not too harsh to suggest that one reason for his criticisms of the New Deal after he left office was simply personal pique that he was not the person in charge of shaping the interventions.

Hoover's relative indifference to the principles of the Constitution explains his mixed record of appointments to the Supreme Court. Hoover appointed three justices. The first was Charles Evans Hughes, to replace Chief Justice William Howard Taft. Hughes had been on the Court before (ironically appointed by President Taft), but had stepped down to run for president in 1916. Hughes was a moderate on the Court in both of his stints as a justice.

Hoover's second appointment was Owen Roberts, and in the early years of FDR's New Deal, Roberts was generally aligned with the Court's conservatives in striking down New Deal legislation for exceeding the Constitution's grant of powers to the federal government. However, Roberts was the key justice who changed sides in the "revolution of 1937," when the Supreme Court buckled under pressure from Franklin Roosevelt and ceased protecting economic liberty from assaults by the federal government.

Hoover's third appointment was the most disappointing: Benjamin Cardozo. Cardozo, a Democrat, was an open proponent of Brandeis-style "sociological jurisprudence" and the Progressive idea of "ordered liberty" that presumes more government supervision of individuals and permits massively expanded federal power. Cardozo wrote the majority opinion in the case that upheld the constitutionality of Social Security, for example.

Between Hoover's weak grasp of constitutional principles and his mixed record of Supreme Court appointments, his constitutional grade is a C-.

Chapter 7

FRANKLIN DELANO ROOSEVELT, 1933–1945

"We have tried spending money. We are spending more than we have ever spent before and it does not work. And I have just one interest, and if I am wrong … somebody else can have my job. I want to see this country prosperous. I want to see people get a job. I want to see people get enough to eat. We have never made good on our promises.… I say after eight years of this Administration we have just as much unemployment as when we started.…

And an enormous debt to boot."

—*Treasury Secretary Henry Morgenthau in 1939*

President Roosevelt's Constitutional Grade: F

As our only four-term president, a chief executive who served through two great national crises—the Great Depression and World War II—it is inevitable that Franklin Roosevelt looms large in the history and development of the modern presidency. While Woodrow Wilson was the intellectual architect of the expansive modern presidency, FDR perfected it and gave it its style, building on and completing the work Wilson had begun, to expand the role of the president and weaken constitutional restraints on government. He also finished Wilson's work of making the Democratic Party a wholly liberal party. He inflated the role of charisma and personality pioneered by his cousin Theodore Roosevelt. He was our first mass media president, making extensive use of radio. Despite his sunny disposition, Roosevelt was also deeply cynical and manipulative about politics. Indeed, it might be said that he regarded the Great Depression

Did you know?

★ Roosevelt ran to the right of Herbert Hoover in 1932, attacking Hoover as a big spender and promising to balance the federal budget

★ FDR argued that government employees should not be allowed to engage in collective bargaining

★ Neither the New Deal nor World War II was actually responsible for ending the Great Depression

Ronald Reagan, a Fan of FDR—with Reservations

"I think that many people forget Roosevelt ran for president on a platform dedicated to reducing waste and fat in government. He called for cutting federal spending by twenty-five percent, eliminating useless boards and commissions and returning to states and communities powers that had been wrongfully seized by the federal government. If he had not been distracted by war, I think he would have resisted the relentless expansion of the federal government that followed him. One of his sons, Franklin Roosevelt, Jr., often told me that his father had said many times his welfare and relief programs during the Depression were meant only as emergency, stopgap measures to cope with a crisis, not the seeds of what others tried to turn into a permanent welfare state. Government giveaway programs, FDR said, 'destroy the human spirit,' and he was right. As smart as he was, though, I suspect even FDR didn't realize that once you created a bureaucracy, it took on a life of its own."

Ronald Reagan

as the ultimate crisis that was too good to waste. Whittaker Chambers called FDR "an artful and experienced ringmaster whose techniques may be studied again and again and again."

There was a certain compelling magnificence about Roosevelt's style that attracted the admiration and emulation of Ronald Reagan among others. It is easy to see how Reagan modeled the style of his own presidency in some ways after FDR's, as Reagan himself suggested in his memoirs: "During his Fireside Chats, his strong, gentle, confident voice resonated across the nation caught up in a storm and reassured us that we could lick any problem. I will never forget him for that." FDR's great contemporary Winston Churchill wrote, "Meeting Roosevelt was like taking your first sip of champagne." But like Reagan, Churchill also expressed serious reservations about FDR's domestic and foreign policies.

Much of what is commonly believed about FDR and his time is wrong, but a revisionist picture of him is slowly emerging, after decades of liberal hagiography that made him out to be the rescuer of the economy and the savior of American democracy. With the passage of time, the weight of scholarship is shifting decisively to the conclusion that FDR's New Deal deepened and *prolonged* the Great Depression, and that far from warding off the specter of socialist revolution, FDR did more than any other president to undermine the Constitution and create the sharply polarized atmosphere of partisan politics that liberals today deplore. Ronald Reagan was absolutely right when he made the controversial remark in 1976 that "Fascism was really the basis for the New Deal."

The Modern Left Is Far Left of FDR

But there are a few conservative aspects of FDR's legacy that belie modern liberals' picture of him. Looking more closely at some of FDR's internal contradictions is a good way of recognizing how much further to the left the Democratic Party has moved since FDR's time. For example, although FDR was the architect of some of the first government entitlement programs such as Social Security, he was a critic of dependency, and suggested that public welfare programs should be sharply limited. Liberals were not happy when Republicans quoted these words back to them in the debates on welfare reform in the 1980s and 1990s.

FDR was the architect of an alphabet soup of government regulatory agencies, though he made it quite clear that while

> ## FDR against Welfare Dependency
>
> PIG
>
> "The lessons of history, confirmed by the evidence immediately before me, show conclusively that continued dependence upon relief induces a spiritual and moral disintegration fundamentally destructive to the national fiber. To dole out relief in this way is to administer a narcotic, a subtle destroyer of the human spirit.... It is in violation of the traditions of America."
>
> Franklin Delano Roosevelt to Congress in 1935

FDR against Bureaucracy

"We need disinterested, as well as broad-gauged, public officials. This part of our problem we have not yet solved, but it can be solved and it can be accomplished *without* the creation of a national bureaucracy which would dominate the national life of our governmental system" [emphasis added].

Franklin Delano Roosevelt

he was in favor of *administration*, he was opposed to *bureaucracy*. This may be a distinction without a difference, but there is some reason to think that the Leviathan government his New Deal set in motion might not meet with his approval if he were alive today. As with welfare, his words on this subject, and the subtle distinctions underlying them, are nearly forgotten by his would-be liberal heirs today.

While Roosevelt thought that many of the agencies set in motion to cope with the emergency of the Depression would be temporary expedients, there isn't a single bureaucracy that today's liberals won't defend and, if possible, enlarge.

FDR was famous for his fierce attacks on big business and "economic royalists." But those who pose as his liberal heirs forget, if they ever knew in the first place, his equal concern for middle class opportunity and his endorsement of individual enterprise. "Let me emphasize," Roosevelt said on this point, "that serious as have been the errors of unrestrained individualism, I do not believe in abandoning the system of individual enterprise." But perhaps the most notable difference between FDR's liberalism and today's is on public employee unions, nowadays the lifeblood of the Democratic Party. In a 1937 letter to a public employees association, FDR wrote: "All Government employees should realize that the process of collective bargaining, as usually understood, cannot be transplanted into the public service.... Particularly, I want to emphasize my conviction that militant tactics have no place in the functions of any organization of Government employees."

FDR, an Episcopalian, made the kind of remarks about religion that send the American Civil Liberties Union into paroxysms of rage. Democracy and Christianity, Roosevelt said, were "two phases of the same civilization." "We cannot read the history of our rise and development as a nation," he said, "without reckoning with the place the Bible has occupied in shaping the advances of the Republic." During World War II FDR wrote a preface for an edition of the New Testament that was distributed to American troops. On the eve of the 1940 election, FDR said in a radio address, "Freedom of speech is of no use to a man who has nothing to say and freedom of worship is of no use to a man who has lost his God." On June 6, 1944, FDR led the nation in prayer for our armed forces on live radio, and in his final inaugural address in 1945, he said, "So we pray to Him for the vision to see our way clearly ... to the achievement of His will." Today's liberals would regard these statements and acts as grounds for impeachment if they came from President George W. Bush or Sarah Palin.

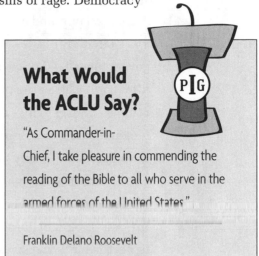

What Would the ACLU Say?

"As Commander-in-Chief, I take pleasure in commending the reading of the Bible to all who serve in the armed forces of the United States."

Franklin Delano Roosevelt

The Paradox of FDR

How can these contradictions be explained? Amity Shlaes, author of one of the best accounts of FDR and the Great Depression, notes that "FDR was not an ideologue or a radical." Rather, he was something more troubling in some ways: he was entirely inconsistent in his thought process, bordering on intellectual instability. One of Roosevelt's top aides compared him to a kaleidoscope: "The bits of brightly colored glass remain the same, but, with every shift, the brilliant and complex pattern falls into new arrangements."

FDR changed his mind frequently and gave conflicting directions to those working for him—which, according to biographer James MacGregor Burns, "produced hurt and bewilderment among his subordinates." His decisions were often arbitrary or even whimsical, such as when he changed the government-fixed price of gold according to his theory of lucky numbers, after confiscating the private holdings of the American people. He surrounded himself with a menagerie of advisers and political operatives—his famous "brains trust"—that included both hard-bitten pols out for partisan advantage and dreamy ideologues, some of whom openly admired fascist and Communist economic planning. Several of FDR's top aides, such as Rexford Tugwell, had toured the Soviet Union and met for hours with Stalin. And several of Roosevelt's advisers and appointees were later revealed to have been Soviet spies; they may have influenced FDR in his dealings with Stalin during World War II.

The pro-Roosevelt histories have always made a virtue of FDR's "pragmatism," often quoting one famous remark: "It is common sense to take a method and try it. If it fails, admit it frankly and try another. But above all, try something." But FDR's "bold, persistent experimentation," as he called it, undermined business and consumer confidence; his punitive taxes and reckless attacks on the rich and prosperous businesses discouraged capital investment; his pro-union policies retarded hiring. His regulatory schemes to manipulate markets, such as the National Recovery Administration (NRA) and Agricultural Adjustment Act (AAA) backfired badly and were struck down by the Supreme Court as unconstitutional. (In the case of the NRA, the Supreme Court was unanimous, which means that

★★★★★★★★★★★★★★

Not Exactly a Resounding Endorsement

"FDR is no crusader. He is no tribune of the people. He is no enemy of entrenched privilege. He is a pleasant man who, without any important qualifications for the office, would very much like to be president."

Liberal columnist Walter Lippmann appraising Roosevelt in 1932, before the New Deal

FDR had gone too far even for the liberal justices Louis Brandeis and Oliver Wendell Holmes. Brandeis told an FDR aide, "I want you to go back and tell the president that we're not going to let this government centralize everything.") These and other New Deal measures represented the expansion of government by nearly a full order of magnitude. Amity Shlaes notes that the National Recovery Act generated 10,000 new pages of law in the U.S. statute books, which had been only 2,735 pages long before FDR took office. "In twelve months," Shlaes points out, "the NRA had generated more paper than the entire legislative output of the federal government since 1789." Whenever a measure failed to work, instead of abandoning it or changing course, FDR always doubled down, seeking more political control over the economy and still higher taxes. When business investment froze under the weight of the uncertainty FDR's policies caused, he responded by proposing an "undistributed profits tax," hoping to either force businesses to invest or confiscate their meager profits.

A Book You're Not Supposed to Read

FDR's Folly: How Roosevelt and His New Deal Prolonged the Great Depression by Jim Powell (Crown Forum, 2003).

Some of Roosevelt's own senior advisers and political supporters came to see the failure of the New Deal. The most lacerating criticism came from Raymond Moley, one of FDR's closest aides in his first seven years in office. Disillusioned, Moley wrote bitterly of the shortcomings of both FDR and the New Deal,

> If this aggregation of policies springing from circumstances, motives, purposes, and situations so various gave the observer the sense of a certain rugged grandeur, it arose chiefly from the wonder that one man could have been so flexible as to permit himself to believe so many things in so short a time. But to look upon these policies as the result of a unified plan was to believe

that the accumulation of stuffed snakes, baseball pictures, school flags, old tennis shoes, carpenter's tools, geometry books, and chemistry sets in a boy's bedroom could have been put there by an interior decorator.

A Book You're Not Supposed to Read

New Deal or Raw Deal? How FDR's Economic Legacy Has Damaged America by Burton W. Folsom, Jr. (Threshold, 2008).

It is often said that it was World War II that finally ended the Great Depression—with some liberals such as Paul Krugman pointing to high wartime spending as the key to reviving the economy. In fact the war required ending the New Deal's war on business and commerce; this explains why the grip of the Depression was finally broken. But FDR didn't give up on class warfare easily. As late as 1942, Roosevelt proposed in his annual message to Congress, "No American citizen ought to have a maximum income, after he had paid his taxes, of more than $25,000 a year," and the Treasury Department proposed a 100 percent income tax rate on incomes above $25,000 (equivalent to about $275,000 today). FDR did not give up his radical egalitarian ways without a fight.

If FDR's admirers—including even Ronald Reagan—are correct in believing that he wasn't a socialist, how can his egalitarian class warfare be understood? Historians who reach for some kind of intellectual synthesis have overlooked Occam's Razor. The simplest explanation is that it was FDR's self-regard and will to power that led him to attack his opponents, and any source of private wealth provided a base from which to oppose his desire to exert complete control over the economy. In his second inaugural address in 1937, FDR asked for "unimagined power to subordinate private interest to the public good."

Roosevelt wanted more and more political power, and he had decided to blame business for the continuing failure of the New Deal to fix the economy. And when the Supreme Court, a co-equal branch of government, exercising its constitutional prerogative to render judgment on Roosevelt's actions, obstructed his designs, he turned on them with equal viciousness and determination to bring them to heel. In the process, he did great harm to the Constitution; the effects of that damage continue to this day.

FDR's Living Constitutionalism

Despite his intellectual incoherence, it is not the case that there was no theory underlying FDR's actions. He did express a political theory, a deeply pernicious one that built in subtle ways upon Woodrow Wilson's attack on the American Founding. Two episodes display FDR's radical break with America's constitutional traditions. The first is his Commonwealth Club speech, given late in the 1932 campaign. The second is the infamous "court packing" initiative of 1937, which is usually and incorrectly understood as a stinging political defeat for FDR.

Historians have tended to overlook FDR's Commonwealth Club speech, in part because historians tend not to take speeches seriously enough as public teachings, and in part because one of FDR's aides who helped write the speech, Rex Tugwell, later wrote that FDR "never saw that speech until he opened it on the lectern." This seems the doubtful boast of a preening speechwriter (and few New Dealers were more preening than Tugwell), but even if accurate, the fact is that the Commonwealth Club speech represents most clearly the bold new liberal public philosophy of New Deal liberalism, and

★ ★ ★ ★ ★ ★ ★ ★ ★ ★ ★ ★

FDR's Not-So-Firm Grasp on American Political Thought

"Roosevelt, himself, familiar though he was with the superficies of American history, had never evidenced, in the years of my association with him, any appreciation of the basic philosophical distinctions in the history of American political thought."

former Roosevelt aide Raymond Moley

deserves to be taken very seriously as the highest expression of FDR's political philosophy—the philosophy of the welfare state.

Unlike Woodrow Wilson's open rejection of the principles of the American founding, FDR's approach to the Constitution was more clever: Roosevelt appeared to embrace the American founding, but was in fact reinterpreting it in radical ways. The rise of the machine age, he said, called for "a reappraisal of values." Referring specifically to Thomas Jefferson's conception of individual rights as bulwarks against government power, FDR said, "The task of statesmanship has always been the re-definition of these rights in terms of a changing and growing social order." The era of Jeffersonian individualism was over, he explained:

A glance at the situation today only too clearly indicates that equality of opportunity as we have known it no longer exists.... Our task now is not discovery, or exploitation of natural resources, or necessarily producing more goods. It is the soberer, less dramatic business of administering resources and plants already in hand ... of distributing wealth and products more equitably, of adapting existing economic organizations to the service of the people. The day of enlightened administration has come.

Making the Democratic Party the Liberal Party

"I believe it is my sworn duty, as President, to take all steps necessary to insure the continuance of liberalism in our government. I believe, at the same time, that it is my duty as head of the Democratic Party to see to it that my party remains the truly liberal party in the political life of America."

Franklin Delano Roosevelt, 1941

The remedy for the new problems FDR saw would be "an economic declaration of rights, an economic constitutional order" that required "new terms of the old social contract." Although FDR did not come right out and say so, he clearly implied that individual property rights must give way to the power of the State to control economic activity.

It was but a short step from this "re-defining" of individual rights to FDR's later idea of, essentially, welfare state rights, whereby the government would provide for you instead of you providing for yourself. In his 1944 State of the Union speech, while the nation was still fighting Germany and Japan, Roosevelt extended the philosophy of the Commonwealth Club address. He talked again about how the Founders' conception of individual rights—the guarantees against government power over the individual—were obsolete, and called for "a second Bill of Rights"—"an economic Bill of Rights" in which the government would guarantee "the right to a useful and remunerative job," along with the right to food, housing, health care, and even recreation: "All these rights spell security."

During his first re-election campaign in 1936, FDR demonized the Republican Party, suggesting that Republicans were anti-American and comparing them to the Tories who left the country at the time of the American Revolution. Clearly FDR was trying to read his political opposition out of the mainstream of American political life. In his 1944 speech outlining the positive "rights" he wanted government to provide for everyone, Roosevelt wasn't satisfied merely to set out his "new principles" of government. He went on to imply that Republican opposition to his novel political philosophy was the equivalent of the Fascism we were fighting

FDR, Self-Admitted Economic Ignoramus

"Thirty-six years ago, I began a more or less intensive study of economics and economists. The course has continued with growing intensity, especially during the last four years. As a result, I am compelled to admit—or boast—whichever way you care to put it—that I know nothing of economics and that nobody else does either!"

President Roosevelt, in a 1936 letter to Joseph Schumpeter, one of the world's most famous economists

against overseas. But he used the clever tactic of attributing this thought to someone other than himself:

One of the great American industrialists of our day—a man who has rendered yeoman service to his country in this crisis—recently emphasized the grave dangers of "rightist reaction" in this Nation. All clear-thinking businessmen share his concern. Indeed, if such reaction should develop—if history were to repeat itself and we were to return to the so-called "normalcy" of the 1920's—then it is certain that even though we shall have conquered our enemies on the battlefields abroad, *we shall have yielded to the spirit of Fascism here at home.* [emphasis added]

In other words, even during wartime, when the country was supposedly united behind the war effort, Roosevelt exploited the war for partisan purposes. Speeches like this are worth remembering when contemporary liberals claim that "divisive" conservatives are "questioning their patriotism."

FDR's Assault on the Judicial Branch

FDR lashed out at the Supreme Court for refusing to rubber stamp his unprecedented New Deal controls on the private sector during his first term. (Though it should be noted that the Court did not invalidate all of FDR's measures. It upheld some of the most dubious of them, including the confiscation and arbitrary revaluation of the price of gold, and the cancellation of mortgage debt—both of which involve a plain violation of the Constitution's Contracts Clause.) After the 9–0 decision that invalidated the National Recovery Administration, Roosevelt complained that the Court was stuck in the "horse-and-buggy" era.

After his landslide re-election victory in 1936, some of Roosevelt's aides proposed that FDR back a series of constitutional amendments to provide Congress and the executive branch with the explicit power to regulate the economy more fully—in other words, that the Constitution should be changed through the mechanism the Founders had provided for just such new circumstances as Roosevelt had claimed now existed. In fact, the Democratic National Platform for the 1936 election had contemplated the possibility of amendments: "If these problems cannot be effectively solved within the Constitution, we shall seek such clarifying amendment as will assure the power to enact those laws, adequately to regulate commerce, protect public health and safety, and safeguard economic security." Roosevelt rejected this idea after the election on the excuse that the amendment process was too "time-consuming"—even though many previous constitutional amendments had passed Congress and been ratified by the states very quickly. There was something insincere about FDR's claim that the American political system could not react quickly in a genuine national emergency.

Instead, FDR decided to try to outflank the Supreme Court politically. He made an unprecedented public attack on the Supreme Court, an institution whose traditions of restraint and aloofness from politics kept the justices from defending themselves. No other president in history had ever attacked the Supreme Court as FDR did. With

★ ★ ★ ★ ★ ★ ★ ★ ★ ★ ★ ★ ★

But He Knew *He* Could Be Trusted

"Fully convinced that he knew best what was needed, Franklin D. Roosevelt conceived it as the function of democracy in times of crisis to give unlimited powers to the man it trusted, even if this meant that it thereby 'forged new instruments of power which in some hands would be dangerous.'"

Nobel Prize winner Friedrich Hayek

no prior indication of his plan during the 1936 campaign, and no discussion with or advance warning to his own party members in Congress, FDR sprang his infamous "court packing" plan in the spring of 1937, its stated intention "to infuse new blood into all our courts" and to correct the current "ill-balanced" Supreme Court. FDR wanted Congress to pass a law stipulating that for every federal judge or Supreme Court justice over the age of seventy, the president could appoint an additional judge or justice. As of 1938, six of the nine justices on the Supreme Court were over seventy; had FDR's plan been enacted, he would have immediately been able to command a Court majority for anything he wanted passed. Raymond Moley said it was "a plan to enable Roosevelt to control the Court" and suborn its independence, plain and simple; it was "a half-baked scheme which commended itself chiefly because of its disingenuousness."

The idea was so unpopular that even FDR's own party rebuked him. The lopsided Democratic majority in Congress not only rejected the proposal handily, but the Senate Judiciary Committee issued a report that harshly rebuked FDR's reasoning and defended the Court from FDR's attack, which it called a "dangerous abandonment of constitutional principle." Seldom has any presidential initiative been so categorically rejected by a president's own party. Preserving our constitutional system intact, the Committee pointed out, is "immeasurably more important ... than the immediate adoption of any legislation however beneficial." The report continued,

> If the Court of last resort is to be made to respond to a prevalent sentiment of a current hour, politically imposed, that Court must ultimately become subservient to the pressure of public opinion of the hour, which might at the moment embrace mob passion abhorrent to a more calm, lasting consideration.... No finer or more durable philosophy of free government is to be found in all the writings and practices of great statesmen than may be found

in the decisions of the Supreme Court when dealing with great problems of free government touching human rights.... It is a measure which should be so emphatically rejected that its parallel will never again be presented to the free representatives of the free people of America.

Roosevelt responded to this defeat with one of the worst temper tantrums in presidential history: he set out to purge the Democratic Party of senators and congressmen who had opposed court packing and other New Deal measures in the 1938 election. For the first and only time in history, a president openly campaigned against incumbent members of his own party, even as the nation's economy began to slump again, with unemployment increasing dramatically. FDR's attempted purge was a total failure and humiliation. Of the Democrats FDR targeted for defeat in primary elections or party caucuses, only one lost. In the November election, Republicans gained eighty-one seats in the House; in the Senate, eight seats, along with a dozen governorships. But for the specter of war, Roosevelt would probably have been defeated in the 1940 election.

The final irony is that the Supreme Court buckled under Roosevelt's attacks, dramatically reversing course in 1937 without any changes in the composition of the Court. The justices suddenly started upholding New Deal measures that were nearly identical to those they had struck down just a few years before. It was called "the switch in time that saved nine." In other words, FDR's court packing initiative actually *succeeded* in its main aim, which was to intimidate the Supreme Court into ceasing to act as a guardian of economic liberty and a limit on the extension of federal government power. Ever since, the Supreme Court

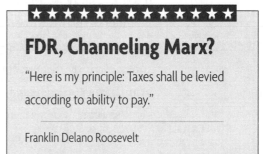

FDR, Channeling Marx?

"Here is my principle: Taxes shall be levied according to ability to pay."

Franklin Delano Roosevelt

has been on a mostly downhill slide, allowing more and more scope to government power, with only limited exceptions. The Supreme Court's abandonment of its role as guardian of constitutional limits to government power and as protector of, especially, economic rights has been called "the revolution of 1937" with good reason.

But the court packing scheme also revealed another flaw in FDR's character—his impatience. The scheme was soon shown to have been utterly unnecessary. Within three years he had been able to reshape the Supreme Court exactly as he wanted it through the conventional appointment process. Between deaths and retirements from the Court, FDR had appointed eight of the nine justices sitting on the Court by the time he died in 1945—the most of any president in American history. They were all liberals who seldom saw an extension of government power they did not approve, or an exercise of executive power they restrained.

FDR's Lasting Legacy: A Supreme Court Unconstrained by the Constitution

FDR's first appointment in 1937 was Hugo Black, who served on the Court for thirty-four years. Black had been a senator from Alabama, and also a member of the Ku Klux Klan. He has a reputation as a liberal justice, though he wrote the majority opinion in *Korematsu v. United States*, the decision that upheld FDR's authority to intern Japanese-Americans during World War II. In a 1967 newspaper interview, Black defended the *Korematsu* decision, saying, "They all look alike to a person not a Jap." Black was a judicial positivist; he upheld government power over economic rights, but not over some individual rights such as free speech. Black was the perfect justice for FDR, as he was totally compliant with liberal aims to extend government control over the economy.

FDR's second appointment was Stanley Forman Reed, in 1938. Reed had served in Roosevelt's administration, first in the Reconstruction Finance Corporation and then in the Justice Department, where he argued on behalf of several New Deal measures before the Supreme Court during FDR's first term. Like Black, Reed was known as a liberal on economics, and he deferred to Congress and the executive branch on all matters of economic regulation.

Felix Frankfurter was FDR's third Court appointment in 1939. A former Harvard Law School professor (where he had been a mentor to Louis Brandeis), Frankfurter was one of the Court's legendary liberals and champions of the idea of the "living Constitution." He served on the Court for twenty-three years.

FDR's appointee furthest to the left was William O. Douglas in 1939, who served longer (thirty-six years) than any other justice in history. Douglas was the justice who "discovered" a sweeping right to privacy in the "emanations of the penumbras" of the Constitution in *Griswold v. Connecticut* in 1965, the precursor case to *Roe v. Wade*, which legalized abortion on demand. He ruled the death penalty unconstitutional (even though it is specified in the Constitution), and stayed the execution of the Rosenbergs in 1953. Republicans attempted to impeach Douglas in the early 1970s.

FDR's appointment of Frank Murphy, the former governor of Michigan, in 1940 gave him what he had sought with his court packing scheme just three years before—a majority on the Court. Murphy served only nine years on the Court, but was pulled into the New Deal slipstream, acquiescing (with few exceptions) in the expansion of government power over the private economy.

A Book You're Not Supposed to Read

The Forgotten Man: A New History of the Great Depression by Amity Shlaes (Harper, 2007).

FDR appointed James F. Byrnes to the Court in 1941, but he served only one year before FDR tapped him to head the War Mobilization Board during World War II. Byrnes later served as secretary of state for Harry Truman, and still later became governor of South Carolina, where he supported segregation.

Robert H. Jackson was FDR's seventh appointment, in 1941. Jackson had been a long-time political aide to FDR and worked in the Justice Department as solicitor general. Jackson had a reputation as a moderate, but he was the author of the majority opinion in one of the Supreme Court's most absurd rulings, the *Wickard v. Filburn* case in 1942 that upheld the federal government's power to prohibit farmers from growing food on their own land for their own personal use. *Wickard v. Filburn* kicked over the last restraint on the ever-expanding Commerce Clause and ratified the liberal view that the government can regulate any private economic activity it wishes to. If Obamacare is not struck down by the Supreme Court, the *Wickard* case may be the precedent for upholding the individual health care mandate.

FDR's last appointment was Wiley Rutledge in 1943. Rutledge had been highly and publicly critical of the Supreme Court's earlier decisions striking down New Deal legislation, and had supported FDR's court packing scheme, so it was not surprising that FDR rewarded him with a Supreme Court appointment when a seat came open—though he had to pass over several more eminent jurists, including Learned Hand, to do so.

Between FDR's radical Progressive views about the principles of the American founding, his court packing scheme, and his left-leaning Supreme Court appointments, it is a shame that he can't be awarded a constitutional grade lower than F. His counterproductive economic policies and hyperpartisanship are just extra credit.

Chapter 8

HARRY TRUMAN, 1945–1953

"If a man is acquainted with what other people have experienced at this desk, it will be easier for him to go through a similar experience. It is ignorance that causes most mistakes. The man who sits here ought to know his American history, at least."
—*Harry Truman on the presidency*

"The only thing new in the world is the history you don't know."
—*Harry Truman*

President Truman's Constitutional Grade: C+

Harry Truman was the perfect embodiment of mid-twentieth-century big-spending, New Deal interest-group liberalism. The product of a corrupt urban machine in his home state of Missouri, Truman was pro-union and generally anti-business, and cautiously supported expanding civil rights protection for blacks. He especially delighted in partisan political battles with Republicans. Whittaker Chambers observed that Truman was "a swift jabber who does his dirty work with a glee that is infectiously impish." He relished using executive power, and proved a decisive president on many occasions, such as his controversial firing of General Douglas MacArthur during the Korean War. Truman was the very embodiment of Alexander Hamilton's call for "energy in the executive," and he did not shrink from what Hamilton called the "extensive and arduous enterprises" that history often demands of our presidents. Winston Churchill took an instant liking to Truman at the time of their first meeting in July 1945 because of what Churchill perceived to be Truman's "precise, sparkling manner and obvious power of decision."

At the same time, Truman is an excellent marker for how far to the left the Democratic Party moved in the post-war years. Indeed, the party began its long slide to the left during Truman's administration, and he battled valiantly against it, fighting off a challenge from the 1948 candidacy of the pro-Communist Henry Wallace, who had been Vice President of the United States during Franklin Roosevelt's third term. (Truman once referred to the pro-Communist elements among American liberals as "the American Crackpots Association.") It may be considered an act of God's ongoing provident care for America that FDR saw fit to replace Wallace with Truman as his running mate in 1944.

Truman would be completely unacceptable to the politically correct Democratic Party today. He embraced Biblical morality. He was a moralistic anti-Communist. He had no trouble understanding the Soviet Union as an evil empire. He routinely referred to the Soviet Communists as "barbarians." He raised hackles in 1941, when a senator, by saying that in the event of war between Nazi Germany and the Soviet Union, the United States might want to aid whichever side was losing so the two tyrannies would fight each other to the death—a remark that the Soviets remembered and resented. Upon becoming president following the sudden death of Roosevelt in April 1945, Truman immediately began taking a harder line against the Soviet Union, at that moment still our ally against Germany and Japan. "I'm tired babying the Soviets," he said.

Now More Popular with Republicans Than Democrats

"Long ago, a young farmer and a haberdasher from Missouri, he followed an unlikely path—he followed an unlikely path to the vice presidency. And a writer observed, 'We grow good people in our small towns, with honesty and sincerity and dignity,' and I know just the kind of people that writer had in mind when he praised Harry Truman."

Governor Sarah Palin, accepting the Republican nomination for vice president, 2008

Truman told his diplomatic team that the lopsided agreements favoring the Soviets had to end, and if the Soviets didn't like it, "they could go to hell." Clearly Truman would not last long in today's Democratic Party.

Truman's decision to drop the atomic bomb on Hiroshima and Nagasaki to bring World War II to a swift and sure end has generated enduring liberal guilt. Truman had not known about the atomic bomb program until he became president. In June of 1945 the American invasion of Okinawa cost the lives of 12,500 American troops, with another 36,000 wounded. The prospective invasion of the Japanese mainland would require almost a million troops. Initial estimates were that America would suffer 50,000 killed and 150,000 wounded in just the first thirty days of an invasion of the Japanese homeland. Japanese losses would surely have been a multiple of these figures, and the fighting would have dragged on into 1946. When Truman learned the news of the atomic bomb project, he immediately grasped the possibility that the war could be ended more quickly and at a much lower cost in lives for both sides, on American terms (unconditional surrender). Truman had served in the Army infantry in World War I over in France and seen action in the trenches. While Truman wrote in his diary that the decision to use the bomb was "my hardest decision to date," he went to bed and slept soundly the night after he gave the order to use it to end the war.

Liberals have never forgiven him for it, and it has been reported that Barack Obama actually wanted to visit Hiroshima and Nagasaki on his 2009 "world apology tour" to make an apology for Truman's act. It required the intervention of Japan's foreign minister to head off this insult to Japan's honor. Truman biographer David McCullough puts the

★ ★ ★ ★ ★ ★ ★ ★ ★ ★ ★ ★ ★ ★

Give 'Em Hell, Harry

Before his first White House meeting with Soviet foreign minister Vyacheslav Molotov, Truman promised to explain America's new attitude toward the Soviets "in words of one syllable." Molotov, taken aback, said to Truman, "I have never been talked to like that in my life." Truman's reply: "Carry out your agreements and you won't get talked to like that."

Not Intimidated by the Office

Truman had a measured attitude about the "burdens" of office and displayed his executive temperament in a letter to his wife Bess after just two months in the Oval Office: "It won't be long before I can sit back and study the whole picture and tell 'em what is to be done in each department. When things come to that stage there'll be no more to this job than there was to running Jackson County and not any more worry." In another letter to Bess he wrote, "Well I'm facing another tall day as usual. But I like 'em that way."

case for Truman's decision to drop the bomb with admirable clarity: "And how could a President, or the others charged with responsibility for the decision, answer to the American people if when the war was over, after the bloodbath of an invasion of Japan, it became known that a weapon sufficient to end the war had been available by midsummer and was not used?"

Despite Truman's big spending ways on domestic policy, his toleration of some Soviet spies still in place inside the government, and instances of corruption during his administration, on the whole he acquitted himself well in the Oval Office, and provides a useful model of some key traits of a successful president. It was not an accident that Ronald Reagan, who campaigned with Truman in the 1948 election (Reagan was still a Democrat then), made prominent reference to Truman as president thirty-five years later, partly as a way of demonstrating how far the post-Vietnam Democratic Party had strayed from its roots. (Reagan was especially fond of one of Truman's jokes: "An economist is a man who wears a watch chain with a Phi Beta Kappa key at one end and no watch at the other.") Sarah Palin also invoked Harry Truman during her vice presidential campaign in 2008—another sign that Truman is now more honored by Republicans than Democrats. To be sure, Truman was an accidental president, chosen in haste to be FDR's running mate in 1944, and president in the first instance because of FDR's death. But his triumphant election in his own right in 1948, after a plucky underdog campaign ("Give 'em hell,

Harry!"), has propelled him to the higher ranks of modern presidents in reputation.

The Self-Taught Statesman

As the only modern president without a degree from a four-year college, Harry Truman was largely self-taught, but also benefited from a traditional education as a young boy, before liberalism ruined public education. Truman showed a high degree of curiosity at an early age. At age ten he read through Charles Horne's four-volume set, *Great Men and Famous Women*; Truman especially enjoyed the essays on military leaders such as Alexander the Great, Hannibal, and Charles Martel. He was a devoted reader of Mark Twain, and in high school read Cicero, Plutarch, Caesar, Marcus Aurelius, Gibbon, and Shakespeare, "learning and never forgetting the vices and virtues of the ancients," in the words of biographer Alonzo Hamby. Late in life Truman reflected on what he took from his education: "I saw that it takes men to make history, or there would be no history.... So study men, not historians. You don't even have to go that far to learn that real history consists of the lives and actions of great men who occupied the stage at the time. Historians' editorializing is in the same class as the modern irresponsible columnist."

Truman's interest in history became a lifelong habit. He read history in the evenings at the White House, in part because it "might help me form an opinion as to the course I had to take." Truman carried in his wallet a copy of Lord Tennyson's poem "Locksley Hall," which begins, "For I dipt into the future, far as the human eye could see...." After he left the presidency, Truman set down that the "three great men in government" whom he most admired were Cincinnatus, Cato the Younger, and George Washington.

Most historians and biographers have ignored Truman's strong religious sentiment. It is easy to miss in part because Truman, though a Baptist, was

modest about public expressions of religion most of his life, and held ecu-
menical attitudes. "I've always believed that religion is something to live
by and not talk about," he wrote as a young man. Early in his political career
he wrote, "If a child is instilled with good morals and is taught the value of
the precepts laid down in Exodus 20 and Matthew 5, 6, and 7, there is not
much to worry about in after years. It makes no difference what brand is on
the Sunday school." (When Truman was sworn in as president, he had the
Bible turned to Exodus 20.)

As president, Truman's Christian piety loomed much larger in his life
than it had previously, in large part because he viewed the challenge of the
Cold War in religious terms—as an assault by Communism on the spiritual
foundations of Western civilization. He began to speak frequently of the
providential mission of the United States, in terms that would find their
most distinct echo in Ronald Reagan thirty years later. "God has created us
and brought us to our present position of power and strength for some great
purpose," Truman said in a speech in 1951, and that great purpose was
defending "the spiritual values—the moral code—against the vast forces
of evil that seek to destroy them." In a 1950 speech Truman was more direct:
"Communism attacks our main basic values, our belief in God, our belief
in the dignity of man and the value of human life, our belief in justice and
freedom. It attacks the institutions that are based on these values. It attacks
our churches, our guarantees of civil liberty, our courts, our democratic
form of government." "To succeed in our quest for righteousness," Truman
said, "we must, in St. Paul's luminous phrase, put on the armor of God."
Truman saw churches as the first line of defense in the war of ideas against
Communism, and was disappointed when a number of denominations
declined to enlist in an international anti-Communist religious campaign.
Truman had asked that churches endorse a statement "of their faith that
Christ is their Master and Redeemer and the source of their strength against
the host of irreligion and danger in the world." (Truman also wanted to

extend formal diplomatic recognition to the Vatican, but had to drop the idea because of Protestant opposition.) Needless to say, liberals ceased using this kind of language beginning in the 1960s.

Truman's Last Great Achievement: Cold War Strategy

Truman had many failures as a president—including the fall of China to Communism in 1949 and the grinding Korean War that began in part because of a diplomatic blunder by his secretary of state, Dean Acheson. The Korean War was one important reason for Truman's growing unpopularity with the American people. He left office in 1953 with some of the lowest public approval ratings in presidential history.

Despite the Korean War stalemate, foreign policy was Truman's main achievement. After World War II ended, the United States found itself in a position it had never been in before—the undisputed leader of the free world, but faced with a new foe that only it could match. War-weary Americans rightly looked forward to demobilization and a return to peacetime preoccupations, but the world situation was not so accommodating. Truman faced the requirement of assembling a long-term international alliance along with a strategic doctrine and defense establishment to carry on

A Book You're Not Supposed to Read

The First Cold Warrior: Harry Truman, Containment, and the Remaking of Liberal Internationalism by Elizabeth Edwards Spalding (University Press of Kentucky, 2006).

the long struggle against Communist expansionism. The U.S. had never before contemplated this kind of high-profile role in global affairs, nor had it ever maintained large-scale armed forces in peacetime. But the Cold War meant there could be no ordinary peacetime.

Truman settled on the doctrine of "containment," assembled the North Atlantic Treaty Organization (NATO), passed the Marshall Plan to help

Europe rebuild, and announced the "Truman Doctrine," according to which the U.S. pledged to aid free nations that were resisting Communist aggression (chiefly Greece in 1946). Truman succeeded in winning substantial Republican support for his grand strategy, so that it become the truly bipartisan foreign policy for almost a generation, until liberal Democrats began to jettison it piece by piece in the 1970s. But even with his own fellow Democrats abandoning the foreign policy architecture he put in place, Truman's design held long enough to find final vindication under Presidents Reagan and George H. W. Bush.

Abuse of Executive Power

Truman, generally sure-footed in his use of executive power, went too far a few times and strayed into unconstitutional territory. In 1952 Truman ordered the government to seize and operate the nation's steel mills, then threatened with a strike that Truman thought might harm the Korean War effort. As there was no statutory authority for Truman's act, he justified the seizure under his broad powers as commander in chief. The Supreme Court did not agree, ruling 6–3 that Truman had exceeded his presidential power under the Constitution and violated the separation of powers in acting without congressional authorization. (The steel industry was represented in the case by John W. Davis—the Democratic nominee for president who had lost to Calvin Coolidge in 1924.)

This was one of the rare direct clashes between the president and the Supreme Court, and a stunning rebuke to the executive branch. Two of Truman's own appointees to the Court, including his former attorney general Tom Clark, joined the majority against him. (Putting that "damn fool from Texas" on the Court was his biggest mistake as president, Truman complained. It would not be the last time a president regretted a Supreme Court appointment.)

Truman made four appointments to the Supreme Court. The first, Harold Burton, was an odd choice, as Burton was a Republican senator from Ohio. (There were no Republicans left on the Court in 1945 when the seat came open, and Truman felt pressure to nominate a Republican for "balance.") Burton was a moderate justice, generally pro-business in his opinions, who left little mark in his thirteen years on the Court. Truman's second appointment was Frederick Vinson as Chief Justice in 1946, following the death of Harlan Stone. Legal historians have regarded Vinson as an undistinguished Chief Justice and even an outright failure in his relatively brief seven years on the Court.

Truman's third appointment, of Attorney General Thomas Clark, prompted charges of cronyism, though Clark was confirmed easily. He seems to have had no clear or consistent judicial philosophy, though he was the author of the famous 1961 opinion that created the "exclusionary rule," making it more difficult for police to gather evidence against criminals. (Clark was also the father of the far left activist lawyer Ramsey Clark, attorney general in the LBJ administration.)

> ★ ★ ★ ★ ★ ★ ★ ★ ★ ★ ★ ★ ★ ★
>
> ## A President Who Saw the Point of Checks and Balances?
>
> "Whenever you have an efficient government, you have a dictatorship."
>
> Harry Truman

Truman's last appointment was Sherman Minton, a former U.S. senator and strong supporter of New Deal liberalism, including even FDR's radical court packing plan. During his brief seven years on the Court, Minton never saw an expansion of government power that he didn't approve.

Truman's Supreme Court appointments seemed to be driven mostly by old-fashioned considerations of political patronage. Neither his judicial appointments nor any of his writings or speeches give much evidence that Truman had any discernable constitutional philosophy. For these reasons he deserves as his constitutional grade a gentleman's C+.

Chapter 9

DWIGHT DAVID ("IKE") EISENHOWER, 1953–1961

"His love was not for power but for duty."
—*Presidential scholar Richard Neustadt on Eisenhower*

President Eisenhower's Constitutional Grade: C

Did you know?

★ Eisenhower's apparent incoherence at press conferences was a deliberate device to mislead his antagonists, both foreign and domestic

★ Ike was the only modern president whose popularity never dropped below 50 percent

★ He kept TV appearances to a minimum because he didn't want to bore the American people

★ Eisenhower said his two biggest mistakes as president "were both sitting on the Supreme Court"

The trajectory of Dwight Eisenhower's presidential reputation is a case study in the wrongheadedness of the dominant modern liberal view of the presidency. During Eisenhower's tenure in office, both intellectuals and the media were nearly unanimous that he was a mediocre president. A 1961 survey of historians ranked Eisenhower below such forgotten nineteenth-century chief executives as Chester Arthur. Eisenhower's towering reputation as commander of the Allied forces that invaded France on D-Day and rolled on to victory over Nazi Germany in World War II did not insulate him from the most contemptuous jokes. He was said to be inarticulate, even though he was known to be a graceful and competent writer. His fondness for golf and backyard barbecue was thought to show a lack of worldly sophistication, despite the fact that he had liberated Europe in the most ambitious military action since Hannibal—one involving extensive delicate political considerations.

Humorists of the time, presidential historian Al Felzenberg reminds us, said that Eisenhower proved that the United States didn't need a president. Then there was the "Eisenhower Doll"—wind it up and it stood there for eight years. Above all, the intellectuals said, Ike was "dumb." ("If he's so dumb," a few unbiased observers replied, "why is he such a good bridge player?") He was thought to be a creature of his staff; one joke went that while it would be bad if Eisenhower died and Vice President Richard Nixon became president, it would be even worse if Ike's chief of staff Sherman Adams died and *Eisenhower* became president. That Eisenhower was consistently popular with the American people throughout his two terms (his average Gallup Poll approval rating was an astounding 64 percent) was an additional insult to elite opinion, and was among the reasons for the contempt for middle class America that intellectuals were expressing ever more openly. The 1950s were gray, conformist, uncreative, stifling. And it was all somehow Ike's fault. They were "the yawning years of Eisenhower," as liberal writer Gary Wills put it.

A Book You're Not Supposed to Read

The Hidden-Hand Presidency: Eisenhower as Leader by Fred I. Greenstein (HarperCollins, 1982).

But in the decades since Eisenhower completed his two full terms in office, his presidential reputation has soared, even among many liberals. Starting in the late 1960s, scholars began reviewing the papers and documents from Ike's White House and were struck by the revelation that this supposedly simple-minded and bumbling man was in fact highly capable—even "cunning"—and was fully in charge behind the scenes. His supposedly inarticulate remarks at press conferences were revealed to have been deliberate devices to mislead the media and his opponents, both foreign and domestic. Derek Leebaert notes that Eisenhower was "one of the few national leaders in the electronic age who seems to have taken a close to malicious delight in his capacity for incoherence."

He has become, in the most famous formulation, the "hidden-hand president." Princeton University's Fred Greenstein, the scholar who came up with that handle, said he had always thought Eisenhower "to be the epitome of a *non*leader," but was astonished to discover that Eisenhower was "alert, politically astute," engaged, and innovative. Ike's thought process, Greenstein concluded, "was hard-headed, rigorous, and well-informed," supplemented by "an impressively coherent advisory process that augmented his own thought and action."

Greenstein, who admits that he doesn't sympathize or agree with many of Eisenhower's policies and decisions, is an excellent case study in the academic cluelessness of liberals. His bias makes him incapable of answering his own excellent question: "How and why could a president who was as politically alert and engaged as Eisenhower was have been judged by his contemporaries to be the opposite?"

The answer is simple: Eisenhower didn't conform to the post-Wilson, post-FDR liberal model of ideal presidents as miracle workers, relentlessly "leading" the American people into a bold new future according to some abstract and ambitious "vision." In style and conduct (though not so much in policy), Ike was the anti-FDR. Eisenhower conducted the presidency much more like a nineteenth-century president, that is to say, more as the Founders intended the office to be conducted. He saw himself as the "presiding" officer, taking care that the laws were faithfully executed. In fact Eisenhower was utterly unique among modern presidents in offering no legislative program at all to Congress in his first year in office, even though the Republican Party had just won a majority in Congress in the 1952 election.

Eisenhower said at the time that he wanted to "restore the balance" between the branches—flying in the face of the received liberal wisdom that the president, rather than Congress (as intended by the Founders), should be the center of gravity in our political system.

Nor did Eisenhower, who was really the first president of the television age, think it advisable to be on TV frequently, or to make continual speeches to the American people. In fact, when pressed by his advisers to make more TV or public speeches, Eisenhower shot back, "I keep telling you fellows I don't like to do this sort of thing. I can think of nothing more boring, for the American public, than to have to sit in their living rooms for a whole half hour looking at my face on their television screens.... I don't think the people *want* to be listening to a Roosevelt, sounding as if he were one of the Apostles, or the partisan yipping of a Truman." On another occasion he remarked, "What is it that needs to be said? I'm not going out there just to listen to my tongue clatter!" Often, if he relented and agreed to speak, he'd say, "All right, but not over 20 minutes." Eisenhower also had a proper disdain for the news media. "Listen," he once told his staff, "anyone who has time to listen to commentators or read columnists obviously doesn't have enough work to do."

A Master Manager

While Eisenhower conducted himself in public as a pre-modern president, in one other very important respect—actual management of the executive branch—he modernized the presidency more than anyone else. He explained to a journalist, "With my training in problems involving organization it was inconceivable to me that the work of the White House could not be better systematized than it had been during the years I had observed it." Eisenhower was the first president to have a formal chief of staff, and he instituted the first White House office of congressional relations. Next to

Harding's innovation of the Bureau of the Budget, Eisenhower is responsible for the most consequential innovation in presidential management in modern times: the formal appointment of a national security adviser, along with a regular consultative process involving the National Security Council (NSC) that has been used by every subsequent president. Truman had actually established the National Security Council, but it was Eisenhower, probably owing to his military career, who made it run smoothly as an important instrument of presidential decision-making. Eisenhower instituted weekly meetings of the council, one of the most important presidential institutions during the Cold War. Over his two terms, Ike presided over 329 of the NSC's 300 meetings.

As Eisenhower wrote in his memoirs, "Organization cannot make a genius out of an incompetent.... On the other hand, disorganization can scarcely fail to result in inefficiency and can easily lead to disaster." Eisenhower believed in a principle that was also central to Ronald Reagan's presidency—delegation: "A President who doesn't know how to decentralize," Ike wrote, "will be weighed down with details and won't have time to deal with the big issues." It is not coincidence that Reagan would receive the exact same misguided criticism—that he was "detached" and "aloof"—that was leveled at Eisenhower.

Eisenhower's deliberate management process may have played a role in one of his most sagacious decisions—the decision in 1954 *not* to intervene in Vietnam when the French were about to be defeated by the Communist

★ ★ ★ ★ ★ ★ ★ ★ ★ ★ ★ ★ ★

He Made It Look Easy

"But Eisenhower had the true professional's instinct for making things look easy. He appeared to be performing less work than he actually did. And he wanted it that way. An air of ease inspires confidence. The singer's hard work on scales should be done at home. On stage, the voice should soar as by natural gift....

"Ike's lack of pretense, his easy charm, made him seem the fulfillment of America's ideal—Everyman suddenly put in charge of the nation's destiny, the good-hearted non-professional with 'common sense.'"

Liberal author Garry Wills

Vietcong. The French collapse, coming only a year after Eisenhower had finally brought the Korean War to an inconclusive end, put enormous pressure on the U.S. to intervene directly, or at least to start an aerial bombing campaign to support a last-gasp French effort. A few advisers recommended using nuclear weapons. In rejecting intervention, Eisenhower showed judgment that eluded his successors in the 1960s, noting that "this war in Indochina would absorb our troops by the divisions."

One of Eisenhower's major foreign policy mistakes, however, shows the limitations of process-oriented structures like the NSC: Eisenhower's decision in 1956 to force the British and French to abandon their military operation to reclaim control of the Suez Canal after Egypt's radical leader Gamal Nasser had seized it. Wanting the U.S. to serve as a neutral "honest broker" in the Middle East, and also wanting America to be popular with Arab nations, Eisenhower demanded that Britain and France withdraw, a demand which had the terrible effects of weakening our closest ally, toppling the conservative British government of Anthony Eden, and strengthening Arab radicalism. Years later Eisenhower told at least two people that he had changed his mind and come to regard Suez as his biggest foreign policy mistake.

The irony is that Eisenhower, a relative anti-interventionist, decided to run for president in the first place at least partly to ensure that the Republican Party would remain committed to internationalism, and the NATO alliance in particular. The leading Republican of the time, Ohio Senator Robert Taft, had expressed isolationist sentiments and was skeptical of NATO. Taft's warnings that U.S. troops would be stationed in Europe for years to come were dismissed as so much alarmism. Eisenhower, on the other hand, had come out of retirement to become the first commander of NATO. He decided to run for president after concluding that only he could defeat Taft for the 1952 GOP nomination and solidify the Republican Party's support for international alliances.

As was the case with Herbert Hoover after World War I, both parties had hoped Eisenhower would be their presidential standard bearer. Truman asked Eisenhower directly about replacing him (Truman) on the Democratic ticket in 1948. (James Roosevelt, FDR's eldest son, also lobbied Ike on behalf of the Democrats.) As late as 1951, Truman was still saying, "My faith in him has never wavered nor ever will," though Truman was bitterly disappointed when Ike declared himself a Republican a few months later. Eisenhower decided to become a Republican in part because of what he saw as the excesses of the previous twenty years under Democratic Party rule, and the corruption of the Truman administration. Eisenhower was perhaps the first candidate to make his central campaign theme a "Crusade to Clean Up the Mess in Washington."

Not an Ideological Conservative

In some ways Eisenhower can be thought of as a small-"c" conservative, rather than an ideological conservative with fully formed views about limited government and the threats liberalism poses to free society. He described himself as a "moderate Republican," and in office he proved that he had no intention of attempting to roll back any of the basic features of the New Deal. In fact Eisenhower expanded some New Deal programs, including Social Security, and he helped to create what became the single largest federal bureaucracy by establishing the cabinet-level Department of Health, Education and Welfare. On the whole, though, Eisenhower was a fiscal conservative. He once told his Cabinet that if he was able to do nothing as president except balance the budget, he would feel that his time in the White House was well spent. Unfortunately, he made no attempt to reduce the high marginal income tax rates (91 percent at the top) that had been adopted during World War II and kept through the Korean War, even though those punitive rates retarded economic growth. The economy grew slowly during the 1950s—about 2.5 percent a year—and suffered three recessions. Eisenhower's greatest domestic legacy is probably the interstate highway system.

Another irony is that despite his foreign policy internationalism, and his own military background, Eisenhower wanted to *reduce* defense spending. Incredible as it may seem today, it was *Democrats* who criticized him for wanting to cut defense, and by the end of his presidency, John F. Kennedy was attacking Eisenhower for an entirely phony "missile gap." Eisenhower's famous farewell address warning of the dangers of a "military-industrial complex" later became a favorite quotation of the left, though in fact Eisenhower was partly trying to warn his young and inexperienced successor, John F. Kennedy, future hero of the left, away from the very adventurism that would lead to repeated disasters in the 1960s and 1970s. Even the far left writer Garry Wills retrospectively noted Eisenhower's steady leadership in contrast to JFK's: "[Eisenhower] took over a nation at war, a people fearful of atomic holocaust and poisoned milk. He left office to a man who cried for more missiles and for shock troops to fight guerrilla wars by helicopter."

No aspect of Eisenhower's presidency disappointed conservatives more than his record on Supreme Court appointments. By the time Eisenhower became president, FDR and Truman had appointed all nine members of the

★★★★★★★★★★★★★★

"The Great Tortoise on Whose Back the World Sat"

"The Eisenhower who emerges [in his memoirs] intermittently free from his habitual veils is the President most superbly equipped for truly consequential decisions we may ever have had, a mind neither rash nor hesitant, free of the slightest concern for how things might look, indifferent to any sentiment, as calm when he was demonstrating the wisdom of leaving a bad situation alone as when he was moving to meet it on those occasions when he absolutely had to.

"He was the great tortoise upon whose back the world sat for eight years. We laughed at him; we talked wistfully about moving; and all the while we never knew the cunning beneath the shell."

Liberal columnist Murray Kempton, writing in 1967

Court, and it was badly out of balance. Eisenhower was able to appoint five justices during his two terms, but he missed the opportunity to reshape the Court's ideology. Three of his appointments—John Marshall Harlan II, Charles Whittaker, and Potter Stewart—were generally judicial moderates with little stomach for arguing for a more rigorous constitutional originalism, though Harlan and Stewart did often dissent from the worst liberal decisions of the Court.

And two of Eisenhower's picks for the Court were complete disasters: Chief Justice Earl Warren in 1953, and Justice William Brennan in 1956. Warren, the former governor of California, led the Court sharply to the left especially in the 1960s, expanding the "equal protection" clause in the Fourteenth Amendment into an all-purpose grant of power for the Judiciary to rectify perceived social injustice. Warren's activism was too much even for some of the old FDR liberals on the Court, such as Felix Frankfurter.

Brennan leaned even more radically left than Warren, ruling for example that the death penalty is unconstitutional in all cases—even though the death penalty is specifically sanctioned in the Constitution. Warren actively collaborated with Brennan to bring about the most liberal possible result in Supreme Court decisions. Brennan is the author of the 1958 decision in *Cooper v. Aaron*, which declared that the Supreme Court is *the* final arbitor of the meaning of the Constitution—which would come as news to the Founders, who thought all three branches had equal claim to interpret the Constitution.

Eisenhower is said to have remarked that his two biggest mistakes as president "were both sitting on the Supreme Court," but he also betrayed a superficial understanding of the Constitution at times. In a letter to his brother, Eisenhower displayed his confusion on this point: "You keep harping on the Constitution; I should like to point out that the meaning of the Constitution is what the Supreme Court says it is. Consequently no powers are exercised by the Federal government except where such exercise is approved by the Supreme Court (lawyers) of the land." This is not the view of Calvin Coolidge or Abraham Lincoln, let alone the Founders.

Eisenhower deserves high marks for general steady leadership in the uncertain postwar decade of the 1950s, for defending the nation ably (one of the most important constitutional responsibilities of the commander in chief), and for sensible modernizations of the office of the president. Above all, Eisenhower's calm, steady leadership enabled America to settle in for the long haul of the Cold War. As the quiet and calm 1950s gave way to the tumultuous 1960s and demoralizing 1970s, Eisenhower's presidency started to look pretty good in retrospect. But for his Supreme Court appointments—especially considering the harm Earl Warren and William Brennan did to constitutional government in America—his constitutional grade must be cut down to a C+.

Chapter 10

JOHN F. KENNEDY, 1961–1963

"A man may die, nations may rise and fall, but an idea lives on."
—*John F. Kennedy*

President Kennedy's Constitutional Grade: C-

John F. Kennedy is the most overrated president. He became a mythical figure—in every sense of the term "myth"—on account of his horrible assassination by a Communist. An entire industry (backed by the Kennedy family fortune) that initially had been assembled to promote JFK to the White House went into overdrive after Kennedy's shooting to burnish his image and create the myth of "Camelot." The JFK glamorization industry still operates and has allowed successive generations of the Kennedy family to stake their own claims to fame, fortune, and political power. John F. Kennedy became the original "hope and change" figure, the tragic would-be conquering hero for liberalism. Liberals' perennial disappointment that utopia never arrives has fueled an extreme nostalgia for JFK: had he lived, liberals tell themselves, he would have delivered the nation into the promised land.

It has been a staggeringly successful marketing campaign. Even though Kennedy only served in office for 1,037 days (the one modern president to serve less time in office was Gerald Ford), opinion polls today often find Americans ranking JFK among our three or four greatest presidents (one 1991 poll had Kennedy tied with Lincoln as our greatest president). But

Did you know?

★ Kennedy was the first president born in the twentieth century and our only Roman Catholic president

★ As president, JFK took mind-altering drugs, many of them prescribed by a physician he called "Dr. Feelgood," who later lost his medical license for malpractice

★ Kenney was assassinated by a Communist

academic opinion, while still dominated by liberals, has started to judge him more clearly. A 1983 survey of historians by *American Heritage* magazine, for example, found Kennedy to be the most overrated public figure in American history.

At age forty-three Kennedy was the youngest man ever elected to the presidency (Theodore Roosevelt was our youngest president at age forty-two, but first reached the office from the vice presidency upon the death of President McKinley). Kennedy had served fourteen undistinguished years in the House and Senate, neither compiling a legislative record of note nor exerting behind-the-scenes leadership. He was known in Congress for dodging key issues; the current joke was that the author of *Profiles in Courage* (the book that had been ghost-written for him) should show more courage and less profile. Eisenhower used to refer to Kennedy as "that young whippersnapper" and "Little Boy Blue." One of JFK's many sympathetic biographers, Richard Reeves, forthrightly concludes, "He was not prepared for [the presidency]." The only modern president with less preparation for the office is Barack Obama, and their cases are similar—in both elections, soaring oratory and carefully presented image disguised the thin background the candidates would be bringing to the job.

A Book You're Not Supposed to Read

Camelot and the Cultural Revolution: How the Assassination of John F. Kennedy Shattered American Liberalism by James Piereson (Encounter, 2007).

The "Kennedy mystique" obscures three key points of interest. First, the Kennedy administration, like Bill Clinton's, underscores the importance of personal character in a president. JFK's reckless behavior, which extended beyond mere womanizing, explains some of his poor performance in office. He made a number of bad decisions impulsively. Second, JFK was not the high-octane far-left liberal that the Kennedy myth-making machine has made him out to be (though there was also disconnect between his rhetoric and his actual decisions, as well as between the reality of his presidency and his posthumous reputation). The contrast between Kennedy's views and actions in office and those of more recent liberals, especially his own younger brother, Senator Ted Kennedy, is stark. Third, Kennedy's assassination essentially caused liberals to lose their minds.

Kennedy's Recklessness

Kennedy's womanizing was on a scale that would have made Bill Clinton blush. His "extracurricular activities" in the White House were frequent and regular; the Secret Service had code names for some of the women with whom he trysted. "Fiddle" and "Faddle," for example, were the code names for two young women on the White House staff that JFK would often see together. One of Vice President Lyndon Johnson's aides remarked, "It was a revolving door over there. A woman had to fight to get into that line."

Among the many women in that line was Marilyn Monroe, whose long-running involvement with Kennedy was one of Washington's worst-kept secrets. Kennedy once requested that Monroe be his birthday present, and Monroe obliged with a breathy rendition of "Happy Birthday" at a party in New York from which Jackie Kennedy was pointedly absent. His relentless sexual escapades were not all just fun and games, though. One of his frequent sex partners was Judith Campbell Exner, who was simultaneously the mistress of Sam Giancana, a kingpin in the Mafia. Kennedy's behavior made him highly vulnerable to blackmail, especially since the news media, which knew much of the behind-the-scenes story, covered up for him—and largely continues to do so to this day. In addition, Kennedy's escapades may have literally put the nation in jeopardy, as he was on at least one occasion separated from the military aide who carried "the football," the president's command equipment for directing the nation's nuclear defenses in the event of an attack. The Kennedy industry has worked very hard and with a high

A Book You're Not Supposed to Read

A Question of Character: A Life of John F. Kennedy by Thomas C. Reeves (Free Press, 1991).

degree of success over the years to suppress critical books, documentaries, and film dramatizations that tell the seamy side of the Kennedy story.

Kennedy's womanizing was not the only aspect of his behavior that should have disqualified him from office. Although Kennedy famously projected an image of youthfulness and "vigor," he was a remarkably unhealthy man for his age. He suffered from Addison's disease, a degenerative hormonal disorder that causes muscle weakness and fatigue and ultimately destroys the adrenal glands. Treatment requires constant use of steroids, which in Kennedy's case may have exacerbated his already out-of-control sexual appetite. But Kennedy didn't stop at conventional treatment; he indulged in quack remedies from dodgy physicians (especially Max Jacobson, whom JFK referred to as "Dr. Feelgood"—Jacobson later lost his medical license for malpractice) who administered high doses of pain killers, amphetamines, and other mind-altering medications, including at least one anti-psychotic drug, in attempts to calibrate Kennedy's mental and physical energy. JFK often wore a back brace on account of severe back pain. There are well-founded rumors that he smoked marijuana and abused other illicit recreational drugs. Had Kennedy escaped assassination, there is a high likelihood that his infirmities and reckless behavior would have made him obviously unfit for office or brought his administration crashing down in scandal. (His medical records were concealed from historical researchers for more than thirty years.)

Character and Performance in Office

It is hard to say exactly how much Kennedy's physical infirmities and uncontrolled appetites for sex and drugs affected his judgment, decisions, and conduct. Kennedy's acolytes always gloss over this question, and, as in the case of Bill Clinton thirty-five years later, insist on compartmentalizing questions of character. But Kennedy's personal weakness found concrete expression in his undisciplined White House management style. Against Eisenhower's direct advice, he abandoned the formal decision-making structure that Ike had set up in favor of informal, chaotic management that more closely resembled a college faculty meeting than an orderly business or military decision structure. This chaotic approach bore bitter fruit early in his presidency with the disastrous Bay of Pigs invasion of Cuba, an operation originally contemplated under Eisenhower, but which the more careful former NATO and World War II commander would surely never have approved. The plan, which called for the U.S. to back a small force of Cuban exiles that would spearhead resistance to Castro, was poorly thought out, but Kennedy compounded his errors with a supreme act of cowardice, cancelling U.S. air support for the invasion after it was launched, thus dooming it to failure.

The Bay of Pigs was the beginning of a series of foreign policy disasters for the tough-talking Kennedy. A few months later Kennedy held a summit meeting with Soviet Premier Nikita Khrushchev, where by all accounts an ill-prepared Kennedy performed disastrously. Kennedy himself knew he had done badly, admitting that the summit was the "worst thing in my life—he savaged me." Between the Bay of Pigs and Kennedy's palpable weakness in Vienna, Khrushchev formed the view that Kennedy was weak and could be pushed around. Khrushchev threatened to go to war over the status of West Berlin, and a few weeks

★ ★ ★ ★ ★ ★ ★ ★ ★ ★ ★ ★ ★ ★

JFK's Cowardice on Berlin

"I want readers to know that Kennedy could have prevented the Berlin Wall, if he had wished, and that in acquiescing to the border closure he not only created a more danger-ous situation—but also contributed to mort-gaging the future for tens of millions of Central and Eastern Europeans. The relatively small decisions that U.S. presidents make have huge, often global, consequences."

Frederick Kempe, author of *Berlin 1961*

after the Vienna meeting decided to build the Berlin Wall instead. It took the Kennedy administration four days to send a note of protest to the Soviet Union after the Wall went up. It was one of the most debilitating retreats by the West in the entire Cold War.

Botching the Cuban Missile Crisis

Kennedy's lack of a serious response to the Berlin Wall egged Khrushchev on to the next bold stroke—the placement of ballistic nuclear missiles in Cuba in 1962, capable of striking the United States homeland in just minutes. The conventional wisdom about Kennedy's handling of the Cuban Missile Crisis is a prime example of the triumph of myth over reality. The resolution of the crisis has been portrayed as a political and diplomatic triumph for the U.S. and for Kennedy. Kennedy is said to have handled the matter "coolly," as he succeeded in getting the Soviets to remove the missiles without having to attack Cuba and risk World War III. In fact the resolution of the crisis was a strategic and political *defeat* for the United States. This fact was not generally recognized at the time only because key concessions from Kennedy were kept secret from the American people and even from most of Kennedy's top advisers at the time. Kennedy secretly agreed to withdraw American missiles from Greece and Turkey, something he had publicly stated he would not do. (When this concession leaked out years later, it was said the missiles had been "obsolete" and unimportant, a view the Soviets did not share at the time.) The biggest public concession, though, was Kennedy's pledge that the U.S. would cease attempting to overthrow the Castro regime in Cuba.

So, in exchange for removing the missiles, the Soviet Union secured the political future of Cuba, which went on to be a major threat to the interests of the United States in Latin America, and weakened the U.S. strategic position in Europe by removing our intermediate-range missiles. This aspect of the Cuban missile crisis became salient in the 1980s, when President Ronald Reagan had to exert enormous political effort to place new missiles in Europe to counter the massive Soviet missile build-up that had occurred in the decade and a half after the Cuban crisis. One wonders whether the outcome of the Cuban missile crisis was the exact outcome the Soviets intended when they put missiles in Cuba in the first place. One of the oddest aspects of the whole story that few people have ever noted is that the Soviet missiles were left out in the open in Cuba, and easily spotted by American reconnaissance. The Soviets were masters of deception and camouflage when it came to their military arsenal. It is almost as if they feared Kennedy so little that they *wanted* the U.S. to see their missiles, knowing they could exact concessions from this weak young president. It is hard to imagine the Soviets risking these moves in Berlin or Cuba during those years if they had faced a President Nixon instead.

These failures highlight the difference between opinion and judgment in a president. One of Kennedy's political virtues is that in principle he was an ardent, Truman-style Cold Warrior. He abhorred totalitarianism, loathed the Soviet Union, and had supported Senator Joe McCarthy while in the Senate. (The fact that JFK's brother Robert Kennedy worked for McCarthy's Senate committee is usually airbrushed from Kennedy histories.) JFK shared none of the self-doubt of the West and the "moral equivalence" between Communism and the free world that became so typical of liberals beginning only a few years later. Kennedy was about the last modern Democrat who sought to bolster America's defense capabilities, and opposition to Communism was his chief reason for sharply increasing defense spending. Today JFK would be counted among conservative Democrats such as Joe Lieberman. (In this he stands in marked contrast, once again, to his far-left brother Ted.) But as we have seen, tough talk was about the best JFK had to offer. His actual performance in foreign policy was weak and vacillating. And his weakness led to his most irresponsible foreign policy decision—to commit the United States to the Vietnam War with an incoherent strategy based on wishful thinking and academic abstractions.

Correctly perceiving that his weakness had called America's reputation for strength into question, JFK told Walter Cronkite that the U.S. needed to restore its credibility and toughness, and that Vietnam was the place to do so. Intervention in Vietnam, flawed from the start, began with Kennedy's impulsive and disastrous decision to approve a coup against South Vietnam's leader, Ngo Dinh Diem, a capable man whose only sin was an unacceptable human rights record and petty corruption entirely typical of Asian governments of the time. The North Vietnamese Communists rejoiced in Diem's murder; they couldn't believe their good fortune that the United States had connived to remove their most formidable political opponent in the South. The Joint Chiefs of Staff called Diem's killing the "Asian Bay of Pigs." Vice President Johnson was also scornful, calling it "playing cowboys and Indians in Saigon." The Vietnam story was all downhill from there, though Kennedy would not be around to see his handiwork collapse in ignominious defeat for the U.S.

JFK, Supply-Sider

One of the ironies of Kennedy becoming the posthumous liberal hero is that many liberals distrusted him both as a candidate and while he was president, and Kennedy had to go to significant lengths to assuage liberal doubts about him, mostly by hiring liberals for high-profile jobs and offering them constant flattery, which usually works on liberal intellectuals. JFK was notably cautious on civil rights and often fretted that the civil rights movement would be politically damaging to him. While much of his voting record on economic issues in Congress followed the main Democratic Party line—pro-union,and for a higher minimum wage—Kennedy did not embrace redistribution or trade protectionism. On the contrary, Kennedy was for economic growth and believed that "a rising tide lifts all boats." During the Eisenhower years the economy had grown at a steady rate of about 2.5 percent a year, slightly below the long-term U.S. average rate of more than 3 percent. And there had been three short and mild recessions. Kennedy felt this rate of growth was too slow, and advocated that the U.S. achieve 5 percent growth in the 1960s. Rather than adopt Keynesian-style government spending like FDR, or President Obama today, Kennedy proposed significant reductions in income tax rates, which were as high as 91 percent when he took office. Kennedy, who had gotten a C in economics at Harvard (probably to his great advantage), understood what came to be known as the supply-side effects of income tax cuts, as he explained in a major speech in 1961:

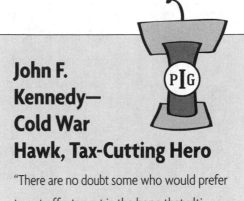

John F. Kennedy— Cold War Hawk, Tax-Cutting Hero

"There are no doubt some who would prefer to put off a tax cut in the hope that ultimately an end to the Cold War would make possible an equivalent cut in expenditures—but that end is not in view and to wait for it would be costly and self-defeating."

President John F. Kennedy, 1963 State of the Union Message

> Our true choice is not between tax reduction, on the one hand, and the avoidance of large Federal deficits on the other. It is increasingly clear that no matter what party is in power, so long as our national security needs keep rising, an economy hampered by restrictive tax rates will never produce enough revenue to balance our budget just as it will never produce enough jobs or enough profits. Surely the lesson of the last decade is that

budget deficits are not caused by wild-eyed spenders but by slow economic growth and periodic recessions, and any new recession would break all deficit records.

In short, it is a paradoxical truth that tax rates are too high today and tax revenues are too low and *the soundest way to raise the revenues in the long run is to cut the rates now*.... The purpose of cutting taxes now is not to incur a budget deficit, but to achieve the more prosperous, expanding economy which can bring a budget surplus. [emphasis added]

John Kenneth Galbraith, one of the leading liberals of the time, mocked JFK's speech advocating tax cuts, calling it "the most Republican speech since McKinley." He warned, "Once we start encouraging the economy with tax cuts, it would sooner or later become an uncontrollable popular measure with conservatives." He was right; twenty years later, Ronald Reagan, Jack Kemp, and other "supply-siders" pointed to Kennedy's example, much to the dismay and outrage of liberals.

The tax cuts didn't pass until shortly after Kennedy's death in 1964, but they worked just as Kennedy had forecast. Gross domestic product (GDP) growth accelerated to more than 5 percent a year following the tax cut—more than a full percentage point above the long-term post-war growth rate of 3.4 percent. Capital spending jumped by a third in the first two years after rates were cut; the personal savings rate increased 50 percent—the amount saved was greater than the cash delivered by the tax cut itself, suggesting that people were indeed reacting quickly to the increased relative reward for savings and investment over consumption. As supply-side theory would have predicted, productivity growth jumped by nearly a full percent. Even though top marginal income tax rates were cut from 91 to 70 percent, taxes paid by those earning more than $50,000 (which would be an income of about $350,000 today) increased nearly 40 percent between 1963 and 1965—a vindication of one of the key tenets of supply-side thinking, and a rebuttal to the main argument against tax cuts. Consumption rose less than predicted. Economist Lawrence Lindsey estimates that the tax cut generated three-quarters of the increase in the growth rate in the 1960s, while Keynesian-style increased demand accounted for only one-quarter of the higher growth. Lindsay concludes, "The tax cuts of 1964 were a major cause of the longest economic expansion then on record, which continued until 1970."

Kennedy was also an ardent free-trader, which distinguishes him from today's liberals, who mainly favor protectionism and resist free trade. He lowered tariffs on a number of products and sponsored a new round of international trade talks aimed at lowering trade barriers around the globe.

But Kennedy's economic performance was also marred by the kind of thuggishness and abuses of power that led British Prime Minster Harold MacMillan to observe that watching the Kennedy family in action was "like watching the Borgia brothers take over a respectable north Italian town." Kennedy himself once said, "My father always told me that all businessmen were sons of bitches," which is curious as his father, Joseph P. Kennedy, had been one of the nation's leading businessmen back in the 1920s and 1930s, when the family fortune was made. President Kennedy often abused his power to harass businessmen and businesses that resisted or criticized his economic policies. When the steel industry raised prices more than Kennedy wished, he used the FBI and the IRS to harass steel company

★ ★ ★ ★ ★ ★ ★ ★ ★ ★ ★ ★ ★

Thieving Kennedys?

When President Franklin Roosevelt appointed millionaire businessman Joseph P. Kennedy (John F. Kennedy's father) to be the first chairman of the new Securities and Exchange Commission, and many leading Democrats objected because of Kennedy's shady business background, FDR replied, "Set a thief to catch a thief."

executives until they rescinded the price increases. These interventions betray a lack of respect for free markets and the limits of executive power alike.

Kennedy's Political Legacy

Our perception of Kennedy is and will always be shrouded by his horrible assassination, which enabled the myth of the young tragic hero whose immense promise was unfulfilled. The romantic haze that came to surround our memory of the man combined with political partisanship to create some frightful results. The increasingly paranoid left embraced wild conspiracy theories (think "Grassy Knoll") on JFK's killing, while the news media strove to blame the assassination on conservatives for supposedly creating a "climate of hate." Neither the left nor the media—nor the Washington establishment for that matter—wished to face up to the unpleasant fact that a dedicated Communist killed Kennedy.

Political scientist James Piereson's penetrating book on the aftermath of Kennedy's killing, *Camelot and the Cultural Revolution*, argues that that fact (as well as the liberal obfuscation of it) is as important for judging the totality of Kennedy's effect on American politics as was his record in office. "The assassination of a popular president by a Communist should have generated a revulsion against everything associated with left wing doctrines," Piereson writes. "Yet something close to the opposite happened. In the aftermath of the assassination, left wing ideas and revolutionary leaders, Marx, Lenin, Mao, and Castro foremost among them, enjoyed a greater vogue in the United States than at any time in our history." Piereson argues convincingly that it was the reaction to the assassination within the mainstream American establishment, as well as among liberal intellectuals, that caused liberalism essentially to suffer a nervous breakdown.

That Kennedy was killed at the hands of a Communist should have had a clear and direct meaning: "President Kennedy was a victim of the Cold

War." But everyone had reasons for averting their gaze from this fact. For Lyndon Johnson, it would have carried frightful implications for foreign policy if it had turned out that Lee Harvey Oswald had links to Castro or the KGB (which Piereson suggests is remotely possible). And liberals didn't want to dwell on this fact for a mix of other reasons, as well—among them, that they would have had to give up their cherished illusion that right-wing extremists were somehow responsible for the assassination. In the early hours after JFK was shot, we didn't yet know of Oswald's Communist background, and the media jumped to the conclusion that Kennedy's killing must have been the work of right-wing extremists. The day after the assassination, James Reston wrote in the *New York Times* that the assassination was the result of a "streak of violence in the American character" and that "from the beginning to the end of his administration, [Kennedy] was trying to tamp down the violence of extremists from the right."

This "meme," as we would say today, took hold so quickly that it could not be shaken, even after Oswald's noxious background began to come out. Indeed, the notion of collective American responsibility for political violence would be repeated five years later after Robert Kennedy was murdered by an Arab radical who professed deep hatred for America. Piereson's analysis suggests that the phenomenon of liberal guilt owes its origin to JFK's assassination: "Once having accepted the claim that Kennedy was a victim of the national culture, many found it all too easy to extend the metaphor into other areas of American life, from race and poverty to the treatment of women to the struggle against Communism."

Besides implanting the idea of the collective guilt of American society, Kennedy's assassination disoriented American liberals in several other ways. "The claim that the far right represented the main threat to progress and democratic order," Piereson writes, "was no longer credible after a Marxist assassinated an American president." The assassination "seemed to call for some kind of intellectual reconstruction" on the left. Instead, the left lost its mind.

JFK's Constitutional Legacy

Kennedy made only two appointments to the Supreme Court, with his first, former labor union lawyer Arthur Goldberg, stepping down from the Court after only four years to become U.S. ambassador to the United Nations. In his brief tenure, Goldberg voted consistently with the liberals.

Kennedy's second appoint was more interesting: Byron White, nicknamed "Whizzer" on account of his athletic career. White had been a college football star, and played for both the Pittsburgh Steelers and Detroit Lions in the NFL, with naval duty during World War II in between his stints with those teams. White, who served for thirty years on the Court, was often described in the media as a "pragmatist"—which means liberals couldn't count on his vote. Indeed, White is the only Democratic appointment to the Supreme Court in the twentieth century who moved to the right while on the Court. He generally voted to uphold civil rights laws, but he voted against racial quotas and the *Miranda* decision, and in favor of the death penalty. Most significantly, he was one of the two dissenting votes in the infamous *Roe v. Wade* decision that legalized abortion on demand. White further disappointed liberals when he wrote the majority opinion in the 1986 case *Bowers v. Hardwick*, which upheld Georgia's statute outlawing sodomy. White's opinion asked whether the Constitution creates "a fundamental right upon homosexuals to engage in sodomy," and concluded the answer was "No": "[T]o claim that a right to engage in such conduct is 'deeply rooted in this Nation's history and tradition' or 'implicit in the concept of ordered liberty' is, at best, facetious."

John F. Kennedy probably put little serious thought into the judicial philosophies of either Goldberg or White, but his accidental pick of White mitigates some of his abuses of executive power, earning him a bump in his constitutional grade to a C-.

Chapter 11

LYNDON BAINES JOHNSON, 1963–1969

"We have the opportunity to move not only toward the rich society and the powerful society, but upward to the Great Society."
—*Lyndon Baines Johnson*

President Johnson's Constitutional Grade: F

L yndon Johnson is a paradoxical figure in American political history, offering useful lessons in the profound differences between legislative skill and executive skill. He was a masterful politician in the U.S. Senate, where he rose quickly to become majority leader in the 1950s, yet his political skills seemed to desert him after he became president following John F. Kennedy's assassination. Johnson was, Daniel Patrick Moynihan pointed out, "the first President to have spent his entire adult life in Washington DC, the company town of the American Republic."

On the level of personal character, Johnson was a mix of hypocrisy and high-octane opportunism. He was the crudest person in American politics since Andrew Jackson. Nearly every description of Johnson employs the adjective "earthy" to describe his crude countenance and his scatological language. Johnson outraged pet lovers everywhere when he picked up his dog by the ears in the presence of reporters on the White House lawn, and similarly offended sensibilities when he lifted up his shirt to display a

Did you know?

★ Johnson earned the nickname "Landslide Lyndon" by stealing a close election for the U.S. Senate in 1948

★ Johnson repeatedly reassured Ho Chi Minh by diplomatic channels that the U.S. had no plans to destroy North Vietnam, or seize its territory

★ Crime rose *20 percent per year* during Johnson's "Great Society" "War on Poverty"

surgical scar on his stomach. "Lucky for us," comedian Dick Gregory commented, "that he didn't have hemorrhoid surgery."

Johnson's definitive biographer, Robert Caro, describes him as power-hungry, cruel, bigoted, ruthless, deceitful, vain, grasping, and even "immoral." During his years in the Senate, he urinated in public, raged at and belittled his staff, used racist epithets with abandon, stole elections, and collected prodigious sums of campaign donations in cash. How much of that money may have ended up in Johnson's own pocket is a matter of speculation, but he eventually retired from politics a multi-millionaire on account of his inside dealings in Washington. Another liberal journalist, Robert Sherrill, described Johnson as "treacherous, dishonest, manic-aggressive, petty, spoiled." And what Johnson wrought in his drive to fulfill his personal ambitions at the expense of the American taxpayer is now threatening to ruin the nation. The fiscal abyss that the United States is facing today can be traced directly to programs Johnson created, especially to Medicare and Medicaid.

Johnson had a voracious appetite for political achievement, and an unquenchable thirst for distinction and adulation. He liked to claim that an ancestor fought at the Alamo—an easily disproven claim—and he exaggerated his modest World War II record. "Johnson's instinct for power," political journalist Theodore White wrote, "is as primordial as a salmon's going upstream to spawn."

Johnson was masterful in the political arts of persuasion, arm-twisting, and horse-trading. Goldwater described two modes of the legendary "treatment"—the "Half-Johnson" (one arm around your shoulder) and the "Full-Johnson" (facing you squarely just a few inches from your face with both

★★★★★★★★★★★★★★★

But Tell Us How You Really Feel about Him

"He couldn't pour piss out of a boot if the instructions were printed on the heel."

a mild (actually printable) example of the kind of language LBJ was known for

arms on your shoulders). He nearly always got his way. Alabama Governor George Wallace, summoned to a White House confrontation over civil rights (at the time, Wallace was captain of the rearguard trying to preserve segregation in the South), emerged from his one-on-one meeting with LBJ saying, "If I hadn't left when I did, he'd have had me coming out *for* civil rights." But despite his forcefulness and political success, Johnson still felt unloved.

There do not appear to have been any political principles at Johnson's core. Johnson once said, "It's not the job of a politician to go around saying principled things." The Constitution, Johnson also remarked, is a series of compromises—but Johnson seemed to have little awareness of or regard for the principles underlying those compromises. For much of his congressional career he was a typical conservative Southern Democrat. In 1948, Congressman Johnson had criticized proposed civil rights laws in terms that made Barry Goldwater look mild by comparison: "This civil rights program about which you have heard so much is a farce and a sham—an effort to set up a police state in the guise of liberty. I am opposed to that program." Johnson wrote to constituents in 1957 and again in 1960 that "I am firmly opposed to forced integration and I firmly believe that the doctrine of states' rights should be maintained." As Senate majority leader, Johnson worked to water down the civil rights legislation that President Eisenhower had proposed to Congress.

It wasn't until Johnson began to have his own presidential ambitions in the late 1950s that he started to become more liberal. In fact, Johnson remarked the day after Kennedy's assassination, "To tell the truth, John F. Kennedy was a little too conservative to suit my taste." But even after Johnson became vice president and then president and swung hard to the left, he still disliked the liberal Eastern establishment. "Bigotry is born in some of the *New York Times* people," he once remarked. When Johnson heard in 1968 that rioters threatened to burn down Washington D.C.'s elite Georgetown, he said gleefully, "I've waited 35 years for this day." The contempt was mutual; Johnson had never been held in much esteem among liberals. William F. Buckley Jr. observed, "If America's liberals had been informed in 1960 that the race in 1964 would be between Lyndon Johnson and Barry Goldwater, they would probably have marched out into the ocean and drowned themselves."

And yet Johnson enacted more liberal legislation than any Democratic president in history, FDR included. LBJ wanted to outdo FDR in social legislation. Senate Majority Leader Mike Mansfield declared, "Johnson has outstripped Roosevelt, no doubt about that. He has done more than FDR ever did or ever thought of doing." And ever since, liberals have come to see Johnson as one of their great unsung heroes, his legacy marred only by the hated Vietnam War. So his biographer Robert Caro, harsh in his descriptions of Johnson's character and behavior, forgives it all: "He was to be the President who, above all Presidents save Lincoln, codified compassion, the President who wrote mercy and justice into the statute books by which America was governed."

The "Great Society" and the "War on Poverty": Johnson Fails at Home

Johnson's chief vehicles for becoming the new FDR were his "Great Society" and "War on Poverty." The first major milestone on the road to Johnson's Great Society was the passage of the 1964 Civil Rights Act. Although

Republicans in Congress actually supported the Civil Rights Act in larger proportion than Democrats (a fact that Republicans seem to forget and Democrats want to deny), some Republicans—such as presidential candidate Barry Goldwater—opposed the Civil Rights Act because they thought it would lead to quota hiring. Johnson and other leading Democrats simply lied about the effect of the law, denying that the Civil Rights Act would lead to quotas. Yet within a year Johnson's administration began the modern "affirmative action" regime that is a thinly disguised racial quota system. Johnson admitted as much in a famous speech at Howard University where he repudiated equality of opportunity and openly called for policies leading to equal results.

Johnson announced the "Great Society" and the "War on Poverty" in speeches shortly after he took over from JFK. The "war on poverty" slogan shows the extravagance of LBJ's political vision. John F. Kennedy's people, who had cautiously described their emerging antipoverty effort the year before as an "attack" on poverty, wanted to start out small and see what might work. Johnson was impatient with this incremental approach. "I was certain we could not start small," Johnson wrote in his memoirs. "It had to be big and bold and hit the whole nation with real impact.... I didn't want to paste together a lot of existing approaches. I wanted original, inspiring ideas."

> ★ ★ ★ ★ ★ ★ ★ ★ ★ ★ ★ ★ ★ ★ ★ ★
>
> ## After 48 Years, Is It Time to Bring the Troops Home?
>
> "This administration today, here and now, declares unconditional war on poverty in America."
>
> Lyndon Baines Johnson in his state of the union speech on January 8, 1964

"All the living principals agree today," journalist Nicholas Lemann has written, "that one thing Kennedy would not have done is publicly declare war on poverty." Several of Kennedy's people who stayed on under Johnson hated the phrase. "I would never recommend to Robert Kennedy or the president of the United States that you could get up and announce to anybody that we're going to solve poverty," David Hackett said later. Notre Dame University President Father Theodore Hesburgh told Johnson that "it's just a terrible title." But Johnson and his inner circle concluded that any more modest phrase was inadequate to the ambition of their policy. It had to be total war. The social scientists raced to start program after program, with ambitious-sounding names like Model Cities, the Community Action Program, and Head Start. One of the poverty warriors, Sargent Shriver, publicly declared that all poverty in America would be abolished within ten years.

What the social engineers got instead was a wave of urban riots, accelerating family breakdown among the poor, and a skyrocketing crime rate. The irony of the "Great Society" "War on Poverty" was that Johnson and the genius social scientists around him thought they were being *conservative*. Johnson himself once said that anti-poverty programs should have "no doles." Instead of simply giving people money or putting people to work in jobs programs, the focus was on "empowerment." Thus the famous "community organizer" Saul Alinsky made use of Johnson administration grant programs to pay for his political activities. Johnson's paradoxical dislike of welfarism boiled to the surface once when he found that money for "illegitimate kids" had been left in a budget proposal after he had demanded

★ ★ ★ ★ ★ ★ ★ ★ ★ ★ ★ ★ ★ ★ ★

But Who's Keeping Score?

Ronald Reagan quipped, "We declared war on poverty, and poverty won."

that it be taken out. To Elmer Staats, the deputy budget director, Johnson exploded in language that could have come straight from the Goldwater campaign: "I told you to cut the damn thing out.... They want to just stay up there and breed and won't work and we have to feed them ... I told you we don't want to take care of all these illegitimate kids and we want to make 'em get out there and go to work.... I don't want to be taking taxpayers' money and paying it to people just to breed." What the Johnson administration did was much worse than simply giving money to poor people. The policies Johnson implemented in pursuit of the "Great Society" effectively destroyed the social capital that was holding together neighborhoods and families in some of the poorest parts of 1960s America.

The reaction of liberals in general and Johnson in particular to the serial failures of their social policy was simple denial. Their refusal to acknowledge the real effects of their policies was seen in no area more clearly than crime. Serious crime, which had been flat since 1950, grew by about 20 percent a year starting in 1964. Johnson's radical attorney general, Ramsey Clark, who would later distinguish himself for embracing every anti-American enthusiasm that erupted anywhere in the world, worked the denial angle hard, saying in 1967, "The level of crime has risen a little bit, but there is no wave of crime in the country." What about the statistics showing crime rising 20 percent a year? a reporter asked Clark. "We do ourselves a great

> ## A Book You're Not Supposed to Read
>
> *Losing Ground: American Social Policy 1950–1980* by Charles Murray (Basic, 1984). Though not narrowly focused on LBJ, this is the best critique of the Great Society welfare state that exploded under the Johnson administration.

disservice with statistics," Clark answered. This stubborn denial of the reality about increasing crime, which the public understood all too well, would prove to be deeply damaging to liberalism—long term, perhaps the liberals' most self-defeating mistake.

Johnson appointed a special commission to inquire about the crime wave and what could be done about it. The commission reported in February 1967 that there was nothing the government could do to reduce crime. "The underlying problems are ones that the criminal justice system can do little about," the commission said. "Unless society does take concerted action to change the general conditions and attitudes that are associated with crime, no improvement in law enforcement and administration of justice, the subjects this Commission was specifically asked to study, will be of much avail." Their prescription was of the "hair of the dog that bit you" type, calling for more of the very policies that Johnson was already pursuing. The commission's report was an endorsement for enlarging the Great Society: "Warring on poverty, inadequate housing and unemployment, is warring on crime. A civil rights law is a law against crime. Money for schools is money against crime. Medical, psychiatric, and family-counseling services are services against crime." The commission endorsed, among other progressive measures, giving convicts furloughs to work in the community during daytime hours. The only measures the commission didn't endorse were the ones the public most strongly desired: money for police protection and more prisons. To the contrary, the commission endorsed leniency toward criminals: "Above all, the Commission's inquiries have convinced it that it is undesirable that offenders travel any further along the full course from arrest to charge to sentence to detention than is absolutely necessary for society's protection and the offenders' own welfare." Another report the following year said the unrest in America came about because the federal government didn't spend enough money on social programs.

The Vietnam War: Johnson Fails Abroad

In his prosecution of the Vietnam War, Johnson was responsible for a disaster that fully matched the wreckage created by his domestic policies. His escalation of the war starting in 1964 began with a deception of the public. Johnson's conduct of the war continued with massive self-deception rooted in his faith in the same kind of expert pretensions that brought about the failures of the War on Poverty.

During the presidential campaign of 1964, Johnson assured voters that America sought "no wider war": "We are not going to send American boys away from home to do what Asian boys ought to be doing for themselves."

But Johnson also privately resolved, "I am not going to lose Vietnam. I am not going to be the President who saw Southeast Asia go the way China went."

Johnson decided to exploit a confusing skirmish involving U.S. navy ships in the Gulf of Tonkin near North Vietnam in the summer of 1964 to obtain congressional authorization to engage in more military action. But this did not mean going to war to defeat an enemy. Johnson and the Pentagon "whiz kids" under defense secretary Robert McNamara regarded Vietnam more as a social science proj-ect in "behavior modification" than as a war. Vietnam was to be the proving ground for the new doctrine of "flexible response." The object

> ### A Book You're Not Supposed to Read
>
> *Lyndon Johnson's War: The Road to Stalemate in Vietnam* by Larry Berman (W. W. Norton & Co., 1989).

of bombing and other military actions was not to achieve victory in the ordinary historical sense, but to "communicate" with the North Vietnamese, in order to achieve a negotiated settlement. In retrospect, diplomatic tele-grams and letters might seem a better method of negotiation than intermit-tent bombing raids and a slow build-up of ground troops with no strategy for victory.

Johnson emphasized that the U.S. wished to "communicate" to North Vietnam that our objectives were narrowly defined, and that our response would be "limited." The word "limited" appeared three times in the draft of the public statement Johnson shared with congressional leaders after the Gulf of Tonkin. Republican Senate Leader Everett Dirksen criticized this rhetorical restraint: "If I had to do it I would put the word 'limited' in deep freeze." Other legislators in the meeting echoed Dirksen. Johnson waved off their criticism, saying, "We are not going to take it lying down, *but we are not going to destroy their cities*" [emphasis added].

These and subsequent statements and actions from Johnson actually reassured the North Vietnamese that they need not fear the destruction of their nation at the hands of the mighty United States. Johnson and his civilian war planners were playing right into the North's hands, a fact that would not even begin to become dimly evident to them for another three years. At the outset of the intermittent and highly ineffective "Rolling Thunder" bombing campaign, McNamara told the Joint Chiefs of Staff that the limitations on the bombing campaign were designed to make sure the North Vietnamese did not get "the wrong signal and think we are launching an offensive." To ensure that neither North Vietnam nor China would misinterpret the "signals" American military force was intended to convey, the U.S. sent a Canadian diplomat, Blair Seaborn, as an intermediary to reassure North Vietnam that the U.S. "had no designs on the territory of North Vietnam, nor any desire to destroy the D.R.V. [the Communist 'Democratic Republic of Vietnam']." Johnson also had the American ambassador to Poland convey a letter to China's envoy to Poland stating that the U.S. had no intention of destroying North Vietnam. "There were men of eminence in the administration," Johnson aide John P. Roche recalled, "who were certain that the first time an American jet flew over Hanoi, Ho [Chi Minh] would come running out with a white flag."

"A great nation," the great British commander the Duke of Wellington wrote, "can have no such thing as a little war." The travail of Vietnam arose from the confusion of the serious business of war and politics with an exercise in crisis management. Turning war into an analytical abstraction violated a basic axiom of Clausewitz against "mistaking war for, or trying to turn it into, something that is alien to its nature."

The North Vietnamese leaders were not programmed according to the whiz kids' game theory. They fully intended to employ the same strategy against the U.S. that they had employed against the French: escalate the war to the point where it became politically unsustainable in the U.S. North Vietnamese Premier Pham Van Dong had prophesied to journalist Bernard

Fall in 1962 that "Americans do not like long inconclusive wars—and this is going to be a long inconclusive war."

How could such an astute politician as Johnson persist for so many years in misjudging the nature of his most determined political enemy, North Vietnam's Ho Chi Minh? Johnson was convinced that North Vietnam would quickly roll over under enough "graduated pressure" from the U.S. At one early point Johnson expressed his confidence in the ill-conceived strategy with one of his typically earthy phrases: "I've got Ho's pecker in my pocket." John P. Roche wrote years later that he could not make Johnson understand that Ho Chi Minh was a dedicated Leninist, intent on complete victory over South Vietnam and the defeat of the United States. Johnson, Roche recalls, kept asking, "'What does Ho want?' as if Ho were a mayor of Chicago holding out for five new post offices." Such a question could only come from a man for whom politics is merely a nihilistic series of deals, utterly without principle.

Besides failing to cow Ho Chi Minh with his scheme of "graduated pressure," Johnson also failed to offer much of a public defense or argument for his Vietnam policy. Johnson did not give a serious public speech about the purpose of the war until September 1967—which was way too late. By 1968, Johnson had lost confidence in the war he had never understood in the first place. There were over 500,000 American troops in Vietnam by the winter of 1968, and although they always prevailed in combat against the Communist Viet Cong guerillas and North Vietnamese regular army, the lack of a victory strategy always left the initiative to the Communists, and they exploited that advantage skillfully in the Tet Offensive in January 1968. Although the Communist attack failed

An Undiplomatic Answer from a Well-Known Diplomat

"Why don't people like me?" a plaintive LBJ asked Dean Acheson. Acheson's answer: "Because you are not a very likeable man."

★ ★ ★ ★ ★ ★ ★ ★ ★ ★ ★ ★ ★ ★

A Victim of the Mob?

"In a sense, he was the first American President to be toppled by a mob. No matter that it was a mob of college professors, millionaires, flower children, and Radcliffe girls."

Daniel Patrick Moynihan

completely in military terms, it was a political triumph for North Vietnam *in the United States*, where the liberal media and the radical left anti-war movement savaged Johnson. Challenged by rival Democrats Robert F. Kennedy and Eugene McCarthy and facing defeat in the primaries, Johnson withdrew as a candidate for re-election in March 1968.

Johnson's costly decision to pursue a non-victory strategy in Vietnam left a bitter legacy. By the time Nixon succeeded him, victory in the war was not a realistic possibility—though Nixon certainly did better than Johnson for a time. Johnson left behind "the Vietnam syndrome," an atmosphere of self-doubt about the efficacy and legitimacy of American power in the world that persists to this day. Every time American forces engage in the world, whether in Bosnia, Afghanistan, Iraq, or Somalia, the reflex of the left is to say it is "another Vietnam"—mostly because the left actually wishes for another American defeat. Sometimes, as in the case of Somalia in 1993, the comparison is justified because American civilian strategists repeat many of Johnson's mistakes.

A Low Point in Judicial History

Johnson made two appointments to the Supreme Court. His first, Abe Fortas, was an old New Deal liberal who had defended Communists from Joseph McCarthy's investigations in the 1950s, so it was not at all surprising that he joined the Court's liberal wing when he arrived in 1965. Fortas saw the Equal Protection and Due Process clauses of the Constitution as a broad writ of power for the Court to pursue "social justice." Johnson tried to make

Fortas Chief Justice in 1968 when Earl Warren announced his intention to resign, but in a surprising turn of events, Fortas was forced to resign in disgrace when it was revealed that he had accepted improper payments from former clients and other outside parties.

Johnson's second appointment was Thurgood Marshall, the first black to serve on the Supreme Court. Marshall had been the lead attorney for the NAACP, and had argued a string of major civil rights cases before the Supreme Court, including the most famous of all, *Brown v. Board of Education*, which ended public school segregation in 1954. Once on the Court, Marshall became one of the most anti-constitutional justices ever to serve. He effectively repudiated the arguments he had made before the Supreme Court that the Constitution should be interpreted in a "color blind" fashion, and defended race-conscious quotas. He opposed the death penalty and dissented in every death penalty case, even though the death penalty is explicitly sanctioned in the Constitution. But the low point came in 1987, when Marshall announced that he would not celebrate the bicentennial of the Constitution because the Founders were racists who sanctioned slavery—an ignorant contrast with the perspective of Frederick Douglass, who always understood the original Constitution to be an anti-slavery document because of its embedded principles. Marshall's attitude was very strange coming from a person charged with a duty of defending and interpreting the Constitution.

★ ★ ★ ★ ★ ★ ★ ★ ★ ★ ★ ★ ★ ★ ★

Too Bad Obama Won't Talk to the Europeans This Way

When France withdrew from NATO in 1966 and ordered all American troops removed from French soil, Johnson instructed his secretary of state, Dean Rusk, to ask French President Charles de Gaulle whether the 60,000 American troops buried at Normandy should be removed and brought home, too.

Lyndon Johnson may have been a disastrous liberal in domestic policy, and a terrible strategist in Vietnam, but at least he didn't go around apologizing for America.

Between his dreadful Court appointments, his heedless expansion of government bureaucracy and the welfare state, and his duplicity in passing a civil rights law that warped constitutional principles of equality under the law, Johnson's constitutional grade is an F.

Chapter 12

RICHARD M. NIXON, 1969–1974

"If an individual wants to be a leader and isn't controversial, that means he never stood for anything."
—*Richard M. Nixon*

President Nixon's Constitutional Grade: C+

Richard Nixon presents a special problem for conservatives. He is rightly honored for his role in exposing the Communist spy Alger Hiss early in his career. Yet he flirted with socialism both abroad and at home, instigating the policy of détente with the Soviet Union that demoralized Cold War foreign policy and emboldened the Soviets, and imposing wage and price controls on the American economy. Nixon despised liberals but largely governed as one, trying relentlessly to ingratiate himself with the liberal establishment even though he knew instinctively that liberals would never respect or accept him.

He had the most complicated character of any modern president—supremely intelligent and visionary, but also petty, vindictive, and paranoid—the latter trait said to be among the reasons his presidency self-destructed in the scandal of Watergate. On the merits, there would seem to be little reason for conservatives to approve of Richard Nixon, and indeed during his presidency many leading conservatives openly attacked him. M. Stanton Evans, chairman of the American Conservative Union at the time, famously said, "There are two things I don't like about President Nixon: his domestic policy, and his foreign policy."

Did you know?

★ The legend that Nixon had a "secret plan" to end the Vietnam War is a media-made myth

★ The infamous "Christmas bombing" of Vietnam actually had one of the lowest casualty totals of any bombing campaign—because the U.S. targeted military sites

★ Under Nixon, federal spending on social issues exceeded spending on defense for the first time in the history of the Republic

★ Federal regulations grew only 19 percent under LBJ, but *121 percent* under Nixon

And yet Nixon deserves to be defended by conservatives because of the viciously unfair attacks on him from the left, and in particular because the standard narrative of the Watergate scandal is in error. Putting Nixon into clearer perspective offers many important lessons: on the distorted media and historical accounts of that turbulent time; on the low character of the left; on the fundamental problems of uncontrollable bureaucracy; and on the constraints facing any modern president who attempts to seriously confront the left and reform the government.

Nixon's Complicated Character and Forgotten Magnanimity

Watergate will forever cloud the talents and supreme ability that brought Nixon to the summit of public life. Henry Kissinger has likened Nixon's complex character and fate to a Shakespearean tragedy; Fred Greenstein thinks him a Dostoyevskian character. Nixon was shy and introverted—not the best traits for a politician—but could also be charming and highly effective with both small and large audiences. Friend and foe alike have testified to his first-class intellect. The Nobel Prize-winning economist Milton Friedman, who met with Nixon on several occasions to discuss economic and social policy, wrote that "few if any [presidents] have had a higher I.Q.... He was also personally pleasant."

There is no doubt that liberal hostility toward Nixon hardened him and aggravated his own animosities. Probably no president of the twentieth century took office with such a fund of hatred among his enemies and critics—most of which arose from his role in the exposure of Alger Hiss, and his supposed "Red-baiting" campaign against Helen Gahagan Douglas in the 1950 California Senate election. Liberals would never forgive these transgressions against good will and good taste. "The hatred he evoked in his political opponents was extraordinary even by the turbulent standards of American democracy," Kissinger observed. "The *New York Review of Books*," political journalist Theodore White noted, "treats him as if he does not belong to the human race." Nixon reciprocated, saying that his enemies should be "kicked in the groin." And historian Paul Johnson has observed, "The Eastern liberal establishment never really admitted the legitimacy of the Nixon administration. From the start, the media interests which spoke for the

★★★★★★★★★★★★★★ Nixon the Eternal Enigma

"I still remain mystified by the personality of the perhaps most complex President of the twentieth century…. It would take a poet of Shakespearean dimension to do justice to the extraordinary, maddening, visionary, and debilitating personality of Richard Nixon."

Henry Kissinger

establishment treated the Nixon presidency as in some metaphysical sense an outlaw regime whose true, unconstitutional character would eventually be exposed."

His greatest election victory, the landslide forty-nine-state sweep in 1972 over George McGovern, left him feeling strangely melancholy—a state of mind Nixon said he could not explain. Nixon's legions of enemies have fixed on a supposed "pettiness" as the core of Nixon's character, and history has forgotten Nixon's great act of magnanimity: not contesting the results of the 1960 presidential election, which Nixon lost to John F. Kennedy by the narrowest of margins.

That the election was stolen from Nixon has never been seriously doubted. Many people, including the outgoing President Eisenhower, urged Nixon to contest the results, demand recounts in Illinois and Texas where the most votes were stolen, and file legal challenges. Nixon refused, because he knew that such an unprecedented political fight would be damaging to the nation. The contrast with Vice President Al Gore's conduct after the close 2000 election is plain to see.

The Embattled President

The most significant fact about the Nixon presidency is that Nixon was a wartime president—arguably the most beleaguered incoming president since Abraham Lincoln in 1860. Like Lincoln, Nixon wasn't just fighting a foreign foe: the antiwar movement of the left openly wished for America's defeat in the Vietnam War Nixon had inherited from President Johnson, and liberal Democrats who had supported the war effort under Kennedy and Johnson were cowed by the revolt of the radical wing of their party. Hence, as Henry Kissinger observed, "The new Nixon Administration was the first of the postwar generation that had to conduct foreign policy without the national consensus that had sustained its predecessors largely since 1947."

By the time Nixon took office in 1969, Vietnam had become the nation's longest war, with war deaths surpassing the Korean War total. The U.S. troop level peaked at 543,000 in the spring of 1969. Nixon shared the nation's frustration, but dared not openly show it. That Nixon had advertised a "secret plan" to end the war during the 1968 campaign is a commonplace of Nixon lore, but this is a myth largely generated by a wire service story. Nixon had said no such thing. The phrase "secret plan" had been used in a question directed to Nixon in a New Hampshire town meeting, but attributed to Nixon in a UPI story that was only belatedly corrected. Nixon had to handle the issue carefully; it would hardly have served his purpose to refute the story and say that he had no plan. Instead Nixon said, quite reasonably, that he didn't want to undercut President Johnson's negotiations through any campaign statements he might make.

Nixon concluded that, although a majority of Americans might back him, he could not prosecute the war with a free hand with the cultural and media establishments of the nation against him. There is considerable evidence that the North Vietnamese understood and exploited the liberal resistance, dragging out negotiations because they recognized that Nixon's secret threats to escalate the war in the fall of 1969 were a bluff. Years after the war, a North Vietnamese official told the *Wall Street Journal*,

> [The anti-war movement] was essential to our strategy. Every day our leadership would listen to world news over the radio at 9 a.m. to follow the growth of the American antiwar movement. Visits to Hanoi by people like Jane Fonda and former Attorney General Ramsey Clark and ministers gave us confidence that we should hold on in the face of battlefield reverses. We were elated when Jane Fonda, wearing a red Vietnamese dress, said at a press conference that she was ashamed of American actions in the war and that she would struggle along with us.

Nixon ultimately settled on a transitional plan of "Vietnamization" of the war, including a phased withdrawal of American troops and training the South Vietnamese to defend themselves, a strategy the Johnson administration had rejected. Nixon finally brought U.S. involvement to an end and secured the release of our prisoners of war, through an act that enraged the left and the media—the "Christmas bombing" of 1972. When the North Vietnamese balked at concluding a peace treaty, Nixon took off the gloves and decided for the first time to attack the North seriously. Nixon, according to his own recollection, told the Chairman of the Joint Chiefs of Staff, Admiral Thomas Moorer,

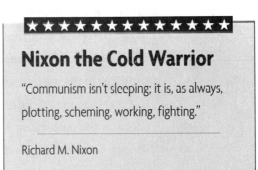

Nixon the Cold Warrior

"Communism isn't sleeping; it is, as always, plotting, scheming, working, fighting."

Richard M. Nixon

"I don't want any more of this crap about the fact that we couldn't hit this target or that one. This is your chance to use military power effectively to win the war, and if you don't, I'll consider you responsible." For the first time in the war, B-52s were used to bomb Hanoi, starting on December 18.

The reaction was ferocious. Opponents of the war, who had by this late date virtually exhausted the vocabulary of accusation and abuse, seized upon the image of the supposed "carpet bombing" of Vietnam to level the most extreme charges of the entire war. The *New York Times* called the bombing "terrorism on an unprecedented scale," and said its first two days alone were the "equivalent of the Hiroshima bomb." (This was wildly inaccurate.) *Times* columnist Tom Wicker said the U.S. had "loosed the holocaust" on North Vietnam. The *Washington Post* also embraced the theme that the bombing amounted to "terrorism," calling it "the most savage and senseless act of war ever visited, over a scant ten days, by one sovereign people upon another." The London *Daily Mirror* said the bombing was "an act of insane ferocity, a crude exercise in the politics of terror." The *Guardian* said, "Mr. Nixon wants to go down in history as one of the most murderous and bloodthirsty of American Presidents." *La Opinion* in Buenos Aries carried the headline, "U.S. Carries Out Most Complete Plan of Destruction in Human History." Congressional Democrats, not to be outdone by the media, engaged in their own hyperbole. Senator McGovern called the bombing "a policy of mass murder ... the most murderous bombardment in the history of the world," and Iowa Senator Harold Hughes said, "The only thing I can compare with it is the savagery at Hiroshima and Nagasaki."

Only months later did information emerge that the media coverage of the Christmas bombing was not simply inaccurate, but bordering on hysteria. In fact, the bombing had one of the lowest casualty totals of any bombing campaign in the history of warfare—because the U.S. had indeed targeted military sites. The Hanoi death toll, the *Economist* noted, "is smaller than the number of civilians killed by the North Vietnamese in their artillery bombardment of An Loc in April or the toll of refugees ambushed when trying to escape from Quang Tri at the beginning of May. That is what makes the denunciation of Mr. Nixon as another Hitler sound so unreal." *New York Times* reporter Malcolm Browne acknowledged that "the damage caused by American bombing was grossly overstated by North Vietnamese propaganda," and the *Baltimore Sun*'s Peter Ward agreed that "evidence on the ground disproves charges of indiscriminate bombing." The critics who claimed the bombing would prolong the war were proved wrong. But the myth that it was a terrible atrocity has persisted ever since.

The peace agreement ultimately did not secure the long-term freedom of South Vietnam—though had Nixon not been damaged by Watergate, it is possible that he would have been able to enforce the agreement and keep the Communist North at bay.

The Folly of Détente

While Nixon was undoubtedly an anti-Communist, he initiated the "détente" with the Soviet Union that undermined America in the Cold War and emboldened the Soviet Union. The arms control treaties Nixon signed, especially the anti-ballistic missile (ABM) treaty of 1972, prevented the U.S. from developing defenses against Soviet missile attack and meant that Ronald Reagan a decade later had to spend considerable political capital to begin to reverse American policy on missile defense (the ABM treaty wasn't finally abandoned until 2001 under President George W. Bush). Meanwhile, the Soviet Union continued a massive arms buildup throughout the 1970s, openly regarding détente as a diplomatic weapon in their "class struggle" against the West. Nixon's opening to Communist China gave rise to the ultimate cliché of counterintuitive politics: "Only Nixon could go to China."

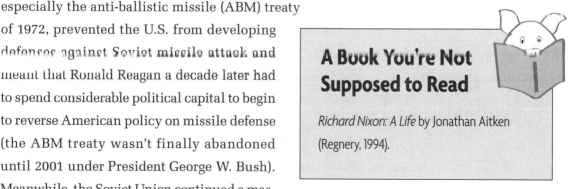

A Book You're Not Supposed to Read

Richard Nixon: A Life by Jonathan Aitken (Regnery, 1994).

The erosion of America's position in the world under détente would escalate during the presidencies of Nixon's successors, Gerald Ford and especially Jimmy Carter. And it is possible to speculate that had Nixon survived Watergate, he might have been in a position to hold a harder line against the Soviet Union. On the other hand, Nixon's similar grand strategy in domestic policy—what might be called his attempt to reach détente with liberalism at home—failed for much the same reason.

Nixon's Liberalism on Domestic Policy

Any other president who had compiled Nixon's domestic policy record would be regarded as standing firmly in the liberal-progressive tradition. President Johnson has gone down in the history books as the big spender on social welfare programs, yet federal spending grew faster during Nixon's tenure than during Johnson's. It was under Nixon that social spending came to exceed defense spending for the first time. Social spending soared from $55 billion in 1970 (Nixon's first budget) to $132 billion in 1975, from 28 percent of the federal budget when LBJ left office to 40 percent of the budget by the time Nixon left in 1974. While Nixon would criticize and attempt to reform welfare, he nonetheless approved massive increases in funding for other Great Society programs such as the Model Cities program and the Department of Housing and Urban Development, despite the fact that top aides had urged him to cut or eliminate many of these programs. Some of the expensive policies that Nixon supported on entitlements, such as the expansion of Food Stamps and automatic cost-of-living increases for Social Security recipients, contributed to runaway spending trends in successive decades.

Federal spending for the arts, which benefited mostly the cultural elites who hated Nixon, quadrupled. Economist Herbert Stein, who served on Nixon's Council of Economic Advisers, summed up his dubious record: "The administration that was against expanding the budget expanded it greatly; the administration that was determined to fight inflation ended by having a large amount of it." Nixon once asked an aide, "What's a balanced budget worth in terms of votes?" "Fifty thousand votes in a national election, that's all." Not surprisingly, the *New York Times* praised Nixon near the end of his first term for his "abandonment of outmoded conservative doctrine."

The explosion in spending was matched by an equally dramatic explosion in federal regulation—from an administration that regarded itself as pro-business. Nixon created a number of the new "alphabet soup" regulatory agencies that are constitutionally dubious, such as the Environmental Protection Agency (EPA), the Consumer Product Safety Commission (CPSC), and the Occupational Safety and Health Administration (OSHA). The number of pages in the *Federal Register* (the roster of federal rules and regulations) grew only 19 percent under Johnson, but a staggering 121 percent under Nixon. In civil rights, Nixon expanded the regime of "affirmative action" racial quotas and set-asides far beyond what Johnson had done. In other words, Nixon consolidated the administrative state of the Great Society in much the same way that President Eisenhower (whom Nixon had served as vice president) consolidated the New Deal. Ronald Reagan would run and govern as much against Nixon's legacy as he would against LBJ's, and a number of Nixon's administrative creations would cause Reagan the most trouble in his attempts to scale back the size and scope of the regulatory state during his White House years.

Nixon's worst deviation from sound domestic policy came in economics. He became the first president ever to impose wage and price controls in

> ★ ★ ★ ★ ★ ★ ★ ★ ★ ★ ★ ★ ★ ★
>
> ## Nixon the Progressive
>
> "We may well have been the most progressive administration on domestic issues that has ever been formed. It was amazing what [Nixon] would say yes to.... It is not likely that the Nixon Administration will ever be credited for what it tried to do."
>
> Daniel Patrick Moynihan, domestic policy adviser to President Nixon

★ ★ ★ ★ ★ ★ ★ ★ ★ ★ ★ ★ ★ ★

Nixon the Apotheosis of Great Society Liberalism

"Looking back on the budget, economic and social policies of the Republican years, it would not be unfair to conclude that the political verdict of 1968 had brought reaffirmation, rather than repudiation, of Great Society liberalism."

Pat Buchanan, speechwriter and adviser in Nixon's White House

peacetime—in another reversal of the conservative principles Nixon had espoused before being elected president. In 1965 Nixon had said, "The lesson that government price fixing doesn't work is never learned." He had attacked wage and price controls in the 1968 campaign, and spoken often of his own frustrations with such controls during World War II. "I will not take this nation down the road of wage and price controls," Nixon had reiterated, "however politically expedient that may seem." But then he did exactly that, in 1971, and at the same time he took the U.S. off the gold standard.

Neither step improved the U.S. economy. On the contrary, these and other moves by Nixon—all in contradiction of the sound conservative principles he had run on—initiated the high inflation that ruined the American economy in the 1970s.

But then Nixon suddenly switched course again after his 1972 landslide election victory and started his second term apparently determined to try to rein in the welfare state and reform the Washington bureaucracy. This is where Watergate comes in.

Getting Watergate Wrong

Nixon's guilt in the Watergate cover-up is a supposedly well-established fact. What might be called the "Standard Heroic Account" of Watergate finds its wellsprings in Nixon's much-exaggerated "paranoia"—that is, Nixon's supposed fixation with the idea that his enemies were out to get him. In the Standard Heroic Account, Watergate was an epic struggle between the truth-seeking crusaders in Congress, the Justice Department, and the media against the villains in the White House trying frantically to cover up criminal political dirty tricks—complete with a "Saturday Night Massacre" (when Nixon fired special prosecutor Archibald Cox and attempted to close down the investigation); crucial evidence that was mysteriously missing or tampered with (the unexplained 18 ½-minute gap in a key Oval Office tape); hush money (cash payoffs to Howard Hunt and others); mystery figures ("Deep Throat," the secret source for *Washington Post* reporters Bob Woodward and Carl Bernstein); and betrayal (by White House counsel John Dean, whose 1973 Senate testimony first implicated Nixon in the cover-up). With Nixon's resignation in August 1974, the two-year Watergate saga ended in a victory for American constitutional democracy. The triumph of a vigilant media and an aroused Congress supposedly showed that "The system works."

There is a certain narrow truth to the Standard Heroic Account of Watergate. Much of Nixon's behavior and many of his decisions are indefensible. But the Standard Heroic Account leaves out some extremely important context, and conceals the fact that Nixon was the victim of a double standard and a witch-hunt atmosphere in Washington. As Nixon noted, previous presidents had bugged and harassed their political opponents. Lyndon Johnson, for example, had bugged Barry Goldwater's campaign in 1964. Nixon was right to complain that he was being held to a different standard. The real reason Democrats wanted to destroy Nixon—and the reason so many Republicans gladly went along—is that Nixon was threatening to take away their political power.

It is on precisely this point that *all* of the accounts of Watergate miss the nature and deeper significance of the political clash that was the backdrop of the affair. Watergate changed the operation of government in subtle but profound ways. While sleuths of history continue to hunt for the tantalizing missing details, it is on Watergate's effect on the structure of government that the most important revisionism remains to be done. The reaction to the *temporary* constitutional crisis brought about by Nixon's misdeeds (temporary because he would have been gone from the White House by 1977 in any case) was a *permanent* constitutional crisis. Congress and the federal bureaucracy were able to usurp powers from the presidency during its post-Watergate weakness—by means of the War Powers Act and the Budget Impoundment and Control Act. Watergate didn't just change our standards of ethics in government; it changed the balance of powers laid out in the Constitution. Far from showing that "the system works," Watergate introduced significant new distortions into our system of government that have hobbled all succeeding presidents.

Nixon had set his sights on a large project in his second term—gaining real control of the executive branch bureaucracy. "We have no discipline in this bureaucracy," Nixon complained to John Ehrlichman on one of the Watergate tapes. "We never fire anybody. We never reprimand anybody. We never demote anybody. We always promote the sons-of-bitches that kick us in the ass." He was starting to refer to many federal programs not as objects to be "reformed," but as "failures" that should be cut. In his second inaugural address, Nixon set out his intention bluntly: "A new era of progress at home requires turning away ... from condescending policies of paternalism—of Washington knows best." His first budget proposal in the second term called for eliminating more than one hundred programs, while holding total spending growth to a relatively parsimonious 8 percent. Nixon was proposing to do nothing less than upend the established political arrangement, according to which Democratic administrations expanded government in exciting new progressive ways, and Republican administrations only slowed, or at best stalled—but *never* rolled back—the encroachment of government bureaucracy, taxes, spending, and regulation onto citizens' lives.

The significance of Nixon's conservative turn was not lost on the liberal establishment. The *New York Times* huffed that Nixon's second inaugural address heralded "a reversion to the do-nothing Federal Government and every-man-for-himself ideology of the Hoover era." Michael Novak, fresh from writing speeches for McGovern running mate Sargent Shriver in the 1972 campaign, wrote that the Establishment "knew that for the first time since Andrew Jackson, a President had arisen who genuinely threatened both the economic and symbolic power of the Eastern elite."

By 1973, Nixon wrote years later, "I had concluded that Congress has become cumbersome, undisciplined, isolationist, fiscally irresponsible ... and too dominated by the media." What was needed, Nixon thought, was to "break the Eastern stranglehold on the executive branch and the federal government." Nixon's plan to break the bureaucracy required that he take Congress on as well. "Armed with my landslide mandate and knowing that I had only four years in which to make my mark," Nixon wrote in his *Memoirs*, "I planned to force Congress and the federal bureaucracy to defend their obstruction and their irresponsible spending in the open arena of public opinion...." Nixon wrote in his diary at the time, "This is going to be quite a shock to the establishment, but it is the only way, and probably the last time, that we can get government under control before it gets so big that it submerges the individual completely and destroys the dynamism which makes the American system what it is."

By declaring his intent to control—and reduce in size—the structures on which the power of the Democratic Party rested, Nixon

Nixon the Small-Government Conservative

"We must always remember that America is a great nation today not because of what government did for people but because of what people did for themselves and for one another."

Richard M. Nixon

would be launching one of the most bitter political fights in American history. Nixon knew that he had "thrown down a gauntlet to Congress, the bureaucracy, the media, and the Washington establishment and challenged them to engage in epic battle."

He started his attack on spending immediately. Nixon froze spending for housing and urban development programs, suggesting that the money be sent back to the states through revenue sharing instead. When Congress overrode his veto of the Federal Water Pollution Control Act, which had appropriated $18 billion for water treatment, Nixon announced that he was going to invoke the presidential power of "impoundment"—he was going to refuse to spend the appropriated money. There is no more direct way of taking on Congress and the bureaucracy than impoundment. The impoundment power had a long pedigree. Presidents going back to Thomas Jefferson had impounded duly appropriated funds. Jefferson had impounded funds for the construction of naval warships because the threat of war with Britain and France had eased. Nixon pointed out that while his impoundments came to 3.5 percent of total spending in 1973, President Kennedy had impounded 7.8 percent of the budget in 1961 and 6.2 percent in 1962, while LBJ had impounded 6.7 percent in 1967.

Nixon signaled that he intended make the widest use of impoundment: "I have nailed my colors to the mast on this issue; the political winds can blow where they may." By the beginning of 1973, Nixon had impounded funds for over one hundred federal programs, each with an interest group or local constituency behind it. More impoundments were promised to follow if Congress did not get runaway spending under control. Members of Congress in both parties rightly feared that scaling back spending might involve being defeated for re-election. Pork-barrel spending was the chief means of assuring their re-election, and a reduced ability to deliver pork diminished the attachments of the interests who helped keep them in office. Hence their fury at Nixon, and hence the reason Watergate quickly became the pretext for destroying the president who was threatening to shut down business as usual in Washington.

Some conservatives at the time perceived what Nixon was up to and fought back against the witch hunt the left unleashed during Watergate.

A joke from the time: a true conservative was someone who didn't support Nixon until *after* Watergate.

Nixon's Constitutional Legacy

Nixon ran for president in 1968 on a platform of "law and order," promising to appoint "strict constructionist" justices to the Supreme Court and signaling that Americans could expect him to reverse the liberalism of Lyndon Johnson's Great Society and the Warren Court's radical jurisprudence. But Nixon's record of judicial appointments is mixed.

The Senate rejected Nixon's first two Supreme Court nominees, Clement Haynsworth and G. Harrold Carswell, because they were thought too conservative and Southern-leaning. When Nixon then appointed Judge Harry Blackmun from Minnesota in 1970, *Time* magazine opined, "There is little likelihood that Blackmun will be criticized for his judicial philosophy or specific decisions." Strict constructionism? "I don't know what it means," Blackmun told a reporter. Blackmun was swiftly confirmed and soon demonstrated that he was no strict constructionist, moving steadily to the left during his time on the Court. He was the author of the worst Supreme Court decision since *Dred Scott*, the 1973 *Roe v. Wade* decision that mandated abortion on demand in all fifty states.

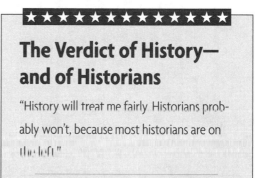

The Verdict of History— and of Historians

"History will treat me fairly. Historians probably won't, because most historians are on the left."

Richard M. Nixon, to NBC's John Chancellor in 1988

Nixon's other three appointees were better, to varying degrees. Chief Justice Warren Burger was a cautious justice, while Lewis Powell, thought to be a conservative at the time of his appointment, often disappointed conservatives in rulings that compromised with liberal doctrine. It was

Powell, for example, who, in the famous *Bakke* case about reverse discrimination in college admissions, promulgated the doctrine that "diversity" was a legitimate criterion for hiring and admissions decisions—a deeply corrupting doctrine that is still with us today.

Nixon's only home run on the Court was William Rehnquist, whom Ronald Reagan later elevated to Chief Justice.

Between Nixon's acquiescence in or even sponsorship of so many constitutionally doubtful expansions of the regulatory statutes—the Endangered Species Act, the creation of OSHA and the EPA—and his botched appointments to the Supreme Court, Nixon's constitutional grade has to be marked down to a C+. If it were not for his abortive attempts to rein in the government in his second term and his vetoes of bad legislation such as the War Powers Act (his veto was overridden), his grade would be even lower.

Chapter 13

GERALD FORD, 1974–1977

"Our constitution works. Our great republic is a government of laws, not of men."
—*Gerald R. Ford*

President Ford's Constitutional Grade: C+

To Gerald Ford fell the job of cleaning up the wreck of Watergate and healing the nation's divisions when he became president in the summer of 1974 following Richard Nixon's resignation. As the nation's only president who was never elected to national office, and facing a large and unruly Democratic majority in Congress, no incoming president has ever had a weaker hand. The lack of an electoral mandate diminished Ford's legitimacy and moral authority in office. Never having won a national election, Ford was at a profound disadvantage against an assertive Congress. But the new president's character was a strength he could draw on in a very weak position.

Ford, Henry Kissinger observed, "did not engage in elaborate maneuvers about who should receive credit" and "was sufficiently self-assured to disagree openly." Only a person with such self-assurance could have stepped into the devastated Oval Office, unelected, with no transition period in which to work out his own priorities, saddled with his predecessor's White House staff, cabinet, and ongoing initiatives, and function as well as Ford did.

The public perception of Ford is at odds with the reality of the man. Ford has always been portrayed as something of a hapless figure: think of how he is called "good ol' Jerry Ford" or how comedian Chevy Chase mercilessly lampooned his many pratfalls. In reality, Ford was far from hapless. He possessed a strong, solid character reflective of the heartland district in Michigan from which he came. "Eisenhower without the medals" is how Ford was often described. It was Ford's misfortune to preside, without benefit of popular election, at a low ebb for America. In many respects the Ford-Carter years were the time of maximum peril for the United States and its allies in the West.

Nixon had reportedly included Ford on his list of potential running mates in both 1960 and 1968, But Nixon may simply have been returning a favor; Ford had been among congressional Republicans who urged Eisenhower not to dump Nixon from the ticket in 1956. The irony of Ford's appointment to the vice presidency following Spiro Agnew's resignation in the fall of 1973 is that Ford, after twenty-five years in the House, was seriously considering retirement from politics in 1974. Nixon's first choice for vice president was John Connally, while party regulars recommended either Governor Nelson Rockefeller or Governor Ronald Reagan. Congressional Republicans suggested Ford. The Democratic Congress was not about to confirm former Democrat Connally, nor Rockefeller, nor Reagan, and provide the Republicans with a possibly strong incumbent president for the 1976 election. The Democratic House Speaker Carl Albert told Nixon that Ford was the only confirmable choice. In other words, Congress dictated its own choice for the chief of the executive branch. Ford accepted, despite the misgivings of his wife, Betty.

Ford's plain-spoken, middle American persona—"I'm a Ford, not a Lincoln," he modestly proclaimed—was a welcome relief to the Watergate-weary nation after Nixon finally resigned. Like most incoming presidents, Ford was greeted with a wave of public support and congressional goodwill, magnified by the fact that he had come from the ranks of the House. Ford, Pat Moynihan wrote, was "the most decent man I had known in American politics." "Our long national nightmare is over," Ford told a relieved nation. But the good mood vanished abruptly when, barely a month in office, Ford pardoned Nixon for any and all crimes he might have committed, even though no indictments had yet been brought. It was a supreme and necessary act of mercy, as even Nixon-hating liberals have come to admit over time. (Three decades after the fact, the Kennedy family gave Ford one of their "Profiles in Courage" awards for the Nixon pardon.)

But the timing of the pardon was awkward for Ford. "Will there *ever* be a right time?" Ford asked when his aides second-guessed him. Congressional Democrats and media cynics, deprived of the culminating satisfaction of seeing Nixon before a jury, thought the fix was in: Nixon must have named Ford to the vice presidency in return for a promise of pardon. Congressional Democrats called for an investigation and darkly hinted that another impeachment might be necessary. Ford denied any pardon deal and took the extraordinary step of testifying before the House Judiciary Committee's Subcommittee on Criminal Justice—becoming the first president since Lincoln to appear before Congress. Perhaps Ford had little choice. His dramatic appearance blunted the congressional uproar and derailed the momentum for an investigation that would have tied the White House in knots for months. But it was also another subtle indication (and encouragement) of congressional dominance.

Ford had already divided and upset Republicans with his choice for vice president. According to one account, the White House had conducted a quiet survey of Republicans leaders, and the leading pick was George H. W. Bush. But Ford decided to nominate Nelson Rockefeller, the most hated liberal Republican in the party. As Pat Buchanan put it, "There was no one who could rattle the cages of the Right like Nelson Rockefeller." Rockefeller's abiding interest in becoming president was no secret. Indeed he was widely thought to have been making plans to run in 1976 against Spiro Agnew with the hope of succeeding Nixon, until Watergate upended everyone's plans. The conservative wing of the Republican Party thought the fix was in. It was feared that Ford, having hinted privately that he was undecided about running for the Oval Office in his own right in 1976, would hand off the nomination to Rockefeller. "Mr. Ford's first big appointment has become his first big albatross," William Safire wrote in the *New York Times*. Even before Congress confirmed Rockefeller, Safire predicted that Ford would have to dump Rockefeller from the ticket in 1976, whereupon "Democratic candidates will charge that Rockefeller is being dumped to 'placate the right wing.'" Lou Cannon pointed out in his chronicle of Reagan's rise, "More than any other single act of Ford's, or indeed all of them combined, it was the selection of Rockefeller which fueled national interest among conservatives in a Reagan candidacy." Though it should be added that Ford's outspoken wife, Betty, contributed mightily to conservative disaffection with her candid comments on *60 Minutes* about her children's potential marijuana use and premarital affairs, as well as with her endorsement of abortion.

But Ford's greatest handicap was that he was not equal to the supreme political demand of the television age—he was not a great communicator. He wasn't even a good one. George Will put the problem succinctly:

> Rhetorical skills are not peripheral to the political enterprise; and they are among the most important skills a person can bring to the presidency.... Ford is a passable head of an administration, but an unsatisfactory chief of state. A President is the chief articulator of collective aspirations, or he is not much. He is articulate, or he is inadequate.... There never has been a great inarticulate President. Ford is the most inarticulate President since the invention of broadcasting.... [A]n inarticulate president is like a motorcycle motor installed in a Mack truck."

And Ford's physical clumsiness didn't help. Ford was arguably the most athletic man ever to be president, but he repeatedly tripped, fell, or bumped his head, usually in the presence of cameras, recalling Lyndon Johnson's slur that "Jerry Ford can't fart and chew gum at the same time." Reporters joked that not only should Ford not have played college football without a helmet, but he shouldn't play president without one, either. Maybe he's trying to sew up the klutz vote, comedians joked. Even major news media made jokes about Ford.

Stagflation at Home

Behind the scenes, the record shows, Ford was a sure-footed and decisive leader, but his physical clumsiness seemed a metaphor for his handling of domestic issues. Ford inherited a rapidly deteriorating economy. Inflation was skyrocketing. Prices jumped 3.7 percent in just the *month* of July 1974. Unemployment was heading toward 7 percent. The deadly and unprecedented combination of rising prices and unemployment came to be known as *stagflation*. The federal deficit was projected to balloon to $51.9 billion (out of a $350 billion budget), at that time an unheard of and alarming level.

Orthodox Keynesian economics held that policy can fight inflation or unemployment, but not both at the same time. Ford's economic advisers, a group that included Alan Greenspan and William Simon, argued that fighting inflation was more important than fighting unemployment, which they viewed as a cyclical phenomenon. Inflation was the more pervasive threat to the long-term health of the economy. Choosing to fight inflation, Ford proposed to get it

★★★★★★★★★★★★★★★★

Sure-Footed Leaders

TIME magazine quipped, "The only thing between Nelson Rockefeller and the presidency is a banana peel." Both Rockefeller and Ford tripped when they walked together into the Senate chamber for Rockefeller's swearing-in ceremony.

under control with the orthodox remedy of a tax increase. He proposed a one-year 5 percent surtax on businesses and upper-income individuals to close the deficit and dampen inflation at the same time. His advisors were undoubtedly right to argue that inflation was a greater danger than unemployment in the long term, but the short-run political cost of addressing inflation ahead of unemployment was heavy for Republicans—especially when Ford, struggling vainly to change the subject from unemployment, denied that the nation was in a recession.

★★★★★★★★★★★★★★

WIN with Ford?

For the announcement of his tax surcharge proposal, Ford wore a campaign-style button that read WIN. The button, Ford explained, stood for "Whip Inflation Now," which was the name of a volunteer organization in which Ford hoped citizens would enroll. Amazingly, over 100,000 did. Millions more requested WIN buttons. It was one of the dumbest stunts in the annals of democratic propaganda.

Weakness Abroad

The sagging economy was the lesser of Ford's major problems. The greatest misfortune of Ford's tenure in office was having to preside over the last chapter of the long Vietnam War saga, including the final collapse of South Vietnam in 1975. What made the episode so ignominious was not simply that a long-suffering American ally was defeated, but the fact that—in the grips of a mood of self-flagellation—the U.S. refused to come to the aid of an ally whose survival had been the bipartisan commitment of five presidents. Ford made a last-ditch appeal for emergency military aid to South Vietnam in a speech before a joint session of Congress, but the heavily Democratic Congress, dominated by anti-war leftists, refused to lift a finger (except the middle digit, figuratively speaking) to help out an ally for whom more than 50,000 American soldiers had given their lives. At least Ford tried. The repercussions of and recriminations over the fall of South Vietnam would last more than a decade, well into the Reagan years. Americans on all sides of the Vietnam controversy have consoled themselves ever since that the fall of South Vietnam was inevitable. But while corruption, military ineptitude, poor leadership, and flagging morale doubtless weakened the prospects of the South Vietnamese, their defeat was by no means foreordained. It required the United States deciding to look the other way. "There is no doubt in my mind," Henry Kissinger wrote, "that, with anything close to an adequate level of American aid, they would not have collapsed in 1975."

While he eventually dismissed most of the staff he inherited from President Nixon to replace them with his own appointees (among them Richard Cheney as his chief of staff and Donald Rumsfeld as secretary of defense), Ford kept Henry Kissinger, the chief architect of détente, as secretary of state until the end of his term. Ford and Kissinger nearly reached a new arms control deal with the Soviet Union, but the biggest milestone of the time was the Helsinki Accords of 1975. The Helsinki Accords, signed at an international meeting in Helsinki, Finland (from whence the name derived), was a bitter compromise that conservatives despised at the time. In exchange for the Soviet Union supposedly recognizing human rights, the West would recognize the legitimacy of Soviet rule over the nations of Eastern Europe. Conservative critics pointed out that a pledge to observe human rights means little in regimes without a free press or a judicial process to secure those rights. The Helsinki Accords prompted Ronald Reagan's first public criticism of Ford: "I am against it, and I think all Americans should be against it."

Henry Kissinger later made a persuasive case that in the long run the human rights provisions of the Helsinki Accords were of use to dissidents behind the Iron Curtain, and some anti-Communist activists such as the Czech Vaclav Havel corroborate this view. But at the time the Helsinki Accords appeared to be an expression of weakness on the part of the West. This perception was deepened by Ford's craven decision around the same time to refuse a meeting with Aleksandr Solzhenitsyn, the Nobel Prize-winning author of *The Gulag Archipelago,* who came to the United States after the Soviet Union expelled him. Solzhenitsyn strongly criticized détente, and Ford, acting on Kissinger's advice, decided against meeting Solzhenitsyn because the meeting would offend the Soviets.

The White House initially said "scheduling problems" prevented a visit, an unpersuasive excuse that was then amended to an even less persuasive one: Solzhenitsyn, the White House said, was in the U.S. "to promote his books," and the president did not wish to lend himself to "commercial purposes." The week before, however, Ford had posed for photographs on the White House lawn with "the cotton queen" and soccer star Pele. Some White House aides muttered about Solzhenitsyn's mental stability, while Ford privately called Solzhenitsyn "a goddamned horse's ass." Finally the White House came clean, admitting that Ford had decided against meeting with Solzhenitsyn "on the advice of the National Security Council," which meant Kissinger. Kissinger issued a statement: "From the point of view of foreign policy the symbolic effect of that [meeting with Solzhenitsyn] can be disadvantageous." Kissinger had lobbied the Soviets to allow Solzhenitsyn to go into exile, and promised Soviet Ambassador Anatoly Dobrynin that the U.S. would not exploit Solzhenitsyn for political purposes. From his point of view, he was only living up to his end of an honest bargain. Solzhenitsyn returned the insult, attacking Ford for signing the Helsinki Accords, which he said represented "the betrayal of Eastern Europe, [and] acknowledging officially its slavery forever."

Ford's snubbing of Solzhenitsyn ignited a firestorm of criticism. "Not even Watergate," George Will wrote, "was as *fundamentally* degrading to the presidency as this act of deference to the master of the Gulag Archipelago." William F. Buckley Jr. poured contempt on Ford: "For a horrible moment one was tempted to wonder whether Mr. Ford knew who Aleksandr Solzhenitsyn was."

Ford's weak handling of foreign policy amazingly enabled the Democratic Party and its 1976 nominee, Jimmy Carter, to run to the *right* of Ford. The Democratic platform in 1976 criticized Ford's détente as little more than "bad bargains, dramatic posturing, and the stress on general declarations.... We must avoid assuming that the whole of American-Soviet relations is greater than the sum of its parts, that any agreement is superior to none, or that we can negotiate effectively as supplicants." Ford's confused and weak approach to the Soviet Union may have ultimately cost him the close election in 1976, when in a debate with Carter, Ford inexplicably said, "There is no Soviet domination of Eastern Europe, and there never will be under a Ford administration."

Say what? Could Ford really be saying that the Captive Nations were no longer captive? Jimmy Carter pounced on Ford's gaffe: "I would like to see Mr. Ford convince the Polish Americans and the Czech Americans and the Hungarian Americans in this country that those countries don't live under the domination and supervision of the Soviet Union behind the Iron Curtain." Over the next few days, Carter compared Ford to George Romney (the present Republican presidential candidate's father, who had dropped out of the 1968 Republican presidential primaries after a gaffe about being "brainwashed" into supporting the Vietnam War), conveying the none-too-subtle double implication that Ford had been brainwashed by Kissinger, and was too dumb to know it. *Newsweek* ran the headline "Jerry Ford Drops a Brick."

A Mixed Record on the Constitution

Facing a very liberal and heavily Democratic Congress intent on expanding its power and adopting bad policies, Ford made strong use of the president's most powerful tool—the veto over congressional legislation. Ford vetoed sixty-six bills in eighteen months—a record. Democrats overrode twelve of those vetoes. Among bills that were passed into law over Ford's veto were the Freedom of Information Act (a statute granting a fishing license for activists to requisition confidential government documents) and several budget-busting spending bills, including one for research on electric cars—sound familiar?

When Ford served as the Republican minority leader in the House, he had led the unsuccessful attempt to impeach the far-left Supreme Court Justice William O. Douglas. So it came as a great disappointment that when Douglas retired from the Court during Ford's presidency, Ford's sole appointment to the Supreme Court was a jurist nearly as liberal as Douglas: John Paul Stevens. Stevens is one of the worst Supreme Court appointments ever made by a Republican president—continuing a string of incompetent appointments going back to Eisenhower. Stevens moved steadily to the left during his nearly thirty years on the Court. He flipped from opposing to supporting affirmative action quotas, supported abortion, and voted against gun rights. He sided with the liberal wing of the Court in *Bush v. Gore* in 2000. His most significant and damaging opinion came in *Chevron v. NRDC* in 1984—the most cited opinion in the history of the Supreme Court—which greatly expanded the constitutionally dubious power of unaccountable administrative bureaucracies to impose rules and regulations. The *Chevron* decision diminished the responsibility and accountability of Congress, and reduced the ability of citizens to rein in arbitrary government power. By farming out unpopular decisions to "swarms of officers" who are just as unelected as and many times more numerous than the ones Thomas Jefferson complained about in the Declaration of Independence, our elected

---

★ ★ ★ ★ ★ ★ ★ ★ ★ ★ ★ ★ ★ ★

Wait a Minute—Wasn't That Ronald Reagan?

"A government big enough to give you everything you want is a government big enough to take from you everything you have."

Gerald Ford

---

representatives have deprived the people of their right to vote their oppressors out of office. Stevens openly scorned interpreting the Constitution according to the original intent of the Founders.

While Ford's use of the veto against a runaway Congress and his general demeanor in conducting himself in office in the aftermath of the Watergate disaster count strongly in his favor, his appointment of Stevens knocks his constitutional grade down to a C+.

Chapter 14

JAMES EARL CARTER, 1977–1981

"Aggression unopposed becomes a contagious disease."
—*Jimmy Carter*

President Carter's Constitutional Grade: F

Nathan Miller, author of a book about America's ten worst presidents, wrote, "Electing Jimmy Carter president was as close as the American people have ever come to picking a name out of the phone book and giving him the job." This is not quite correct. Although he had a thin record as an undistinguished one-term governor of Georgia, Carter's successful drive to the presidency in 1976 was a work of political genius and determination—though his campaign is responsible for lengthening the presidential election cycle to the endless and expensive process we have today. It was Carter who transformed the Iowa caucuses, until then a minor, sleepy affair that most candidates ignored, into the high-profile, first-in-the-nation contest it is now.

Carter skillfully exploited the nation's post-Watergate mood of disenchantment with Washington. His one shrewd political insight: after the disappointment of Vietnam, the failure of the Great Society, and the scandal of Watergate, what Americans most wanted in a president was someone who taught Sunday school, which Carter did at his Baptist church in Plains, Georgia. He promised never to lie to the American people. But he concealed his soft liberal ideology and projected a persona that

Did you know?

★ Jimmy Carter was the first president born in a hospital

★ Carter is the only president who ever filed a UFO sighting report with the U.S. Air Force

★ He also directed the government to consult a psychic to help locate a missing airplane

★ Carter's vice president, Walter Mondale, nearly resigned because he had lost confidence in President Carter's leadership ability

Segregation Forever?

"I see nothing wrong with ethnic purity being maintained. I would not force a racial integration of a neighborhood by government action."

Jimmy Carter in Pennsylvania, during the 1976 campaign

concealed the nasty and hypocritical side of his character. He was a high-minded practitioner of low blows.

Carter's Character

Both as president and in his long, self-aggrandizing career as a former president, Carter has represented himself as a racial healer. But his political career in Georgia, and even some of his appeals in the 1976 campaign, reveal him to have been a typical Southern race-baiter. Sociologist Kenneth Morris, whose study *Jimmy Carter, American Moralist*, is generally favorable to Carter, observes that the "not-so-subtle racism" of Carter's 1970 campaign was "blatant ... the chicanery had been more than accidental; it had been systematic."

Longtime NBC and ABC broadcaster David Brinkley observed of Carter, "Despite his intelligence, he had a vindictive streak, a mean streak, that surfaced frequently and antagonized people." Eleanor Randolph of the *Chicago Tribune* wrote, "Carter likes to carve up an opponent, make his friends laugh at him and then call it a joke.... [He] stretched the truth to the point where it becomes dishonest to call it exaggeration." And Gary Fink, author of a generally favorable study of Carter's governorship, notes that "Carter usually claimed the moral and ethical high ground" but "practiced a style of politics based on exaggeration, disingenuousness, and at times outright deception."

The man with the legendary smile could be unfriendly and cold. "There were no private smiles," said one disgruntled campaign aide in 1976. His personal White House secretary, Susan Clough, recalled that Carter rarely said hello to her as he walked by her desk. Not a "Happy Thanksgiving," or a "Merry Christmas." Nothing, she said. Arthur Schlesinger Jr. judged Carter to be a "narcissistic loner." "Carter was never a regular guy," his speechwriter Patrick Anderson observed. "The sum of his parts never quite added up to that.... Carter talked his way into the presidency, yet in some profound way he never learned the language of men."

Was Carter a liberal? A Southern conservative? A moderate? He presented himself as all of the above. One poll before the election found that Carter "comes across as more conservative to conservative voters, more middle-of-the-road to middle-of-the-roaders, and more liberal to liberals." And Carter's own pollster Pat Caddell found that *on election day in 1976*, "fifty percent of the public still does not know where Carter stands on the issues." It may have been a winning formula for the election, but it was a disaster for Carter once he took office.

★ ★ ★ ★ ★ ★ ★ ★ ★ ★ ★ ★ ★ ★

Adultery in His Heart

"I've looked upon a lot of women with lust. I've committed adultery in my heart many times. This is something that God recognizes I will do—and I have done it—and God forgives me for it. But that doesn't mean I condemn someone who not only looks at women with lust but who leaves his wife and *shacks up* with somebody out of wedlock. Christ says, 'Don't consider yourself better than someone else because one guy screws a whole bunch of women while the other guy is loyal to his wife.'"

Jimmy Carter to *Playboy* magazine, 1976

Domestic Policy Disasters

Carter began his presidency with an attitude of fiscal conservatism, rebuffing many proposals from the liberal Democratic Congress to expand spending. Liberals were certain that Carter would acquiesce in new activist government programs once in office, and were shocked to discover that Carter had *really meant it* when he pledged to balance the budget. Carter relished the discomfort he caused liberals on fiscal matters. "I wish you could have seen the stricken expressions on the faces of those Democratic leaders when I was talking about balancing the budget," Carter told biographer Peter Bourne. It wasn't just members of Congress that Carter upset. Carter charged his secretary of Health, Education, and Welfare, Joseph Califano, with the task of coming up with a welfare reform plan. Califano didn't take Carter's condition that any reform plan had to be accomplished at current funding levels seriously. When Califano presented Carter a set of options that all cost billions more, Carter exploded: "Are you telling me that there is no way to improve upon the present system except by spending billions of dollars? In that case, to hell with it! We're wasting our time."

But what most upset liberals, especially Senator Ted Kennedy, was Carter's refusal to back a comprehensive national health insurance plan that would have cost upwards of $100 billion a year. During the campaign Carter had endorsed national health insurance, but in office he proposed a slow, piecemeal approach to the issue. The government "cannot afford to do everything," Carter said, postponing even the introduction of a bill until 1979. What Carter eventually proposed in 1979 was a hospital cost-containment measure that went nowhere.

★★★★★★★★★★★★★★★

The Cat Got Your Energy Policy?

When Carter, clenching his fist for dramatic effect, called his energy policy the "moral equivalent of war," people noticed that the phrase yielded the acronym "MEOW."

Energy policy was Carter's most frivolous misadventure. At a time when government regulation and price controls were wreaking havoc in the energy market and causing soaring prices for consumers, Carter proposed *more* government regulation of energy, subsidies for "alternative" sources that never work very well, and higher taxes.

While Carter had a measure of fiscal conservatism, his general handling of the economy—especially of the most serious problem of the time, inflation—was disastrous. True to form, Carter tried to explain inflation as a moral problem afflicting the American people: "It is a myth that the government itself can stop inflation." Rather, inflation was a reflection of "unpleasant facts about ourselves," of "a preoccupation with self" that retards the willingness of Americans "to sacrifice for the common good." At no time did Carter mention the money supply, or the government's role in running the Treasury printing press. The Carter administration proceeded to fight inflation through "jawboning," which meant giving an official scowl to businesses and labor unions who sought price and wage increases. In 1979, inflation soared further, to more than 12 percent. With the prime rate nearing 20 percent and signs that inflation might begin spiraling to Latin American levels, Carter finally reversed course and appointed Paul Volcker to head the Federal Reserve. But by then the pain necessarily involved in fighting the inflation was considerably more acute than if Carter had governed more sensibly when he took office. Volcker immediately jacked up interest rates to curb monetary growth.

President Malaise

The economic problems of the nation reached their nadir in the summer of 1979, providing the occasion for the worst presidential speech ever given: Carter's famous "malaise" speech. The president never actually used the term "malaise" in his speech, but he said the nation suffered from a "crisis of confidence," and in his own notes he used the term "malaise" to describe the nation's condition.

There were credible rumors that Carter had suffered a nervous breakdown in the days before the speech, as he fled to the presidential

★ ★ ★ ★ ★ ★ ★ ★ ★ ★ ★ ★ ★ ★ ★

The Gloom Merchant

"I think it's inevitable that there will be a lower standard of living than what everybody had always anticipated, constant growth.... I think there's going to have to be a reorientation of what people value in their own lives. I believe that there has to be a more equitable sharing of what we have.... The only trend is downward."

Carter to visitors to Camp David before the 1979 "Malaise" speech

retreat at Camp David for ten days to figure out what to do. At one point before the speech, Vice President Walter Mondale bluntly told Carter that

a speech based on the "malaise" idea would be "political suicide," and that he doubted he would be able to defend it. "You can't castigate the American people," Mondale told Carter, "or they will turn you off once and for all." Mondale almost resigned in protest over the speech.

Carter had built up great expectations for a redemptive presidency during his 1976 campaign. Having run for office on the promise of "a government as good as the people," Carter was now saying, in effect, that the people were no good.

Jimmy and the Extraterrestrials

"I don't laugh at people any more when they say they have seen a UFO because I've seen one myself."

Jimmy Carter, 1975

The net results of Carter's erratic economic policies were high inflation, slow productivity growth, stagnant personal incomes, and persistent unemployment. But those were the least of Carter's troubles as his term progressed. Carter oversaw a ruin in foreign policy to match the ruin of the domestic economy. By 1980, Americans' anxiety about the prospect of war would reach its highest level since the Cuban missile crisis.

Foreign Policy Disasters

Henry Kissinger observed that by 1980 Carter had achieved a rare trifecta: "The Carter administration has managed the extraordinary feat of having, at one and the same time, the worst relations with our allies, the worst relations with our adversaries, and the most serious upheavals in the developing world since the end of the Second World War."

Carter had campaigned for the presidency as a critic of détente and a champion of human rights, but he ended up embracing a détente even more appeasing than under Nixon and Ford, and undermining the cause of democracy and human rights around the world. According to the annual Freedom House survey of democracy and liberty around the globe, there was almost no increase in freedom during Carter's presidency. Meanwhile, both Iran and Nicaragua, principal targets of Carter's human rights policy, became human rights disasters when revolutions replaced pro-American rulers with despotic anti-American rulers (Communists in the case of Nicaragua). And the fall of the Shah in Iran was a powerful impetus to the explosion of terrorism that is still convulsing the world today. America's allies in the Middle East, especially Saudi Arabia, were alarmed at the outcome of the Iranian revolution and appalled by the ineffective American response. The lesson drawn was that it was not necessarily advantageous to be too close to the United States.

Carter's foreign policy was sentimental rather than hardheaded or principled—a heavy dose of liberal guilt combined with the fashionable view that the "bipolar" world of the Cold War should give way to a "multi-polar" world. Four months into his administration, Carter made explicit his departure from the post-war foreign policy consensus. In a May 22, 1977, commencement address at Notre Dame University, Carter declared, "Being confident of our own future, we are now free of that *inordinate fear of communism* which once led us to embrace any dictator who joined us in that fear.... The unifying threat of conflict with the Soviet Union has become less intensive..." [emphasis added].

Two years later, the Soviet Union invaded Afghanistan—the first time the Soviets had invaded a nation outside their sphere of influence in Eastern Europe—and threatened the Middle East. Carter said the invasion had opened his eyes to the Soviet menace, and he announced a new policy—the "Carter doctrine"—that any attack on a Middle Eastern nation constituted an attack on American interests, and would draw a U.S. military response. Then he sent unarmed airplanes to the Middle East to show his new "toughness."

Robert Tucker of Johns Hopkins University wrote in *Foreign Affairs'* annual survey of the world, "After almost three years, it is reasonably clear that the Carter Administration's foreign policy has been a failure."

By the beginning of 1980, the bottom had fallen out of Carter's presidency. Khomeini's triumph in Iran turned out to be not the end but the beginning of America's agony in the Middle East. In November 1979, Iran seized the American embassy in Tehran, holding fifty-two Americans hostage, in violation of every diplomatic tradition and international law. The hostage-taking plunged America into a war-like crisis, except that the United States never credibly threatened Iran with war. Some of the Iranians who participated in the hostage-taking said subsequently that they expected the affair to last only as long as it took the U.S. to make credible threats of military action against Iran, and they were startled that Carter quickly and publicly disavowed the use of force (though Carter did send a private warning to Iran threatening severe but unspecified consequences if the hostages were harmed). Within days it was evident that the crisis would drag on for months. The Palestine Liberation Organization (PLO), looking for a way to ingratiate themselves with the U.S., offered to intervene—Arafat had been one of the first foreign visitors to Iran after Khomeini's return in February—but Khomeini bluntly told Arafat to stay out of the matter. Carter later turned to Libya's Muammar Qaddafi for help, asking his brother Billy Carter, who had accepted a $200,000 dollar "loan" from Libya that would become an embarrassment to Carter in the summer of 1980, to intercede with the anti-American tyrant of Tripoli. Khomeini was not impressed. Carter inexplicably decided to send former Attorney General Ramsey Clark, than whom there was no finer example of an accuser of America before the world—Clark had already written to an Iranian official offering advice about how to seek damages for the "criminal and wrongful acts committed by the Shah"—as an envoy to Iran, but Clark received the same treatment as the PLO. All U.S. attempts to make any kind of productive diplomatic contact with Iran hit a stone wall. Even freezing billions of dollars of Iranian assets in the U.S. and packing the Shah off to Panama did nothing to alter the deadlock.

President Carter's Constitutional Grade

Jimmy Carter is the only president of the twentieth century who did not appoint a single justice to the Supreme Court, so he doesn't have a legacy in the third branch of government comparable to those of other presidents. He deserves an F grade for his respect and defense of the Constitution, nonetheless, for an unusual reason: his unprecedented and outrageous behavior as an ex-president. Carter does not seem to understand that the nation has only one president at a time. He has consistently undermined his successors in ways both direct and indirect.

On the surface it is astonishing that someone whose four years in the presidency are widely judged to have been a disastrous failure continues to attract front-page headlines and exert influence on the world stage more than thirty years later. Carter, *Time* magazine's essayist Lance Morrow once observed, has established himself as "America's anti-President: a psalm-singing global circuit rider and moral interventionist who behaved, in a surreal and often effective way, as if the election of 1980 had been only some kind of ghastly mistake, a technicality of democratic punctilio." Carter has assembled a record of egregious behavior that is invariably forgiven and forgotten. The most notable instance came in late 1990 and early 1991, as the United States was assembling the coalition to expel Saddam Hussein from Kuwait. In the U.S., Carter opposed the prospective Gulf War, saying it would

A Book You're Not Supposed to Read

The Real Jimmy Carter: How Our Worst Ex-President Undermines American Foreign Policy, Coddles Dictators, and Created the Party of Clinton and Kerry by Steven F. Hayward (Regnery, 2004).

be "a massive, self-destructive, almost suicidal war." But he didn't stop there. In November 1990 Carter wrote to several heads of state represented in the UN Security Council, including Francois Mitterrand, Margaret Thatcher, Mikhail Gorbachev, and more than a dozen others, appealing for "negotiations" and deploring President George H. W. Bush's "line in the sand" rhetoric. The UN Security Council, Carter said directly, could stop the United States from launching a military campaign. The Arab League, not the U.S., should be the agent to work out a diplomatic solution. Carter sent out his irenic missives without the knowledge of the Bush administration, which didn't learn of Carter's activities until Canadian Prime Minister Brian Mulroney telephoned Defense Secretary Dick Cheney to ask him what Carter was up to. Cheney was shocked, later telling Carter biographer Douglas Brinkley that Carter's actions were "reprehensible, totally inappropriate for a former president."

In the day preceding the UN's January 15 ultimatum for Hussein to leave Kuwait, Carter continued his behind-the scenes meddling. Carter wrote on January 10 to Saudi's King Fahd, Egypt's Hosni Mubarak, and Syria's Hafez Assad urging them to break from Bush's painstakingly assembled coalition. "I urge you," Carter wrote, "to call publicly for a delay in the use of force while Arab leaders seek a peaceful solution to the crisis. *You have to forgo approval from the White House, but you will find the French, Soviets, and others fully supportive*" [emphasis added]. While Carter had belatedly informed the Bush administration of his November communiqués, he kept his January missives secret from Bush, who did not find out about them until several years later. Carter never apologized to Bush for his interference. Carter also opposed President George W. Bush in the run-up to the Iraq War in 2003, at one point going as far as to question President Bush's own Christian faith. It is episodes of this kind that prompted Lance Morrow to comment that "some of his Lone Ranger work has taken him dangerously close to the neighborhood of what we used to call treason."

Any lingering doubts about Carter's political failings were removed once and for all when he was awarded the Nobel Peace Prize in 2002, explicitly as an anti-American gesture on the part of the Nobel committee.

Chapter 15

RONALD WILSON REAGAN, 1981–1989

"Freedom is never more than one generation away from extinction."
—*Ronald Wilson Reagan*

President Reagan's Constitutional Grade: A-

Ronald Reagan's achievements are so massive that even his political adversaries have grudgingly come to acknowledge them. One liberal historian, John Patrick Diggins, wrote in 2007 that Reagan deserves to be considered among the greatest American presidents alongside Washington, Lincoln, and Franklin Roosevelt.

After more than ten years of high inflation, slow economic growth, and rising pessimism, Reagan—the first two-term president since Eisenhower—successfully turned the nation around, broke the back of inflation, stimulated rapid economic growth that saw the creation of 20 million new jobs, and restored the nation's self-confidence and optimism about the future.

His greatest and most long-lasting achievement was winning the Cold War over the Soviet Union—"without the firing of a single shot," in the words of British Prime Minister Margaret Thatcher. Princeton University historian Sean Wilentz, a liberal, wrote of Reagan, "His success in helping finally to end the cold war is one of the greatest achievements by any president of the United States—and arguably the greatest single presidential achievement since 1945."

Did you know?

★ The nearsighted Ronald Reagan cheated on his eye exam to gain admittance to the U.S. Army cavalry reserve in the 1930s

★ Reagan was afraid to fly, and took almost no airplane flights for thirty years before beginning his political career

★ Reagan's respect for the office of the presidency was such that he would not take off his suit jacket in the Oval Office

In both domestic and foreign policy, Reagan reached these achievements despite the fierce opposition and non-stop criticism of liberals and the news media. Just as today, liberals in the 1980s opposed reducing taxes and deregulating the marketplace. In foreign policy, liberals opposed Reagan's strategy of "peace through strength" as well as Reagan's tough talk and clear statements about the Soviet Union as an "evil empire." Most everyone (including some on his own senior staff) thought Reagan was foolish to say in Berlin in 1987, "Mr. Gorbachev—tear down this Wall!" But two and a half years later, the Berlin Wall came down.

The indubitable proof of Reagan's success is that today even liberals want to claim his legacy—though they can do so only by distorting his ideas. But there is one part of Reagan's legacy that liberals can't distort, and that conservatives have tended to overlook in recent years: Reagan's devotion to the Constitution, and his desire to move the nation closer to the Founders' views of limited government.

Reagan the Restorer

Reagan was the first president since FDR to speak frequently and substantively about the Founders and the Constitution, and he was the first president since Calvin Coolidge to criticize the administrative state that modern liberal constitutionalism has created. This is a remarkable and telling fact. It is largely overlooked today that FDR spoke often about the Founding and the Constitution, and quite differently from Woodrow Wilson. While Wilson was openly critical of the Founding and the Constitution, FDR's references to the Founding were mischievous—he appeared to be defending or proposing a restoration of the principles of the Founding while in fact attempting a wholesale modification of the meaning of our constitutional order. After FDR, our presidents practically ceased making reference to the Founding or the Constitution—until Reagan arrived.

In a 1979 letter from Reagan to Ben Shaw, publisher of the Dixon, Illinois, *Evening Telegraph* newspaper, Reagan wrote,

> The permanent structure of our government with its power to pass regulations has eroded if not in effect repealed portions of our Constitution. I have been speaking particularly in my talks around the country about the 10th article of the Bill of Rights. The federal government is performing functions that are not specified in the Constitution and those functions should be returned to the states and to the people. Of course the tax sources to fund them should also be turned back.

★ ★ ★ ★ ★ ★ ★ ★ ★ ★ ★ ★ ★

Reagan's Central Insight

"There is a threat posed to human freedom by the enormous power of the modern state. History teaches the dangers of government that overreaches—political control taking precedence over free economic growth, secret police, mindless bureaucracy all combining to stifle individual excellence and personal freedom."

President Reagan, Westminster Hall, London, 1982

Reagan's first inaugural address included the most significant discussion of America's founding principles since Harding and Coolidge. In that speech Reagan declared, "In this present crisis, government is not the solution to our problem. Government *is* the problem.... It is no coincidence that our present troubles parallel and are proportionate to the intervention and intrusion in our lives that result from unnecessary and excessive growth of government."

He continued, "It is time to check and reverse the growth of government, which shows signs of *having grown beyond the consent of the governed*" [emphasis added]. Note here that Reagan didn't rest his argument against the growth of government on the ground of efficiency or effectiveness, but on the constitutional ground of *consent* as explained in the Declaration of Independence. This had been a constant theme of Reagan's political rhetoric

★ ★ ★ ★ ★ ★ ★ ★ ★ ★ ★ ★ ★ ★

Why More Government Is Always So Great for the Economy

"The government's view of the economy could be summed up in a few short phrases: if it moves, tax it. If it keeps moving, regulate it. And if it stops moving, subsidize it."

Ronald Reagan

for more than twenty years, but one that was rarely heard from America's political class—even from other conservatives. Reagan criticized the size of government, but he was careful to qualify his critique:

It is my intention to curb the size and influence of the Federal establishment and to demand recognition of the distinction between the powers granted to the Federal Government and those reserved to the States or to the people.... Now, so there will be no misunderstanding, it is not my intention to do away with government. It is rather to make it work—work with us, not over us; to stand by our side, not ride on our back.

While this was not really revolutionary, it was controversial—as it challenged the basic premises of the modern centralized administrative state. Liberals had never expected to hear such heresy from the presidential podium. Although many liberals had been shaken by the disasters of the preceding fifteen years, from Vietnam and the Great Society through President Carter's ineffectual rule, there had never been a point at which the fundamental premises of modern liberalism were attacked from the pinnacle of American power.

It is significant that Reagan rejected the liberal reformist theme, very popular at the time of his election, that the presidency—or our democracy in general—was inadequate to the times.

From time to time, we have been tempted to believe that society has become too complex to be managed by self-rule, that government by an elite group is superior to government for, by, and of the people. But if no one among us is capable of governing himself, then who among us has the capacity to govern someone else?

Reagan had so fully internalized the thought of his political forebears—including Jefferson, Lincoln, and Roosevelt—that it is not clear whether he knew he was paraphrasing them. But the origin of the ideas Reagan was expressing is no mystery. In his first inaugural address in 1801, President Thomas Jefferson had said, "Sometimes it is said that man can not be trusted with the government of himself. Can he, then, be trusted with the government of others? Or have we found angels in the forms of kings to govern him? Let history answer this question."

As president Reagan fought valiantly, and with some success, to roll back big government and reestablish sensible limits on its power and reach. But he was often stymied by opposition from Congress and adverse court rulings. He also perceived that his successors might not be as resolute as he was in curbing government growth and holding the line on government spending. Reagan concluded that restraining government in the long run might require constitutional reform.

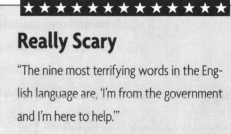

Really Scary

"The nine most terrifying words in the English language are, 'I'm from the government and I'm here to help.'"

Ronald Reagan

Reagan's Unfinished Agenda

There were two important initiatives in Reagan's second term that have tended to be forgotten over the years, but that deserve to be remembered today.

First, starting in 1985, and working chiefly through his second attorney general, Edwin Meese, the Reagan administration picked a major fight with

A Book You're Not Supposed to Read

The Age of Reagan: The Conservative Counterrevolution, 1980–1989 by Steven F. Hayward (Crown Forum, 2009).

liberalism. Meese and Reagan began making speeches and publishing articles arguing that the judiciary (mainly the Supreme Court) should interpret the Constitution according to the "original intent" of the Framers, and that federalism and "coordinate review"—that is, the idea that all three branches, not just judges and lawyers, have a duty and a right to interpret the Constitution—should be revived. After all, the Preamble begins "We the people," not "We the judges." As Attorney General Meese put it,

> The Supreme Court, then, is not the only interpreter of the Constitution. Each of the three coordinate branches of government created and empowered by the Constitution—the executive and legislative no less than the judicial—has a duty to interpret the Constitution in the performance of its official functions. In fact, every official takes an oath precisely to that effect.

In launching a high-profile debate on interpreting the Constitution, Reagan and Meese reopened a fundamental question that liberals thought was settled. No prominent Republican since Coolidge had seriously advanced such an argument. The public fight Meese picked over original intent, legal scholar Jonathan O'Neill wrote, "constituted the most direct constitutional debate between the executive branch and the Court since the New Deal." Reagan and Meese were attempting nothing less than to wrest the Constitution away from a self-appointed legal elite and return it to the people. The reaction not just of the usual suspects such as the *New York Times* editorial page, but also of sitting Supreme Court justices—two of them made speeches criticizing "original intent"—and of many prominent voices in the legal academy assured that this issue would not go away. Indeed, it is still very much with us.

Second, starting in 1987 Reagan argued for a package of five constitutional amendments he called his "Economic Bill of Rights." This represented another way in which Reagan was trying to turn back the liberal legacy of FDR, whose own "economic bill of rights" of 1944 consisted of more things the government would give you by redistributing wealth (such as a right to a job, a right to health care, and a right to housing and food). Reagan wanted to restore the older understanding that individual rights are limits on the government's power over you, rather than claims you can make against your fellow citizens through expanded governmental power.

Reagan's first two amendments were very familiar: a balanced budget amendment, and an amendment granting the president a line-item veto over spending bills, which most state governors have and which enables the executive to reduce spending for individual programs that is often included in large budget bills that the president can't veto, such as defense appropriations. Reagan had asked for both of these amendments in nearly every state of the union speech during his presidency.

But Reagan's other three proposed amendments were different and interesting. His third proposal was a requirement for a two-thirds supermajority vote of Congress for all tax increases. The fourth was a constitutional spending limit, so that the federal government couldn't just slowly (or quickly, as under Obama) increase its share of the nation's income step by step and year by year. Finally, Reagan's fifth proposed amendment was a constitutional prohibition on wage and price controls. This last one is the most curious—and an indication of Reagan's farsightedness. By the late 1980s, inflation had come down, and there was no one arguing that the U.S. would ever want to consider wage and price controls again. Nearly everybody across the political spectrum at that time agreed that the wage and price controls of the 1970s hadn't been very successful—that, in fact, such price controls could not

★ ★ ★ ★ ★ ★ ★ ★ ★ ★ ★ ★ ★ ★ ★

"A Conservative Camelot"

"The Reagan years will be for conservatives what the Kennedy years remain for liberals: the reference point, the breakthrough experience—a conservative Camelot. At the same time, no lesson is plainer than that the damage of decades cannot be repaired in any one administration."

Governor Mitch Daniels of Indiana

work. But Reagan knew that times change. Perhaps he anticipated the kind of fiscal situation we have today, with enormous budget deficits and a Federal Reserve Bank running the government printing presses overtime. If inflation returned, a big-government liberal like President Obama might want to bring back wage and price controls as a remedy.

Constitutional amendments are by design difficult to pass, and Reagan's economic bill of rights got nowhere in the Democratic Congress of the late 1980s. But in the last two years, the Tea Party has revived Reagan's economic bill of rights, and various versions have been proposed in Congress since the inauguration of Obama and the 2010 election of a Republican House.

These were not the only constitutional changes Reagan supported. He also supported constitutional amendments allowing prayer in the public schools and restrictions on abortion. The anti-abortion amendment was blocked by a Senate filibuster. But that wasn't the end of Reagan's constitutional arguments on the issue.

The Pro-Life President

One of Reagan's great regrets is that he signed a liberal abortion law in California when he was governor back in 1967. He later changed his mind, and was firmly pro-life by the mid-1970s. His administration did what it could to reduce abortion within the limits of the *Roe v. Wade* decision, attempting to stop federal funding for abortion clinics and to require parental notification when any underage girl sought an abortion (both of these steps were blocked by federal judges), and to restrict medical research on aborted fetuses.

To mark the tenth anniversary of the *Roe v. Wade* decision, in the spring of 1983 Reagan published a long article in the *Human Life Review*, republished in 1984 as a small book entitled *Abortion and the Conscience of the Nation*. Reagan's political advisers were nervous about publishing such an article so close to his reelection campaign. Reagan replied, "I might not be reelected. We're going with it now." Reagan was the first sitting president to publish a book, and seldom has any president since Lincoln spoken so openly and forcefully about such a contentious moral issue. He was just as direct and unequivocal as Lincoln was about slavery. "Make no mistake, abortion-on-demand is not a right granted by the Constitution." *Roe* was an act of "raw judicial power," Reagan said, quoting Justice Byron White's scorching dissent, comparable to *Dred Scott*: "This is not the first time our country has been divided by a Supreme Court decision that denied the value of certain human lives." Some of Reagan's language was bracing: "The abortionist who reassembles the arms and legs of a tiny baby to make sure all its parts have been torn from its mother's body can hardly doubt whether it is a human being." The media said such a controversial article by a sitting president was "rare" and "unusual."

The President's Prerogative Power

The first and most important responsibility of the federal government under the Constitution is to defend the nation from its foreign enemies, and the most important responsibility of the president as "commander in chief" is to see to that defense. This is the central issue in what became known as the "Iran-Contra" scandal, in which the Reagan administration sought to provide covert military aid to the freedom fighters (the "Contras") fighting to overthrow the Communist Sandinista dictatorship in Nicaragua. Because the issues about the president's powers under the Constitution that arose during this controversy returned in almost the same form in the controversies that shadowed President George W. Bush after September 11, 2001, Iran-Contra is worth discussing at some length.

The Iran-Contra scandal was a tangled affair that involved some mistakes in judgment by Reagan and his senior advisers—most particularly the decision to attempt indirectly to ransom American hostages that Islamic extremists were holding hostage in Lebanon through arms sales to Iran, still ruled by the Ayatollah Khomeini. Some of the proceeds from the arms sales were diverted to support the Contras in Nicaragua. While the arms sales to Iran were unwise, neither the arms sales nor the diversions of funds to Nicaragua were clearly violations of existing laws, in large part because some of the laws that pertained to these actions were poorly written or ambiguous. In fact, in the subsequent independent counsel investigation, no one was directly charged with crimes for either the arms sales or the diversions of money in this politically charged scandal.

The fact is that Congress, acting inconsistently and irresponsibly for most of Reagan's presidency, had attempted to tie the president's hands in the conduct of foreign policy in ways that were at the very least constitutionally dubious. More than once Reagan had complained that it was not possible to carry out foreign policy with 535 secretaries of state on Capitol Hill in the House and Senate.

During the course of the Iran-Contra affair, numerous scholars and intellectuals dusted off John Locke's *Second Treatise of Government*—the text that had been the primary inspiration for the Declaration of Independence. Locke's understanding of the nature of prerogative in the executive was equally important to the Founders as they designed the office of the presidency. Locke had defined prerogative simply as *"nothing but the power of doing public good without a rule"* (emphasis in the original). Why "without a rule"? Because, Locke explained, "many things there are which the law can by no means provide for.... many accidents may happen wherein a strict and rigid observation of the laws may do harm." Indeed, Locke went as far as to say that "it is fit that the laws themselves should in some cases give way to the executive power.... [The executive must have] the power to act according to discretion for the public good, without the prescription of the law, *and sometimes even against it."*

Locke's idea of prerogative power is plainly a holdover, preserved and amplified, from the historically preexisting power of monarchs under the against which the institutions of parliamentary democracy arose—to check its too frequent abuse and aggrandizement. Executive prerogative is a concept that cannot by its very nature be delimited through formal legal means. And executive prerogative sits uneasily with the formal constitutionalism of American republican thought. No modern constitutional lawyer can accept it easily (though the federal judiciary has been very reluctant to intervene to limit or define it, dismissing several lawsuits brought by members of Congress to clarify the matter). In the scheme of the Founders, the abuse of executive prerogative was meant to be checked by the separation of powers, and congressional oversight is both necessary and proper. But even within congressional assertion of its own prerogative in the positive law, there is clearly scope for the president to exercise his prerogative. The National Security Act, for example, recognizes the general need for secrecy and discretion by providing that the president must notify Congress about covert operations "in a timely manner." What is "timely"? There are no legislative or judicial parameters of timeliness. Reagan never notified anyone in Congress of the Iran arms sales initiative during the year prior to its exposure in November 1986. But obviously had Reagan notified Congress of the arms transactions with Iran, it would have been on the front page of the *Washington Post* the next day.

Examples of presidential use of prerogative power in American history would include Jefferson's decision to consummate the Louisiana Purchase despite his own constitutional doubts; Lincoln's suspension of *habeas corpus* in 1861 (the Constitution expressly stipulates that suspension of *habeas* "in times of rebellion" is a congressional, not executive, power); Theodore Roosevelt's sailing of the Great White Fleet in 1907 in the absence of congressional authorization; and Franklin Roosevelt's various transgressions of the Neutrality Act, among others. These and other examples fit Alexander Hamilton's conception in *The Federalist* of the presidency as the locus of the government's "extensive and arduous enterprises." Jefferson, channeling Locke, argued in 1810 that there are "higher" duties than "strict observance of the laws." But Nixon showed the limits of presidential prerogative when he infamously argued that

---

★ ★ ★ ★ ★ ★ ★ ★ ★ ★ ★ ★ ★ ★ ★

Jefferson Defends Presidential Prerogative

"The question you propose, whether circumstances do not sometimes occur, which make it a duty in officers of high trust, to assume authorities beyond the law, is easy of solution in principle, but sometimes embarrassing in practice. A strict observance of the written laws is doubtless one of the high duties of a good citizen, but it is not the highest. The laws of necessity, of self-preservation, of saving our country when in danger, are of higher obligation. To lose our country by a scrupulous adherence to written law, would be to lose the law itself, with life, liberty, property and all those who are enjoying them with us; thus absurdly sacrificing the end to the means."

Thomas Jefferson in a letter to John Colvin in 1810

"If the president does it, it's not illegal"—an assertion the American public rejected.

As between Jefferson and Nixon, how is this delicate matter to be judged? While scholars and constitutional lawyers will argue for bright-line standards, the example of Nixon suggests the answer that Locke gives explicitly: the people shall judge. "The people," Locke wrote, observing the whole tendency of their actions to be the public good, contested not what was done without law to that end, or, if any human frailty or mistake—for princes are but men, made as others—appeared in some small declinations from that end, yet it was visible the main of their conduct tended to nothing but the care of the public. The people, therefore, finding reason to be satisfied with these princes whenever they acted without or contrary to the letter of the law, acquiesced in what they did....

The outcome of the constitutional struggle over the Iran-Contra matter would be decided in that exact way: by public judgment of the political clash in Washington. The joint House-Senate committee investigation of the Iran-Contra affair—an investigation Democrats likened to Watergate and hoped would end with Reagan's impeachment—took a turn President Reagan's critics had not expected when Lieutenant Colonel Oliver North appeared and delivered a devastatingly effective attack on liberals in Congress for their irresponsible meddling in foreign policy. Public opinion decisively shifted in Reagan's favor, and the liberal dream of driving another Republican president from office died quickly. In other words, the people judged, just as Locke said they should, and judged that Reagan had acted properly, if not necessarily wisely.

One Bull's Eye and Two Close Shots

During the 1980 campaign Reagan told the *Wall Street Journal*, "I think for a long time we've had a number of Supreme Court Justices who, given any chance, invade the prerogative of the legislature; they legislate rather than make judgments, and some try to rewrite the Constitution instead of interpreting it." Reagan set out to appoint conservatives to the judiciary in a more serious and systematic way than any administration in history.

But Reagan had promised in the 1980 campaign that he would make a woman "one of his first" appointments to the Supreme Court, and when Justice Potter Stewart retired from the Court in 1981, Reagan decided to fulfill this campaign promise immediately. In 1981 there were precious few Republican women with the judicial qualifications for such a high appointment; women accounted for fewer than 5 percent of all law school graduates ages 45 to 60 in 1981, and among them was Arizona Court of Appeals Justice Sandra Day O'Connor.

There were doubts about O'Connor at the time, but Reagan was satisfied that she would be a sound constitutional justice. In a personal letter to evangelical writer Harold O. J. Brown, Reagan wrote, "She has assured me that she finds abortion personally abhorrent. She has also told me she believes the subject is one that is a proper subject for legislation.... I have full confidence in Mrs. O'Connor, in her qualifications, and in her philosophy."

O'Connor would later become a disappointment to conservatives, but Reagan's confidence in O'Connor was initially justified. During her first years on the Court she was a solid conservative, voting with her Stanford Law School classmate and fellow Arizonan Justice Rehnquist in 92 percent of the Court's decisions. Throughout her tenure on the Court she generally remained a champion of property rights, writing the strong dissent in the infamous *Kelo* case in 2004 that upheld the power of local governments to take private land to give to other private land owners, in clear violation of the plain language of the Fifth Amendment's "takings" clause. In the first case about abortion to reach the Court after O'Connor joined, she voted with the dissenters in criticizing *Roe v. Wade* for forcing courts "to pretend to act as science review boards." *Roe* "is clearly on a collision course with itself.... there is no justification in the law or logic for the trimester framework adopted in *Roe*," O'Connor said. But she changed her mind in later abortion cases, and also voted to uphold affirmative action racial quotas in college admissions.

Reagan's second appointment to the Court in 1986 was Antonin Scalia, the first Italian-American to serve on the Supreme Court. He was a grand-slam home run for defenders of constitutional originalism, and he was confirmed by a vote of 98–0 in the Senate.

Reagan's third appointment to the Court was Anthony Kennedy, in 1987. Kennedy has often been a disappointment to conservatives; he is a very inconsistent Justice. But this appointment deserves an asterisk, like Roger Maris's home run record. Kennedy was Reagan's third and last choice for the Supreme Court seat that came open in 1987. His first choice was the stellar Robert Bork, whose nomination was expected to sail through the Senate with little difficulty. Even Senate Judiciary Committee chairman Joe Biden said he'd vote for Bork. But after a scurrilous attack led by Ted Kennedy and the entire apparatus of the left, Democrats in the Senate voted down Bork's nomination—and in doing so changed judicial politics forever. The incident even gave rise to a new transitive verb in many dictionaries: "Borking, to Bork," meaning to scuttle a nomination by means of a campaign of relentless public attacks on the character and opinions of the nominee.

Reagan was so angry that he said he was tempted to appoint no one and leave the seat empty until the next president took office, but then he decided to name someone "they'll object to just as much as the last one." That person was Douglas Ginsburg, a jurist of strong libertarian credentials whose appointment was scuttled when it was revealed that he had smoked mari-juana as a Harvard professor. That left only Anthony Kennedy on the list of potential appointees who had been reviewed by the Justice Department. Reagan knew that Kennedy was a weak choice from his point of view. For-mer Attorney General William French Smith told Reagan, "I know Anthony Kennedy, and he won't be there in the trenches." But with no other nominee in reserve, Kennedy got the nod.

With the defeat of Bork and the weakness of O'Connor, Reagan lost his chance to reshape the Supreme Court decisively. Still, his appointments—

including even Kennedy on many issues—did move the Court in a more conservative direction. And Reagan was very successful in placing principled conservatives throughout the district courts and the federal circuit courts of appeals.

Because of Reagan's overall record of understanding, articulating, and implementing principled constitutionalism, the two disappointing Supreme Court appointments only lower his constitutional grade to an A-.

Chapter 16

GEORGE H. W. BUSH, 1989–1993

"I want a kinder, gentler nation."
—*George H. W. Bush*

President Bush's Constitutional Grade: B

After serving loyally as Ronald Reagan's vice president for two terms, George Herbert Walker Bush won election in his own right in 1988. He had a well-earned reputation as a decent and generous man, with a moderate Republican ideology. The ups and downs of his single term show the inadequacies of both decency and moderation in modern presidential politics. The first Bush presidency is also an object lesson in how to squander the successful legacy of a predecessor—in this case, the legacy of Ronald Reagan.

The most important political fact of the Bush presidency was the manner in which he won the election—a lesson Bush largely forgot after taking office. The 1988 election was in many respects a referendum on the Reagan presidency; Bush ran, in effect, for a third Reagan term. Bush reassured conservatives at the Republican convention in 1988 when he declared his fealty to Reaganism with the pledge: "Read my lips: No. New. Taxes." The man who had derided tax cuts as "voodoo economics" in 1980 now offered his own supply side fillip: Bush proposed to cut the capital gains tax from 28 to 15 percent. In the fullness of time George Bush lived up to this pledge—just not *this* George Bush. Conservatives felt betrayed when George H. W. Bush broke away from Reagan's policies and principles.

And liberals will never forgive Bush for pointing out the deep liberalism of their 1988 nominee, Massachusetts Governor Michael Dukakis. Dukakis had tried to conceal his liberalism behind the veneer of managerial "competence," and liberals cried foul when Bush pointed out his furloughs for murderers, vetoes of bills calling for public school children to recite the Pledge of Allegiance, opposition to the death penalty, support for gun control, and membership in the American Civil Liberties Union. Liberals howled because liberals think such appeals to fundamental cultural values should be out of bounds. They do not appreciate that presidential elections are about character and value questions above all. And by 1988 most Americans disliked liberalism. As political journalist William Schneider wrote at the time, "Why has liberalism become such a scare word? The reason is that Reagan has changed the shape of American politics." Instead of defending their unpopular positions, liberals attacked Bush for "running a negative campaign." This has become the template for liberal interpretations of national elections ever since (especially in 2004). But as political scientist Aaron Wildavsky observed, "A negative campaign is one in which the wrong candidate loses."

Squandering the Reagan Legacy

Despite owing his election largely to the legacy of Reagan, Bush went to some trouble to distance himself from Reagan, most pointedly in his convention speech, with language about seeking to bring about "a kinder, gentler nation." ("Kinder and gentler than whom?" Nancy Reagan is reported to have asked.) After the election the first order of business for the Bush transition was turning out all of the Reaganites as quickly as possible. It was said of Bush appointees that (unlike Reaganites), they had mortgages rather than ideologies. Paul Weyrich said that he had always feared that the election of Bush meant the arrival of "country club Republicans who couldn't wait for the end of the Reagan administration." George Shultz's top aide at the State Department, Charles Hill, recalled, "It was suddenly clear that this would be an adversarial transition. The new people were not friendly. The signals were: get out of here as fast as you can." Newt Gingrich cautioned, "We are not Bush's movement."

In domestic policy Bush abandoned Reagan's caution about extending government regulation. Both regulation and federal spending began rising rapidly after the years of restraint under Reagan. Bush sponsored several new statutes that expanded federal regulation and litigation—including especially the Americans with Disabilities Act, a well-meaning but poorly drafted statute. He also sponsored a new Clean Air Act that extended the reach of the Environmental Protection Agency and set in motion the ethanol boondoggle. And Bush signed on to a new civil rights law that Congress passed after the Supreme Court ruled that some forms of racial preferences were unconstitutional. He also increased federal education spending because he had promised to be the "education president."

> ★ ★ ★ ★ ★ ★ ★ ★ ★ ★ ★ ★ ★
>
> ## A Man of Principle?
>
> "I'm conservative, but I'm not a nut about it."
>
> George H. W. Bush

But Bush's biggest mistake was raising income taxes to fight the federal deficit. He abandoned his "no new taxes" pledge in the worst way possible— both agreeing to raise income tax rates and giving in the Democrats' demands that he drop his call for a cut in the capital gains tax. Bush later regretted the deal, but by then it was too late. By 1992, Bill Clinton was able to run to Bush's *right*, hitting Bush for raising taxes and promising to "end welfare as we know it" (welfare was an issue Bush had ignored). Bush not only lost the conservative base that forms the core of the Republican Party, but he lost independents, too. In the 1992 election, two-thirds of voters who voted for Bill Clinton told the exit polls that Bush's abandonment of his "no new taxes" promise was a "very important" factor in their decision to support Clinton.

If Bush's tax increase and domestic policy generally conceded too much ground to liberalism, one aspect of his economic policy deserves praise. When the economy entered a mild recession in 1991, Bush and his team wisely decided that the best course was to do nothing—to let the natural economic cycle play itself out without some kind of counter-productive government intervention or "stimulus." Bush was the first president since Harding to adopt this course—and to refrain from repeated public pronouncements explaining how his administration was working to revive the economy. The wise decision not to intervene in the economy came at a high political cost, though; Bush's laissez-faire policy and silence about the economic crisis contributed to his fall in popularity, and left Bill Clinton an opening to campaign on the theme, "It's the economy, stupid." Bush would have been better served by a more forceful economic message, even if it had been just an explanation of why the government would only make things worse if it intervened. Instead, he offered no defense of his policy.

Bush Abroad

One reason Bush performed poorly on domestic affairs is that, by his own admission, he lacked "the vision thing." The one area where he was something of a visionary was foreign policy—which is not surprising, given Bush's extensive background in foreign affairs. He had served as UN ambassador and director of the CIA before he became vice president. Unfortunately, Bush embraced an internationalist vision, in his own words, "a new world order"—a description that rightly raised Americans' suspicions that their president put too much confidence in the "world community."

It was unfortunate that Bush chose this ill-conceived phrase and failed to grasp how unpopular it was outside the Beltway, for his management of foreign affairs during his one term was generally laudable. When the Berlin Wall came down suddenly in November 1989, Bush was wary of inflaming a potentially unstable situation and issued a statement so low-key it made people wonder if he was on valium.

Bush's management of the dissolution of the Soviet Union in 1990 and 1991, while uneven and vulnerable to numerous criticisms, was generally capable, and he played a central role in easing the way for the reunification of West and East Germany, which was a very sensitive issue for all of Europe.

The most memorable foreign episode of Bush's presidency was the 1991 Gulf War, "Operation Desert Storm," for which Bush assembled a large international coalition to reverse Saddam Hussein's invasion of Kuwait. The swift and decisive victory of American arms in the Gulf War was vivid testimony to the rebuilding of American military capabilities and morale under President Reagan over the previous decade. The Gulf War, however, ended inconclusively. While Iraq was forced out of Kuwait, the offensive stopped short of dislodging Saddam Hussein from power in Iraq. Bush and his team miscalculated, believing that Hussein would be overthrown by his own people in the aftermath of the war. Instead, the United States had to return to finish the job twelve years later.

> ★★★★★★★★★★★★★★
> ## Playing It Cool
> Reporter to the president, on the fall of the Berlin Wall: "You don't seem elated."
> President Bush: "I'm not an emotional kind of guy."

A Split Decision

President Bush made two appointments to the Supreme Court, and the contrast between them shows the hazards of the often careless appointments many Republican presidents have made over the decades. Bush's first appointment, David Souter, was one of the very worst Republican appointments ever made to the Court, while his second, Clarence Thomas, was one of the best.

Bush appointed David Souter to replace the radical liberal William Brennan in 1990; Souter was chosen precisely because he had no "paper trail," and Bush wanted to avoid a confirmation fight like the one that had brought down Robert Bork in 1987. Bush had been assured that Souter would be a "home run" on the Court, but he should have been wary when Souter revealed that his model justice was Oliver Wendell Holmes. (In fact, any prospective judicial appointee who admits to admiring Holmes should be disqualified from appointment by any conservative administration that is awake.) Liberals were suspicious of Souter, with many groups like the National Organization for Women opposing his confirmation. They needn't have worried. Once confirmed, Souter quickly lurched to the left, voting to uphold abortion on demand and joining the liberal bloc in almost all major cases that reached the Court. According to the *Wall Street Journal*, retired New Hampshire Senator Warren Rudman, one of Souter's chief sponsors for the appointment, later took "pride in recounting how he sold Mr. Souter to gullible White House Chief of Staff John Sununu as a confirmable conservative."

Bush made up for this blunder with his second appointment in 1991: Clarence Thomas. As Thomas was a conservative black and only the second black to be appointed to the Supreme Court (Thomas was replacing Thurgood Marshall), the left went all-out to defeat his confirmation. Bush's support for Thomas wavered briefly when the left rolled out a trumped-up sexual harassment charge against him, but Bush ultimately held firm and Thomas was confirmed. He has gone on to be the strongest voice on the Supreme Court for reestablishing the Founders' understanding of constitutional interpretation.

President Bush 41 (as he is often called to distinguish him from his son) deserves credit for a steady hand in conducting foreign policy—which satisfies the president's most important constitutional duty: defending the nation. His appointment of Clarence Thomas to the Supreme Court is also a very large factor weighing in Bush's favor. But his major blunder with Souter and his acquiescence in expanding government regulation knock Bush's constitutional grade down to a straight B.

Chapter 17

WILLIAM JEFFERSON CLINTON, 1993–2001

"It depends on what the meaning of the word 'is' is. If the—if he—if 'is' means is and never has been, that is not—that is one thing. If it means there is none, that was a completely true statement."

Bill Clinton

"Bill Clinton never should have won the 1992 Presidential election."

—*Martin Walker, the* Guardian *(a left-wing paper)*

President Clinton's Constitutional Grade: F

Did you know?

★ Bill Clinton was the first Democrat since FDR to be elected to two terms

★ Bill Clinton was the first to offer a "two-for-one" presidency

★ Bill Clinton was the second president to be impeached

★ Bill Clinton was the first president to grant clemency to terrorists

★ Bill Clinton was the first president to pardon a family member

Bill Clinton was by universal agreement a highly intelligent man and a supremely gifted politician, and yet he has to be judged as having squandered his gifts and achieved far less than he might have because of his deep character flaws. The news media and the Democratic Party establishment, who both knew of Clinton's impulsive womanizing and reckless behavior, did not merely cover it up. They argued that character doesn't matter in a president. But the main lesson of the Clinton catastrophe is that in reality *personal character matters* to the presidency as well as the nation.

Womanizing was just one of Clinton's flaws. Another aspect of his character was a volcanic temper, which occasionally burst out in public, such as when he lied directly to the American people about not having "sexual relations with *that woman*—Miss Lewinski," or the time he angrily stormed

237

out of a press conference after only a single unsympathetic question from a network news reporter. Clinton, a former professor of constitutional law at the University of Arkansas, stretched and pulled at the Constitution's limits on executive power, and arguably exceeded them.

Bill Clinton was the first baby boomer to hold the nation's highest office, but only the third-youngest president. He was the first Democrat since FDR elected to two terms and the first president to serve after the Cold War had been won, so in one key sense he got a free ride. By the account of novelist Toni Morrison, Bill Clinton was the nation's first black president, displaying "every trope of blackness"—raised in a single parent household, playing the saxophone, liking junk food, and displaying an "unpoliced sexuality." On the last score he followed in JFK's footsteps, but he outdid his hero; Bill Clinton was the first, and to date only, president to have his anatomy described on national television, by his lawyer, as "a normal man" in terms of "size, shape, direction."

Bill Clinton was the first to offer a co-presidency—himself and Hillary Rodham Clinton in a two-for-one special. The Constitution of the United States knows nothing of such an arrangement, but the ambitious Hillary welcomed it. As advisor George Stephanopoulous noted, Hillary "established a wholly owned subsidiary within the White House, with its own staff, its own schedule and its own war room called 'the Intensive Care Unit.'"

Other first ladies had not exactly been wallflowers. Edith Wilson guided her husband's hand in signing bills after his stroke. Eleanor Roosevelt was a leading cheerleader for the New Deal. Florence Harding was instrumental in Warren's rise. Rosalynn Carter sat in on Jimmy's cabinet meetings, and Nancy Reagan was blamed for engineering the dismissal of chief of staff Don Regan.

★ ★ ★ ★ ★ ★ ★ ★ ★ ★ ★ ★ ★

The Presidential "We"?

"I'm not going to have some reporters pawing through our papers. We are the president."

Hillary Clinton

Barbara Bush, a shrewd judge of character, was clearly an unofficial advisor to George H. W. Bush. But no First Lady can be compared to Hillary in her influence on the president's policy and personnel decisions.

"If Hillary makes a stupid suggestion, who's going to call her on it?" said Ben Wattenberg, a former aide to President Lyndon Johnson. LBJ had been disturbed by JFK's appointment of his brother Robert as Attorney General, and subsequent legislation had made it impossible for presidents to appoint a relative to a position over which Congress exercises jurisdiction. So the Clinton arrangement had to be unofficial, but it proceeded nonetheless, with FLOTUS in charge of health care reform.

Bill Clinton was not, like Woodrow Wilson, openly contemptuous of the Constitution, at least in word. His actions were another matter, particularly in areas where the president wields unalloyed power: pardons, monuments, and executive orders.

By Order of the President

President Clinton made especially heavy use of one particular presidential power: the right to issue executive orders. The first five presidents, doubtless mindful of the abuse of power by royalty, were reluctant to issue such orders. In fact, George Washington, John Adams, Thomas Jefferson, James Madison, and James Monroe issued a total of only fifteen executive orders. The first by Washington was to proclaim a national day of thanksgiving. (The actual term "executive order" was not used until Abraham Lincoln's presidency, and most executive orders remained unpublished until the modern era, when the State Department began to number them.)

Franklin Delano Roosevelt, a president Bill Clinton admired, was the Pete Rose of EOs, racking up 3,522—567 in 1933 alone. Ronald Reagan was no match, with only 381 in eight years, and neither was George H. W. Bush, with only 165 in four years. Clinton logged in at 364 EOs, but numbers alone do not tell the whole story. Consider Clinton's practice of using executive orders to cancel previous executive orders by other presidents, with Ronald Reagan a primary target.

On February 17, 1981, Ronald Reagan had issued EO 12291 "to reduce the burdens of existing and future regulations, increase agency accountability for regulatory actions, provide for presidential oversight of the regulatory process, minimize duplication and conflict of regulations, and insure well-reasoned regulations." To that end, the order subjected new regulations to cost-benefit analysis, a sensible measure by any standard. A Clinton EO revoked that order.

Reagan's EO 12612 sought "to restore the division of governmental responsibilities between the national government and the States that was intended by the Framers of the Constitution and to ensure that the principles of federalism established by the Framers guide the Executive departments and agencies in the formulation and implementation of policies." Therefore bureaucrats were to exercise restraint in taking action that would result in federal preemption of state laws. A Clinton executive order revoked that one, too.

Government zeal to grab private property prompted Reagan's executive order 12630, which called for caution when "constitutionally protected property rights" were in play. "Executive departments and agencies should review their actions carefully to prevent unnecessary takings and should account in decision-making for those takings that are necessitated by statutory mandate." A Clinton executive order revoked Reagan's EO on takings.

Ronald Reagan issued executive order 12606 "in order to ensure that the autonomy and rights of the family are considered in the formulation and implementation of policies by Executive departments and agencies." Actions were to be evaluated as to whether they strengthened the family and parental rights or "substitute government action" for the function of parents.

The impact on family earnings and budget was also to be considered. Bill Clinton duly revoked that order. On his watch federal bureaucrats did not need to consider the consequences of their actions on the American family.

Clinton's own EO 12836 targeted regulations requiring employers who contracted with the federal government to inform their employees of their rights under *Communication Workers v. Beck*, a Supreme Court ruling that had limited unions' ability to collect the money of workers and use it for political purposes. His proclaimed goal was to "eliminate executive orders that do not serve the public interest," but in effect Clinton's order meant that more workers would make involuntary political contributions to Democrats. Further, federal contractors were no longer required to post a notice that workers are not required to join unions.

The president's order on homosexuals in the military instituted a policy of "Don't ask, don't tell," prompting gay adviser David Mixner to hail Bill Clinton as "the Abraham Lincoln of our movement," though Clinton's own preference was decidedly for women (more about that in due course). Other Clinton executive orders allowed abortions on U.S. military bases overseas and racial profiling in hiring—a government-imposed quota policy known by the euphemism "affirmative action." Both abortion and racial quotas highlighted Clinton's hypocrisy: he claimed he wanted abortion to be "safe, legal, and rare," but always supported measures to expand abortion; he even vetoed a law that would have restricted partial-birth abortion. On affirmative action, Clinton claimed he wanted to "mend it, not end it," but this was nothing more than a smokescreen to obscure his determination to derail any reform of racial quotas.

A Clinton executive order also banned roads in more than 50 million acres of wilderness, a "stroke of the pen, law of the land" action taken without any cost-benefit analysis but duly hailed by environmental activists. It was just one of many Clinton EOs that belied his proclamation that the era of big government was over.

Clinton's Monument Valley

The personal touch also extended to Clinton's mania for monuments. The California coastline is under the jurisdiction of scores of duly elected local governments (and the California Coastal Commission, an unelected body that manages to combine mafia-style corruption with Stalinist regulation). Yet Bill Clinton declared the entire California coast, more than 800 miles, a national monument.

That particular proclamation illustrates what Barbara Olson described as Clinton's "pharaonic magalomania." The Antiquities Act of 1906 calls for national monuments to embrace the "smallest area compatible with proper care and management of the objects" protected by the Act—originally supposed to be historic and pre-historic ruins and monuments. Thus the Statue of Liberty—not all of New York Harbor—is a national monument. But "smallest" does not fit the Clinton style.

He authorized the Grand Staircase-Escalante National Monument in Utah, a full 1.7 million acres, and the Grand Canyon-Parashant National monument, covering 1,104,000 acres. On January 17, 2001, with the clock ticking down to the end of his presidency, he created, count 'em, nine new national monuments: the Carrizo Plain, 204,107 acres; Buck Island Reef, 135 acres; Kasha-Katuwe Tent Rocks, 4,148 acres; Minidoka Internment, 72.75 acres; Pompey's Pillar, 51 acres; the Sonoran Desert, 486,149 acres; the Upper Missouri Breaks, 377,346 acres; the Virgin Islands Coral Reef, 12,708 acres; and Governor's Island, 20 acres. Clinton's grand total comes to 5,686,767 acres of new national monuments, and we should not forget the 50 million acres of national forest that are off limits to logging and road building.

I Beg Your Pardon

Clinton's most flagrant abuse of his constitutional power was his use of the presidential pardon. The Constitution of the United States gives the president "power to grant reprieves and pardons for offenses against the United States." As Charles Krauthammer has observed, this is the most sacred power of the president, and as such should be exercised with the greatest caution. Alexander Hamilton explained in Federalist No. 74 that the American Founders made the president's pardon power absolute because "the sense of responsibility is always strongest in proportion as it is undivided," and this would "inspire scrupulousness and caution."

> ## A Book You're Not Supposed to Read
>
> *The Final Days: The Last, Desperate Abuses of Power by the Clinton White House* by Barbara Olson (Regnery, 2001).

It has not always seemed to be used scrupulously and cautiously, even in the early days of the republic. George Washington pardoned two leaders of the Whiskey Rebellion, and James Madison pardoned pirate Jean Lafitte. Andrew Johnson issued amnesty for ex-Confederates willing to take an oath to the United States. Theodore Roosevelt issued amnesty for followers of Philippine guerrilla leader Emilio Aguinaldo. More recently Gerald Ford pardoned Richard Nixon for crimes he may have committed in office. Jimmy Carter provoked a furious controversy by pardoning Vietnam War draft evaders and deserters. Carter also pardoned Patricia Hearst, the kidnapped heiress who became the submachine gun-toting "Tanya" in the Symbionese Liberation Army. George Bush pardoned Caspar Weinberger for the Iran-Contra scandal. But all these presidents could make some kind of case that these pardons, even if not scrupulous and cautious, were in the national interest.

I am going to go out on a limb here. Bill Clinton is not a naturally cautious man. In fact, even in elected office he has always been reckless to a fault, exhibiting what Michael Kinsley, a supporter, called "a frightening lack of self control." An attractive woman named Cyd Dunlop once caught Clinton's eye, and he called her in her hotel room while she was in bed with her husband, attempting to persuade the woman to step out, right then, and hook up with him. And of course, he let Monica Lewinsky, the eager, thong-flashing "assistant to the president for blow jobs" (APBJ), perform her tasks in his office, where others could—and apparently did—walk in.

More than simple recklessness was in play, however, in Clinton's treatment of terrorism. This was a development his administration should have seen coming, and not just from the Islamic side. U.S. presidents have been prime targets for some time, with more than twenty attempts against their lives—some successful, as in the cases of Lincoln, Garfield, McKinley, and Kennedy. The unsuccessful attempts also provide a warning. On November 1, 1950, Oscar Collazo and Griselio Torresola attempted to assassinate U.S. President Harry Truman at Blair House, where Harry and Bess Truman were living while the White House was being renovated. The attempt failed, though Torresola and Secret Service agent Leslie Coffelt died in the brief gun battle. That failed attempt to kill a president did not end the terror campaign for Puerto Rican independence. Rather, the movement turned to easier targets in cities such as New York, Chicago, and Washington, D.C.

The *Fuerzas Armadas de Liberacion Nacional* (FALN) is a violent group seeking an independent Marxist-Leninist Puerto Rico on the Cuban model. The group was responsible for no fewer than 130 bombing attacks in the United States from 1974 to 1983. These attacks killed six Americans and wounded scores of others.

Apprehended FALN terrorists remained unrepentant, and Carlos Romero-Barcelo, Puerto Rico's delegate in Congress, wrote to President Clinton requesting that he keep the FALN members imprisoned. The FBI opposed their release on the grounds that they were criminals and represented a threat to the United States. Even Attorney General Janet Reno of Waco fame considered them a threat. And Eric Holder, then a deputy Attorney General, wanted consideration for the victims.

Clinton, however, chose to bypass the Justice Department and failed to consult with any victims, or relatives of victims, of FALN terrorism. In September of 1999 Clinton gave clemency to fourteen of sixteen imprisoned FALN members. This was the first case of presidential clemency for terrorists.

One can see here the hand of Co-President Hillary, whose politics were shaped by Liberation Theology—orthodox Marxism-Leninism tricked out in Christian vocabulary which, as Michael Novak (*Will It Liberate?*) has pointed out, never liberated anyone or anything. Hillary also interned for Robert Treuhaft, a lawyer for the Communist Party USA and husband of Jessica Mitford. Both were Stalinists and so slavishly pro-Soviet that even the New Left and Black Panthers shunned them.

On his last trip on Air Force One, Clinton strode into the press room and asked, "You got anybody you want to pardon?" He had already been flooded with requests, and he was disposed to grant them—largely because of a personal issue that in due time would highlight an important constitutional principle.

The Constitution of the United States nowhere elevates the president above the law of the land. That fact emerged with crystal clarity in the case of Paula Corbin Jones, a secretary with the Arkansas Industrial Development Commission. She was twenty-four when she caught the eye of Governor Clinton at a May 1991 management conference. Clinton tasked a state trooper to bring Jones to his room. There, a year before he would become president of the United States, Bill Clinton dropped his pants and invited Paula Jones to "kiss it." She declined and fled, later suing the president for sexual harassment. President Clinton had his political hit squad smear Jones as a white-trash slut and dupe of Republicans. He fought Jones all the way to the U.S. Supreme Court, contending that he should not have to defend himself against Jones's suit as a sitting president—and lost in a 9–0 shutout.

Clinton wound up paying out an $850,000 settlement, a large amount for a case that supposedly had no merit.

The Jones lawsuit revealed the existence of Monica Lewinsky, the APBJ barely older than Chelsea Clinton—and ultimately brought on Clinton's angry denial that he never had sex with "that woman." George Stephanopoulos described the performance as Clinton "lying with true conviction." True to form, the Clinton machine smeared Monica as a mental case and sexual predator. Hillary Rodham Clinton, on national television, blamed the whole thing on a "vast right-wing conspiracy."

On December 19, 1998, in the wake of the 445-page Starr Report, Bill Clinton became only the second U.S. president to be impeached. He was already the first to give his blood for a DNA test, which helped expose his falsehoods. He vowed to carry on, and did, but if he wanted to avoid prosecution for false testimony in the Paula Jones case, he had to finalize a deal with independent counsel Robert Ray before leaving office:

> ★ ★ ★ ★ ★ ★ ★ ★ ★ ★ ★ ★ ★ ★
>
> ## A One-Track Mind
>
> "You know, if I were a single man, I might ask that mummy out. That's a good-looking mummy."
>
> ---
>
> Bill Clinton, on seeing an ancient Inca mummy on display at the National Geographic Society

I will not seek any legal fees incurred as a result of the Lewinsky investigation, to which I might otherwise become entitled under the Independent Counsel Act. I have had occasion, frequently, to reflect on the Jones case. In this consent order, I acknowledge having knowingly violated Judge Wright's discovery orders in my deposition in that case.

I tried to walk a fine line between acting lawfully and testifying falsely, but I now recognize that I did not fully accomplish this goal, and that certain of my responses to questions about Ms. Lewinsky were false.

It was vintage Clinton—"I did not fully accomplish this goal"—but to no avail. The president of the United States had fought the law, and the law won. The system worked, as they said in the wake of Watergate.

This admission—not to mention the five-year suspension of his license to practice law—would have been a humiliation for any lawyer, let alone the president of the United States, the most powerful person in the world,

Living in His Own Alternative Reality?

"It depends on how you define alone.... There were a lot of times when we were alone, but I never really thought we were."

Bill Clinton in grand jury testimony

who took a solemn oath to defend the Constitution and uphold the laws. That it left Bill Clinton in a foul mood, disposed to break more records before he left office has to be taken into account when we consider the pardons.

The president may wield absolute authority to grant pardons, but modern presidents have seen fit to develop a careful review process and firm guidelines to prevent the power from abuse or the appearance of corruption. Before a presidential pardon is granted, the case must pass through the office of the Pardon Attorney in the Department of Justice. The offense in question must be federal, not a violation of state laws, and a five-year period must have elapsed. Those on probation, parole, or supervised release are not eligible. The FBI and other agencies are supposed to be consulted. Other presidents may have occasionally waived or overridden the formal pardon review process, as in Gerald Ford's pardon of Richard Nixon. Clinton ignored the process altogether.

Clinton even pardoned some criminals who had not applied for a pardon, including Dan Rostenkowski, the Illinois Democrat who had chaired the House Ways and Means Committee. In 1996 "Rosty" was indicted for mail fraud and sentenced to seventeen months in prison. He had not asked for a pardon and the required five years had not elapsed, but Clinton pardoned him anyway in December 2000. The Christmas pardons at the end of Clinton's term included Archie Schaffer III, chief spokesman for Tyson Foods, who had been convicted for trying to influence Agriculture Secretary Mike Espy. This was doubtless a partisan payoff.

Jonathan Pollard, who spied for Israel (see *Territory of Lies*, by Wolf Blitzer), did not make the list, despite support for a pardon from Benjamin Netanyahu. Leonard Peltier, serving two life sentences in Leavenworth for the murder of two FBI agents, drew support from Desmond Tutu, Jesse Jackson, Susan Sarandon, and other luminaries. Even so, Peltier failed to make the cut with Clinton. So did junk-bond king Michael Milken.

As his second term wound down, the Clinton White House badgered the Justice Department to find more pardon cases, and was taking applications from all comers. He saved the worst for last.

From Odometers to Anteaters

True to form, the 140 pardons and 36 commutations on Clinton's last day in office included Arkansans brothers Art and Doug Borel, convicted of rolling back the odometers on cars. Larry Lee Duncan of Branson, Missouri, committed the same crime and also got a presidential pardon. The president of the United States also pardoned Billy Wayne Warmath, sixty-two, of Walls, Mississippi, who had committed $123.26 of credit card fraud in 1965, when Lyndon Johnson was president. Warmath, a Republican, said he was happy about the pardon. The president also deployed his power to pardon Howard Winfield Riddle, a smuggler of banned anteater skins used in cowboy boots. Almon Glenn Braswell had promoted fake cures for baldness and also dabbled in mail fraud and perjury. Braswell got a Clinton pardon and the next day wired $200,000 to the law firm in which Hugh Rodham, the co-president's brother, was a partner.

Clinton showed a soft spot for frauds. On January 20, 2001, he pardoned Charles D. Ravenel, a former Democratic candidate for the U.S. Senate. Ravenal had looted Citadel Federal Savings Bank in one of the biggest frauds in the history of South Carolina. As Alec Guinness said in *Star Wars,* "You will never find a more wretched hive of scum and villainy." Bill Clinton was up to the challenge.

Things Go Better with Coke

Clinton also commuted the sentences of twenty-one drug offenders. Some had received long sentences for minor offences, but not all fit this pattern. Manhattan lawyer Harvey Weinig, for example, had helped launder money for the Cali Cartel. The Colombian government denounced his presidential pardon. As it happened, Weinig was related by marriage to a former senior aide in the Clinton White house. What a cozy world.

Bill Clinton became the first president to pardon a family member when he cleared Roger Clinton Jr., his half-brother (Secret Service name "Headache"), of a 1985 cocaine conviction that had landed him in jail for year. Ironically, Roger had been busted in a sting operation authorized by Governor Clinton. Roger was once a driver for Dan Lasater, a restaurant magnate and cocaine distributor Clinton had pardoned as governor. While Lasater was in prison, the executive vice president of his business was Patsy Thomasson, whom the Clintons brought to Washington where she directed the Office of the Administration and managed a White House drug-testing program.

President Clinton also commuted the sentence of Carlos Anibal Vignali, who had shipped nearly half a ton of cocaine to Minneapolis for processing into crack sold in poor neighborhoods. Vignali is the son of Horacio Vignali, a wealthy Los Angeles developer and major donor to Democratic politicians.

Xavier Becerra, Antonio Villaraigosa, and others formed a phone bank to plead with the president for a pardon for Vignali. Horacio also prevailed on Clinton's U.S. attorney in Los Angeles, Alejandro Mayorkas, to call the White House on behalf of the imprisoned drug dealer, whose pardon, like many others, bypassed the usual channels. Hugh Rodham charged the Vignali family $200,000 for work on the pardon.

This presidential pardon prompted a U.S. attorney to resign and sparked outrage among law enforcement. The Clintons ignored the scandal.

Close Enough for Government Work

President Clinton pardoned Henry Cisneros, the former San Antonio mayor he had put in charge of Housing and Urban Development. In Clinton style, Cisneros had pleaded guilty to false statements in a case involving a former mistress. Richard Wilson Riley Jr., son of Clinton's Secretary of Education Richard Riley, was convicted of conspiring to sell cocaine in 1993. Clinton gave him an unconditional pardon.

Bill Clinton also pardoned John Deutch, former CIA director, who had gotten in trouble for putting classified information on his home computer. The president pardoned Samuel Loring Morison of Naval Intelligence, who had leaked classified photos. Clinton commuted the sentence of Ronald Henderson Blackley, chief of staff for Mike Espy, who had made false statements in the Clinton style.

Jesse Jackson, another friend, lobbied the president to pardon Mel Reynolds, a former Chicago congressman who had resigned after a conviction for sex with a sixteen-year-old campaign worker and also been prosecuted on fraud charges. Clinton commuted his sentence and also pardoned Dorothy Rivers of Jackson's PUSH (People United to Save Humanity) organization, who stole $1.2 million in government grants.

Connections did not always carry the day. Susan McDougal, the Clintons' Whitewater partner, got a pardon; but Webster Hubbell, associate attorney general, did not. This doubtless reflects the president's preference to go the second mile for women. Jimmy Carter had already pardoned Patty Hearst, but her bank robbery conviction remained on record. Bill Clinton made it go away.

Family Values

Susan Rosenberg was a member of the Weather Underground, a domestic group of bomb throwers in league with the May 19 Communist Organization, the Black Liberation Army, the Red Guerrilla Resistance, and others, known collectively as "The Family." Like Bonny and Clyde, they robbed banks, killed police officers, and bombed the U.S. Capitol, the Naval War College, the FBI office in Staten Island, and other targets.

Rosenberg was apprehended with 740 pounds of explosives and an arsenal of weapons. She was sentenced to fifty-eight years in prison and became a celebrity of the left, with Noam Chomsky, William Kunstler, and others lobbying for her release. They got it on the last day of the Clinton presidency, when he not only granted Rosenberg clemency but also commuted the sentence of Linda Sue Evans, convicted in the 1983 plot to bomb the Capitol. The president's actions provoked outrage from Charles Schumer, senator from New York, and from Rudolph Giuliani, then mayor of New York, who had prosecuted a Family attack on Brink's. Like the victims, these politicians had no recourse.

One can see the hand of FLOTUS in the Rosenberg and Evans pardons, which gave hope to terrorists everywhere. For all their flair, however, Rosenberg and Evans took a back seat to another case right out of Ian Fleming's *Goldfinger*.

Rich and Pinky

Marc Rich, born in 1934 in Antwerp, Belgium, became a U.S. citizen in 1947 and by 1977 had become the world's biggest trader in aluminum. He also shipped oil to pariah nations such as South Africa, traded with Iran and Libya, and swapped oil for sugar with Cuba. In 2000, his operations took in some $7 billion. U.S. officials charged him under the RICO statute in a case they called the largest tax fraud in U.S. history, but Rich and his partner Pincus "Pinky" Green fled the country. While Rich was a fugitive, one of his companies, Clarendon, sold more than $4 million of nickel and copper to the U.S. Mint, a division of the very Treasury Department Rich had defrauded.

Marc Rich had all the money and power anyone would want, but these did not suffice. He also sought a pardon. He gave away money to worthy causes, gaining himself high-profile allies such as Ehud Barak and Abe Foxman. Rich was aiming for an unconditional pardon, turning down all deals that involved surrender to U.S. authorities. He opted to play on Clinton's dislike of prosecutors, and deployed his former wife Denise to lobby the president. She gave at least $1.5 million to causes related to the Clintons at the very time former White House counsel Jack Quinn was pressing Bill Clinton for a pardon. She loaded the Clintons with gifts, including a gold saxophone for the president. Rich got his pardon, along with "Pinky" Green.

In a *New York Times* op-ed, Clinton denied the pardons were due to Denise Rich's contributions to the Clinton library foundation. These stories were "utterly false" claimed the president, and "there was absolutely no quid pro quo." The *Times*'s own editorial, in contrast, said the pardon "begins and ends with money and the access afforded by money" and was a "gross misuse of a solemn presidential responsibility."

Clinton's piece was "in almost every important way a lie," according to Michael Kelly, who had covered Clinton's 1992 campaign for the *Times*.

"No other president ever did what Clinton did," wrote Kelly. Clinton "sought to corrupt the pardoning process on a wholesale basis. None set up a secret shop to bypass his own government and speed through the special pleas of the well connected and well heeled. None sent the Justice department dozens of names for pardon on inauguration morning, too late for the department to run even cursory checks." Concluded Kelly, "Eight reasons, four lies. Not bad, even for the old master himself."

Jimmy Carter went on record that "large gifts" played a role in the pardons, which he called "disgraceful." Carter's own pardons and commutations, by the way, included Oscar Collazo, who tried to kill Harry Truman; Jefferson Davis, president of the Confederate States of America; and G. Gordon Liddy of Watergate fame.

In February 2001, the Senate Judiciary Committee held hearings on the Clinton pardons. According to Charles Schumer, senior senator from New York, "To my mind there can be no justification for pardoning a fugitive from justice. It does not matter that the fugitive believed the case against him was flawed or weak. It does not matter that the fugitive was enormously philanthropic. Pardoning a fugitive stands our justice system on its head and makes a mockery of it."

For Tom Harkin, left-wing Iowa Democrat, "There's no excuse for what he did for Marc Rich. This should have not been done." Joe Biden said, "I think the president had an incredible lapse in memory or was brain dead." For Barney Frank, "It was a terrible thing he did. It was just abusive. These are people who forgot where the line was between public service and what was personally convenient for them." Clinton defender Bob Herbert noted that some of the pardons "fit neatly with the standard definition of a bribe."

Good point. The Constitution gives the president the power to pardon, but nowhere authorizes the president to sell pardons. Clinton critic Charles Krauthammer said the president was as oblivious to the special nature of the pardon power "as he was to the reverence due every other power of his office.... It was not bad judgment. It was sacrilege."

California governor and presidential aspirant Jerry Brown hinted that the Rich pardon might be a crime. As for Bill Clinton, Brown said, "he must have sugar plums dancing in his head," adding, "President Clinton did not start out with a lot of scrupulosity. Here we are talking about money and venality."

Descent to the Murky Bottom

As far as the Clinton legacy is concerned, I will let liberals, Democrats, editors, and former Clinton defenders have their say.

"Some of Mr. Clinton's closest associates and supporters are acknowledging what his enemies have argued for years—the man is so thoroughly corrupt it's frightening," wrote Bob Herbert of the *New York Times*. "The president who hung a 'for rent' sign on the Lincoln Bedroom also conducted a clearance sale on pardons in his last weird sleepless days in the White House."

For former *New Republic* editor Andrew Sullivan, "In Bill Clinton we had for eight years a truly irrational person in the White House, someone who, I think, lived on the edge of serious mental illness. He was and is a psychologically sick man." Further, "Clinton was not psychologically healthy enough to have been president of the United States."

According to the *Economist*, Clinton was "too dishonest an individual to be trusted with the presidency, however clever he might be."

"He was an arrogant, no-good son of a bitch," wrote John Robert Starr, managing editor of the *Arkansas Democrat-Gazette*, "a dirty rotten scoundrel."

Clinton critics had been right all along, said the *New York Observer*: "Mr. Clinton was, in fact, an untrustworthy low-life who used people for his own purposes and then discarded them."

Hamilton Jordan, former chief of staff for Jimmy Carter, attacked the Clintons in an op-ed titled "The First Grifters." The Clintons' only loyalty, he wrote, was "to their own ambitions."

Chris Matthews of *Hardball* had a different take. "The loser in this deal is the country," he wrote. "Before this, we laughed at poor little countries that drug dealers and international crooks could buy. We mocked the Third World capitals where a little money in the fingers of a certain family member would open doors or close eyes. Thanks to Bill and Hillary Clinton, we have now forfeited that small national vanity." The subtext here is that the Clintons were a milestone en route to Third World status for the United States—a rather dubious legacy.

"Ask yourself, what did Bill Clinton get done?" wrote Forrest McDonald, historian and author of *The American Presidency: An Intellectual History.* "Was there any major legislation he was responsible for? Welfare reform came from the Republican Congress. Health care was a disaster. He simply didn't get much done. He was a comedy of errors."

A Book You're Not Supposed to Read

Legacy: Paying the Price for the Clinton Years by Rich Lowry (Regnery, 2003).

Bill and Hillary Clinton were sixties (and thirties) re-enactors who showcased no ideas that had not been tried and found wanting. They found true reform difficult and left it untried. The Clinton administration is evidence that people can possess glittering academic qualifications and personal charisma yet remain professionally, psychologically, and morally unfit for public office, especially the nation's highest office. The Clintons, in effect, came to Washington, dropped their drawers, and told the nation to "kiss it." For the most part, the nation did. There's a lesson in there somewhere.

As Clarence Thomas might put it, beware of emanations from a penumbra. The Clinton Presidential Center containing the Clinton Presidential

Library and Museum is located near the Arkansas River in an old warehouse district known locally as Murky Bottoms. At least one tour guide sees the fearful symmetry with the Clinton legacy, which travel writers like Melissa Roth were touting as early as 2001: "Two hours west of Graceland, Little Rock is becoming a mecca for American scholars, European tourists, and kitsch-collectors, all thanks to the South's other pelvis-proud king."

The High Cost of Bad Character

The tragedy of the Clinton presidency is that Clinton held some moderate policy views and from time to time proved himself amenable to compromises with Republicans that advanced conservative goals, such as on welfare reform, balancing the budget, and even, late in his second term, tax cuts. Whether he was willing to work with Republicans on these issues out of sincere conviction or political expediency is hard to know, though it is worth pointing out that his famous rebuke of the rap artist "Sister Souljah" in the 1992 campaign had been preceded by public criticisms of Jesse Jackson as far back as 1984.

In the middle of his second term—we learned subsequently—Clinton and House Speaker Newt Gingrich were secretly negotiating a large deal to reform Social Security and Medicare, which even a decade ago were known to be on a long-term course to insolvency, threatening the nation with fiscal ruin. The outline of the deal was a classic Washington compromise that would have left both sides unhappy to some extent, but also would have advanced both sides' goals. Clinton was willing to agree to private accounts for both Social Security and Medicare—the main conservative reform proposal—and Gingrich was willing to consider some tax increases to shore up the program for existing beneficiaries. A Clinton-appointed special study commission had recommended just such a course.

Whether such a compromise reform could have passed Congress became a moot point when Clinton was impeached for perjury and obstruction of justice in 1998. Liberals in Congress supported Clinton against the impeachment charges on the condition that he abandon any talk of reforming Social Security and Medicare. In other words, the price of keeping Clinton in office was "no more welfare reforms." Today, over a decade later, the future fiscal imbalance for Social Security and Medicare has grown to more than $100 trillion, saddling future generations with either crushing tax increases, sudden program cuts that will affect low income seniors who depend on those programs, or economic collapse. In other words, Clinton's reckless personal behavior didn't just soil his own reputation and our respect for the Oval Office; in retrospect, his lack of character was a multi-trillion dollar catastrophe for the nation.

Summing It All Up for Posterity

"I may not have been the greatest president, but I've had the most fun eight years."

Bill Clinton

Radicals in Black Robes

In addition to Clinton's aggressive use of executive orders and abuse of the presidential pardon power, his judicial appointments also showed a lack of respect for the Constitution. His first Supreme Court appointment, in 1993, was Ruth Bader Ginsberg, whom Jimmy Carter had previously placed on the D.C. District Court of Appeals, the second-highest court in the nation. Ginsberg is a radical feminist, having founded the *Women's Rights Law Reporter* journal while a law professor at Rutgers University. She later directed the ACLU's Women's Rights Project, where the primary "woman's right" of concern was unrestricted abortion. About the *Roe v. Wade* decision that legalized abortion on demand in 1973, Ginsberg said later: "Frankly, I had thought at the time *Roe* was decided, there was concern about population growth and particularly growth in populations that we don't want to have too many of." Ginsberg has also been an advocate of appealing to foreign law when deciding cases before the Supreme Court.

Clinton's second appointment, in 1994, was Stephen Breyer. Breyer, a former aide to Massachusetts Senator Ted Kennedy, taught at Harvard Law School before becoming a federal judge. Breyer is openly contemptuous of interpreting the Constitution according to the original intent of the Founders, and instead supports an activist judicial philosophy he calls "active liberty," which in practice means consistently ruling in behalf of expanding government regulatory power and the welfare state. Like Ginsberg, Breyer supports appealing to foreign law when deciding cases. He has voted consistently to uphold abortion on demand—including partial-birth abortion—and he doesn't believe that the Second Amendment establishes an individual right to keep and bear arms.

Clinton clearly knew what he was doing when he chose as his Supreme Court nominees justices who would defend and expand the liberal agenda. If there were a lower constitutional grade than F, Clinton would deserve it.

Chapter 18

GEORGE WALKER BUSH, 2001–2009

"Make no mistake, we will show the world that we will pass the test."
—*George W. Bush*

President Bush's Constitutional Grade: B+

President George W. Bush, the son of the forty-first president, presents conservatives with a problem similar to the one posed by Richard Nixon. Bush had conservative inclinations and advanced a number of important conservative policies and principles. But he was a disappointment to conservatives on a number of important fronts. As with Nixon, most of the attacks from liberals and the media were unfair, when they weren't flat-out wrong. Unlike his father, George W. Bush was a genuine Washington outsider, deliberately at odds with the Eastern cultural establishment—right down to his cowboy boots and Texas mannerisms. Bush genuinely disliked Washington his entire life, and the annoyance he caused the cultural elite delighted him. For these reasons, but above all for defending the nation in the uncertain and dangerous years after September 11, 2001, conservatives owe Bush a serious defense.

Calling Bush's presidency controversial is like saying the sky is blue. Bush had the distinction of seeing some of the highest public approval ratings ever recorded, and also the lowest—a testimony to the turbulent decade in which he served, and to some of the unprecedented conditions he faced, starting with the disputed election of 2000 in which Bush lost the popular vote to Al Gore but won the Electoral College, which is the constitutional majority that counts.

Bush's legacy won't come into full focus for many years to come, for the same reason that it took many years to judge Harry Truman's strengths and weaknesses more accurately. (Both were wartime presidents, and both in unconventional wars.) But the fact that his successor, Barack Obama, has kept or expanded so many of President Bush's key policies in the war on terror, after having harshly criticized those very policies during the 2008 election campaign, suggests that Bush built well for the new era of asymmetric warfare the nation found itself in after September 11.

"Events, Dear Boy"

One of the most famous statements in politics is British Prime Minister Harold MacMillan's answer to the question of what factors are most likely to blow a government off course: "Events, dear boy, events." There is probably no president in all of American history about whom this statement is more telling than Bush. Bush ran for office in 2000 intending to be chiefly a domestic policy president, and he specifically criticized the "nation building" enterprises of the Clinton administration, suggesting that the United States should be more reticent ("humble" was the term Bush used on several occasions) about committing military forces abroad. Yet foreign policy came to dominate Bush's presidency, and Bush's foreign policy became largely defined by nation-building efforts in Iraq and Afghanistan and by extensive military deployments to carry out the democratization of these nations. Bush articulated a

A Book You're Not Supposed to Read

Rebel-in-Chief: Inside the Bold and Controversial Presidency of George W. Bush by Fred Barnes (Crown Forum, 2006).

new policy of pre-emptive action against potential terrorist states, which became known as the "Bush Doctrine"—putting himself in the illustrious company of the handful of presidents with long-term foreign policy precedents attached to their names (such as the Monroe Doctrine, the Truman Doctrine, and the Reagan Doctrine).

But despite having to meet the challenge of the September 11 attack—the most serious attack on the continental United States since the War of 1812—Bush still compiled a substantial domestic policy record, as well as advocating for a number of other domestic reforms that failed to come to fruition because of liberal opposition.

More Compassionate Than Conservative?

Bush campaigned for the presidency in the 2000 election under the general banner of "compassionate conservatism"—perhaps a necessary tactical concession to the political atmosphere Bill Clinton had created with his successful "triangulation" strategy. Clinton had partially restored public confidence in the federal government by a partial embrace of conservative ideas—especially on welfare reform and a balanced budget—and Bush perceived that a purely conservative campaign would fail to attract independent voters. But this was not mere politics on Bush's part. He believed in "compassionate conservatism," saying on one occasion that "when somebody hurts, people are hurting, government has got to move."

But a compassionate government will have difficulty being a limited government because needs are infinite and compassion has no clear limiting principle. "Compassionate conservatism" represents a massive concession to the liberal view that government exists to alleviate every instance of suffering—as long as the sufferers can organize themselves into a grievance group. One of Bush's main legislative achievements, the creation of

Medicare Part D, the prescription drug benefit, is a good example of the problems with his compassionate conservatism. While the cost of prescription drugs is a valid problem, Medicare Part D created an unprecedented new Medicare entitlement program without a dedicated funding source. Medicare was already trillions of dollars out of balance, and the new prescription drug benefit was paid for wholly with deficit spending—that is, with borrowed money.

Bush's other major social policy accomplishment—if accomplishment it can be called—was the No Child Left Behind (NCLB) Act, which required states to adopt achievement standards and regular testing for public schools. The idea of requiring greater accountability for the performance of public schools is reasonable in the abstract. But NCLB represents a new level of federal intrusion into what has always been and should remain a state and local responsibility, and it will provide an excuse for the education lobby to press for more federal spending for education. Bush had hoped that some school choice and charter school pilot programs might flow from the NCLB law, but so far there has been only a small amount of progress with either idea.

There were other disappointments in Bush's domestic policy. Federal domestic spending grew faster than at any time since the Johnson-Nixon years, though this was partly the fault of a Republican Congress that lost all spending discipline (a factor that contributed to Republicans losing both the House and Senate in the 2006 mid-term election). Among other budget-busters, Bush signed a huge increase in farm subsidies that was passed purely to gain favor with farm state voters in the close mid-term elections of 2002. Bush also imposed steel tariffs that benefited a handful of U.S. steel producers but harmed many more businesses (and their customers) that had relied on lower-cost imported steel. And he signed the Sarbanes-Oxley law, a massive and ill-conceived expansion of the regulations governing public corporations that Congress passed in an overreaction to the accounting frauds associated with the collapse of Enron and a handful of other companies at the end of the Internet bubble. This cost-heavy law did nothing to prevent the housing bubble and banking crisis that exploded just a few years later. (Bush's attempt to get Congress to enact an amnesty for illegal immigrants as part of a "comprehensive" immigration reform fortunately failed.)

Other aspects of Bush's economic policy were stronger. In 2003 he succeeded in persuading Congress to pass a significant tax cut, reducing income tax rates and cutting the capital gains and stock dividend tax rate to 15 percent, their lowest rate in decades. From a supply-side point of view, these cuts were more substantial even than the rate cuts under President Reagan. Under modern budget rules, however, they will automatically expire at the end of 2012 unless Congress acts, after which time income and capital gains tax rates will return to their Clinton-era levels.

Following his re-election in 2004, Bush pushed hard for most of 2005 for fundamental reform of Social Security. He traveled the nation giving numerous speeches arguing for allowing private retirement accounts in lieu of the current Social Security system, but was met with a timid response from congressional Republicans, and determined opposition from Democrats. Chances for his reform proposal were already slim when Hurricane Katrina devastated New Orleans in September 2005, and public anger at the administration's sup-

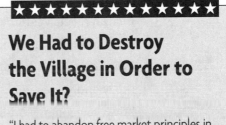

We Had to Destroy the Village in Order to Save It?

"I had to abandon free market principles in order to save the free market system."

George W. Bush, defending TARP

posedly slow response derailed his political momentum for the rest of his second term. (In fact, it was the failure of Louisiana's state and local governments that created the catastrophic conditions in New Orleans. The criticism of Bush was totally unjustified.)

In the closing weeks of Bush's second term, there occurred the financial crisis that accelerated the recession that had begun in late 2007. In great haste Bush and his treasury secretary Henry Paulson pushed Congress to pass the $700 billion Troubled Asset Relief Program (TARP) to prevent a banking crisis from bringing the economy to a grinding halt. Congress passed this unprecedented bailout without any hearings or significant floor debate. Economists will argue forever whether the government needed to backstop the banking system to prevent a catastrophic collapse of the nation's credit, but the palpable panic of the Bush administration surely made the situation worse, eroding consumer confidence and probably deepening the economic downturn.

The Bush administration's panicky reaction contrasts markedly with President Reagan's response to the stock market crash in October 1987, when the market fell a record 22 percent in one day. Amidst similar panic conditions and fears the crash would be a re-run of 1929 and the Great Depression, Reagan reacted calmly, and the Federal Reserve issued a one-sentence statement assuring the financial community that it would provide adequate liquidity for credit markets. Markets calmed down within a few days, and the economy resumed its steady growth. We shall never know whether or how the economy might have gone in the absence of the TARP bailout for the banks, but the TARP bailout set the stage for the Obama administration's nearly $1 trillion "stimulus" bill a few months later, which certainly has prolonged our economic woes.

On one part of this story Bush deserves credit. Early in his term Bush and Republicans in Congress tried to impose closer scrutiny on Fannie Mae, Freddie Mac, and the rest of the government-related housing finance system. Democrats in Congress, especially Representative Barney Frank, consistently blocked their efforts to increase oversight and enact reforms that might have prevented or lessened the severity of the housing bubble and its subsequent collapse.

Defending America, Enraging the Left

President Bush's response to Osama bin Laden's attack on the United States on September 11, 2001, will always dominate historical accounts of his presidency, but it should not be forgotten that in the months prior to September 11, Bush had already taken several wise steps to reassert the primacy of American interests in foreign policy, reversing the Clinton administration's watery and deferential multilateralism. First, Bush announced that the United States would not abide by the unratified Kyoto Protocol, which would have imposed draconian reductions in energy use on the U.S., supposedly to fight global warming. Second, Bush gave notice to Moscow that the United States would withdraw from the 1972 Anti-Ballistic Missile (ABM) Treaty, which was obsolete in the aftermath of arms reductions Reagan and the first President Bush had achieved, but was also a dangerous prohibition on missile defense in an age of rogue states such as North Korea and Iran developing nuclear weapons and missile technology. Shortly thereafter, Bush announced the first deployment of a new missile defense system in Alaska to counter the growing missile threat from North Korea. Finally, Bush ended the Clinton administration's favoritism toward Yasser Arafat and the Palestine Liberation Organization. All of these moves produced howls of outrage from Europeans and American liberals.

The Al Qaeda attack on the U.S. on September 11 finally awakened the U.S. to the need to fight the threat of Islamic terrorism that had been growing steadily for the previous thirty years. Like Harry Truman facing the development of nuclear weapons and the threat of the Soviet Union right after World War II, Bush found the United States in a new situation that required new doctrines and policies to meet the threat. Bush's first decision was his

★ ★ ★ ★ ★ ★ ★ ★ ★ ★ ★ ★ ★ ★

Not Just a Crime, an Act of War

"After the chaos and carnage of September 11th, it is not enough to serve our enemies with legal papers."

George W. Bush

most important—to treat the attack and the threat of future terrorism as warfare, rather than a police matter. The fundamental division between Bush and liberals was made evident the very next day, on September 12, 2001, when Senator majority leader Tom Daschle recoiled from Bush's use of the term "war" to describe our response. "War is such a powerful word," Daschle told President Bush. It was a preview of Bush's successor, whose administration refuses to acknowledge Islamic terrorism publicly, calling terrorist acts "man-caused disasters" instead.

Not surprisingly, liberals opportunistically attacked Bush's policies in the fight against terrorism after 9/11. Liberals predicted that an attack on Afghanistan, where Al Qaeda had planned 9/11, was doomed to fail and that Afghanistan would become "another Vietnam." Afghanistan fell to American forces in three weeks. Bush had to decide how to treat terrorists who had been captured on the field of battle but were not uniformed troops of a nation state. Correctly noting that such non-state combatants were not covered by the Geneva Convention rules of war, which nearly all nations have agreed to, Bush decided to send many of the enemy combatants to a special facility at the American base in Guantanamo, Cuba, where they would face trial by military commission, and many others suspected of terrorism to third nations which had their own legal claims against the suspects.

★ ★ ★ ★ ★ ★ ★ ★ ★ ★ ★ ★ ★

No Regrets

Asked after he left office about waterboarding, Bush said, "I'd do it again to save lives."

Most controversial was Bush's decision to allow "enhanced interrogation" (which meant "waterboarding") of terror suspects who had been trained to withstand conventional interrogation techniques. Only three captured terrorists were ever subjected to waterboarding, including Khalid Sheikh Mohammed, the tactical mastermind of the 9/11 attacks. The Bush administration also moved to monitor communications between foreign nations through an aggressive electronic surveillance program. Liberals howled about all of these decisions, preferring to have terrorists treated like ordinary criminals with full American civil rights and prosecuted through American civilian courts, and wanting to constrain the president's power to pro-actively investigate terrorist threats through electronic eavesdropping.

Also controversial was Bush's decision to invade Iraq to displace the regime of Saddam Hussein, based on what has become known as the "Bush doctrine" of preemptive action against potential threats. Hussein's desire for, and past record of, developing weapons of mass destruction were well known, but intelligence about his current stockpiles turned out to be faulty. Bush and his military planners misjudged the nature and extent of the insurgency that followed, and the American military commitment ended up being longer and costlier than hoped. One of President Bush's more courageous decisions was to approve the "surge" in 2007, after the American public had largely lost confidence in the Iraq enterprise.

> ★ ★ ★ ★ ★ ★ ★ ★ ★ ★ ★ ★ ★
>
> ## No Smoking Gun?
>
> "Facing clear evidence of peril, we cannot wait for the final proof, the smoking gun that could come in the form of a mushroom cloud."
>
> George W. Bush

Iraq was the starting point for an important corollary to the Bush doctrine: spreading democracy to the Middle East. Bush called this the "freedom agenda." It is doubtful that most Middle Eastern nations, dominated by tribal and religious factions, have the civic culture and political experience for genuine multi-party democracy. And in practice Bush had to rely on the U.S. State Department and our aid bureaucracies such as the Agency for International Development (AID)—whose representatives were, to put it mildly, not 100 percent on board with the Bush agenda—to implement this democratization. We should not be surprised if the results were chaotic.

Bush and the Constitution

Bush's constitutional performance was very strong, with a couple of important exceptions. The controversies about President Bush's handling of the terror threat opened a new chapter in the long-running controversy over the nature and limits of presidential power, especially in wartime. Bush argued that his actions were fully consistent with the constitutional understanding of the president having full executive power and responsibility for national security. (Many of the same issues about executive prerogative that had come into play in President Reagan's handling of the Iran-Contra scandal came up again in the war on terror.) In addition, Bush defended the theory of the "unitary executive," that is, the idea that, constitutionally, executive responsibility resides exclusively with the president and could not be shared with Congress or the judiciary. Bush's understanding is entirely consistent with that expressed by the Founders, especially with Alexander Hamilton's description of the president as the only organ of the national government that can conduct "arduous" enterprises.

President Bush used so-called "signing statements" to spell out how his administration would interpret and implement laws that Congress had passed and sent to the president for his signature. Signing statements have been used by presidents since James Monroe, usually to assert objections to intrusions on executive branch power, or to attempt to clear up ambiguities in the legislation being signed. But never has the use of signing statements been so controversial as under President Bush. Controversial or not, Bush's use of signing statements was an entirely justified means of exercising his responsibility to defend the Con-

★ ★ ★ ★ ★ ★ ★ ★ ★ ★ ★ ★ ★ ★

Waiting for History to Catch Up

"You can't worry about being vindicated, because the truth of the matter is, when you do big things, it's going to take a while for history to really understand."

President Bush, 2009

stitution. President Obama, who strongly criticized Bush's signing statements during the 2008 campaign, has continued the practice.

One place where Bush's strong defense of the president's constitutional responsibilities lapsed was his decision in 2003 to sign the McCain-Feingold campaign finance law, which imposed dramatic new limits on political speech in election campaigns. President Bush said that he thought the law was unconstitutional but signed it anyway, claiming the law's constitutionality was a matter for the Supreme Court to decide. This view breaks with the precedent established and upheld by most earlier presidents and with the clear intent of the Founders, who understood that it was the president's duty to veto laws he judged to be unconstitutional. Saying the constitutionality of McCain-Feingold was a matter for the Supreme Court offered support for the theory of judicial supremacy in constitutional interpretation, in contrast to the view that all three branches have the equal right to interpret the Constitution in the discharge of the functions of their branch. (The Supreme Court subsequently struck down several key features of the McCain-Feingold law because of its encroachment on the First Amendment right of free speech, but upheld other parts of the law.)

President Bush's two Supreme Court nominations, of John Roberts and Samuel Alito, were superb. Roberts was named chief justice following the death of William Rehnquist in 2005, and Samuel Alito replaced Sandra Day O'Connor a few months later. Bush had originally appointed his White House counsel, Harriett Miers, to the O'Connor seat, but opposition from conservatives—alarmed at Miers' opaque legal record and alarming statements that she (like Justice Souter) admired Oliver Wendell Holmes—caused Bush to drop her nomination and substitute Alito instead. So far Roberts and Alito have proved to be solid conservative votes on the Court.

For his vigorous defense of the president's constitutional power to defend the nation against the threat of terrorism and for his two solid Supreme

Court appointments, Bush deserves a top grade for presidential performance. But his regrettable signing of the McCain-Feingold bill after saying he thought it was unconstitutional knocks him down half a grade to a B+.

Chapter 19

BARACK HUSSEIN OBAMA, 2009–?

"Change will not come if we wait for some other person or some other time. We are the ones we've been waiting for."
—Barack Obama

President Obama's Constitutional Grade: F*

Barack Obama is exactly the kind of demagogic president the Founding Fathers feared would undermine the stability of the American republic, trading on personal charisma and employing what Alexander Hamilton called "the little arts of popularity." In addition to practicing a style of politics that would be abhorrent to the Founders, Obama is the most ideologically leftist president in American history, more radical by several orders of magnitude than either FDR or Lyndon Johnson.

Obama shrewdly exploited the nation's unhappiness in the sudden economic catastrophe of the fall of 2008 to win an election with vague and empty appeals to "hope and change," but offered few specifics on how he would govern. His drive for the presidency was less an election campaign than the creation of a cult of personality, complete with the first-ever logo for a presidential candidate. Obama deliberately encouraged preposterous conceptions of his own greatness, telling the American people in his

Did you know?

★ Obama is the first cigarette smoker in the White House since Lyndon Johnson—though he conceals this fact, like much of his record

★ The "stimulus" was a bid to permanently increase the size of government by raising the baseline for government spending

★ President Obama wanted to include Hiroshima and Nagasaki on his "apology tour," but the Japanese government said no thanks

---

* Of course the final report card on Barack Obama's presidency cannot be issued until, at the earliest, January of 2013 (or, worst case scenario, January of 2017). But the current president is in the position of a student who has a solid F on his progress report and shows absolutely no signs of bringing up his grade before the end of the semester.

nomination acceptance speech in 2008, for example, that his name, Barack, means "blessed."

In presenting himself literally as a messiah figure, he raised unrealistic and unhealthy expectations for what he could deliver in office. Obama's advanced narcissism led him to grandiosities such as his claim, upon securing the Democratic nomination, that history would record that "this was the moment when the rise of the oceans began to slow and our planet began to heal"—as though he seriously believed that he could command the waves to stop, as King Canute is said to have done ironically. While his personality and charisma sufficed to win election to office, his reliance on these very same attributes is now degrading his own presidency and the majesty of the office itself. According to the Gallup Poll, Obama has become the most politically polarizing president in the sixty-year history of presidential polling.

★ ★ ★ ★ ★ ★ ★ ★ ★ ★ ★ ★ ★ ★ ★

Has Any President Ever Encouraged Such Unrealistic Hopes?

"Many spiritually advanced people I know (not coweringly religious, mind you, but deeply spiritual) identify Obama as a Lightworker, that rare kind of attuned being who has the ability to lead us not merely to new foreign policies or health care plans … but who can actually help usher in *a new way of being on the planet*, of relating and connecting and engaging with this bizarre earthly experiment. These kinds of people actually help us *evolve*. They are philosophers and peacemakers of a very high order, and they speak not just to reason or emotion, but to the soul."

Mark Morford, online columnist, 2008

★ ★ ★ ★ ★ ★ ★ ★ ★ ★ ★ ★ ★

"I believe in our ability to perfect this nation."

Barack Obama

Obama came to the presidency with the thinnest record and least governing experience of any modern president, justifying the view that he should
be considered America's first affirmative
action president, who won the election largely
because of his race. Indeed, many independent
voters undoubtedly chose him as a means of
proving they were not racists. Liberal columnist Joan Walsh wrote that Obama makes
white voters "feel better about themselves for
liking him." Many voters—and certainly the
mainstream media that was openly supporting
Obama—averted their gaze from the evidence
of his radicalism and unfitness for office, and particularly from his association with violent revolutionaries such as William Ayers and radical
anti-Americans such as his church pastor, the Reverend Jeremiah ("God
damn America!") Wright, who openly proclaims Marxist-inspired "black
liberation theology" from the pulpit.

> ★★★★★★★★★★★★★★
> ## Great Expectations
>
> "I won't have to worry about putting gas in
> my car. I won't have to worry about paying
> my mortgage. If I help him, he's going to help
> me."
>
> Obama supporter Peggy Joseph, October 2008

Obama's "Fourth Wave" Ambitions

The Obama administration should be seen as the culmination of Woodrow Wilson's design to transform the president from his intended role as
the chief magistrate of the government to the visionary "leader" who moves
America to new and different places according to his ambitious "vision."
Obama successfully concealed his deep radicalism in the campaign, and
has continued to obscure his essentially socialist goals since taking office,
but it is clear from his two autobiographies and from tell-tale signs in his
background that he is ambitious to be the agent of the fourth great wave of
liberal reform of modern times. Wilson and the Progressives represented
the first wave of liberal reform; FDR and the New Deal were the second;

and LBJ's Great Society was the third. Each one of those waves of liberal reform led to steep increases in the size and reach of the federal government, with more spending, regulation, and higher taxes. And those previous waves of liberalism created electoral realignments in favor of Democrats. Obama hoped to achieve another realignment that would give Democrats a durable majority in Congress, and it appeared that the 2008 election, which delivered large Democratic majorities, represented a possible realignment like the 1932 election, but the 2010 midterm election showed that the American people do not support Obama's agenda.

Each past wave of liberal reform also entailed a weakening of the Constitution, and the Obama agenda is no exception. Only the checks and balances of the separation of powers between the branches—the feature of the Constitution that Woodrow Wilson hated the most because it constrained visionary presidents like himself and Obama—have contained Obama from implementing more of his radical agenda. Still, he has made considerable strides in forcing the nation to the left. Embracing the slogan of his first chief of staff, Rahm Emanuel, that we should "never let a good crisis go to waste," Obama used the banking crisis of 2008 to enact a nearly $1 trillion "stimulus" bill on the basis of the (previously discredited, but now revived) Keynesian theory that the government can heal the economy simply by spending borrowed money. The "stimulus" bill failed, prolonging the recession and saddling the nation with an unprecedented and truly threatening level of new debt. Obama had promised that the stimulus bill, by spending money for "shovel ready" projects around the country, would limit unemployment to 8 percent. But unemployment soared to more than 10 percent

A Book You're Not Supposed to Read

Radical-in-Chief: Barack Obama and the Untold Story of American Socialism by Stanley Kurtz (Threshold, 2010).

and has remained stubbornly high. Obama later admitted that there weren't many "shovel-ready" projects. Much of the money went to reward favored Democratic Party constituency groups and to expand the left's favorite government programs, such as the Energy Department's loan guarantee program for "green energy" that resulted in the Solyndra calamity and other corrupt boondoggles.

But to focus on just the economic results of the stimulus is to miss the most important aspect of the stimulus bill, which was political rather than economic. Adding $1 trillion of new spending in one shot increased the "baseline" for federal spending across the board, program by program. The stimulus was a bid to increase the size of the federal government

> ★ ★ ★ ★ ★ ★ ★ ★ ★ ★ ★ ★ ★ ★ ★
>
> ## Obama, Economic Genius?
>
> "The true engine of economic growth will always be companies like Solyndra."
>
> ---
>
> President Obama, May 26, 2010
>
> Solyndra filed for bankruptcy on September 6, 2011, after having been awarded more than half a billion dollars in loan guarantees from the federal government.

permanently. Some spending programs will shrink a bit with the formal end of the stimulus period, but overall the size of government and of most spending programs will be much higher than before Obama took office. Prior to Obama, federal spending in peacetime averaged around 20 to 22 percent of Gross Domestic Product (GDP). The stimulus bill bumped the federal government's spending level to a new plateau of around 25 percent of GDP, and Obama's health care plan will increase that level further. (During the campaign, incidentally, Obama promised that he would deliver a *net spending cut.* He was obviously lying.) By deliberately creating a huge federal deficit—the largest in peacetime by almost a factor of two as a proportion of GDP—Obama has created massive political pressure for tax increases. Permanently higher taxes are the necessary condition for a larger government, as new programs require a larger share of taxpayers' income and wealth.

Obama made clear during the 2008 campaign that redistributive egalitarianism is his core principle—both in his answer to a question from ABC News's Charlie Gibson in a primary debate, and in his famous answer to "Joe the Plumber" during the fall campaign. When Gibson pointed out that cuts in the capital gains tax rate usually *raised* revenue, and asked Obama why he would want a tax increase that might depress revenue, Obama answered, "Well, Charlie, what I've said is that I would look at raising the capital gains tax for purposes of fairness." *Fairness* is, of course, a liberal code word for redistribution and punitive taxation of the successful, regardless of its negative economic effects. Even more revealing was Obama's off-the-cuff answer on the campaign trail in October 2008, when "Joe the Plumber" Wurzelbacher challenged Obama about his plans to tax "the rich." Obama replied that "I think when you spread the wealth around, it's good for everybody." As his presidency has proceeded, it has become clear that Obama differs from previous liberals like JFK in preferring redistribution to economic growth.

The Nature of Obama's Radicalism

Obama carefully maintains what the spy trade calls "plausible deniability" of the fact that he is a socialist—for example, pointing out that he did not nationalize the banking sector as many leftists such as Paul Krugman wanted him to do. Obama and his supporters are correct in making the argument that his program is not socialism in the narrow, formal sense of government ownership of the means of production. But it is something actually worse: Obama's variety of socialism can be regarded as welfare statism on steroids, or maybe even fascism—state control of private resources—if that term weren't so widely misunderstood. Obama proudly pointed out to Wall Street bankers in 2009 that "my administration is the only thing standing between you and the pitchforks" of an angry people. (This hasn't stopped Obama's political allies from exploiting the "Occupy Wall Street" movement to whip up support for tax increases.) But Obama's essentially socialist orientation can be seen in the bailout of General Motors, which involved abrogating debt contracts under threats of coercion, closing car dealerships based on political considerations, and awarding equity in the company to the president's labor union allies that had done so much to make the company unprofitable. This is the erosion of the rule of law that is typical under the classical form of socialism.

Obama's not-so-hidden agenda can be seen in his approach to his signature issue—universal health care. Speaking to a union audience in 2003, Obama said,

> I happen to be a proponent of a single-payer universal health care program.... a single-payer health care plan, a universal health care plan. And that's what I'd like to see. But as all of you know, we may not get there immediately. Because first we have to take back the White House, we have to take back the Senate, and we have to take back the House.

"Single-payer" universal health care is a euphemism for fully socialized, government-run health care. During the 2008 campaign Obama specifically repudiated single-payer, but what has come to be known as "Obamacare" seems designed to facilitate an eventual government takeover of the entire health care sector. Just as Obama was something of a "stealth" candidate concealing his true views, Obamacare is a stealth takeover of health care, designed to fail in ways that will require *more* government power to remedy.

Obama's Contempt for the Middle Class

At bottom, like most liberal elitists, Obama holds the American middle class in contempt. He betrays this contempt in both small and large ways. One small but telling way was his response to the successful candidacy of Scott Brown to replace Ted Kennedy in the Senate in Massachusetts following Kennedy's death in 2009. Brown ran on the slogan, "I'm Scott Brown, I'm from Wrentham [a working class town], I drive a truck, and I'm asking for your vote." In an off-the-cuff comment, Obama derided Brown by saying, "Anyone can buy a truck." This dismissal of the iconic conveyance of so many working Americans no doubt comes naturally to Prius-driving elites in Cambridge and Hyde Park, but it shows Obama's remoteness from the real lives of most working Americans.

> ★★★★★★★★★★★★★★
>
> ### He Doth Bestride the Narrow World Like a Colossus
>
> "I mean in a way Obama's standing above the country, above—above the world, he's sort of God."
>
> *Newsweek* magazine "reporter" Evan Thomas, 2009

But Obama's most egregious display of his contempt for and assumed superiority over middle class America came in his remarks before a San Francisco audience caught surreptitiously on tape during the 2008 campaign, when he offered the following explanation of how working class Americans have responded to a changing economy that has cost jobs in their communities:

> You go into these small towns in Pennsylvania and, like a lot of small towns in the Midwest, the jobs have been gone now for twenty-five years and nothing's replaced them. And it's not surprising, then, they get bitter, they cling to guns or religion or antipathy to people who aren't like them or anti-immigrant sentiment or anti-trade sentiment as a way to explain their frustrations.

There is no better distillation of the alienation of liberalism from middle class American life. The embedded assumption is that Americans worship God and engage in hunting not from conviction or for genuine enjoyment, but purely out of resentment.

This contemptuous elitism comes directly from Obama's background in elite academic institutions and his subsequent career as a "community organizer" in the mold of his radical inspiration, Saul Alinsky. As political scientist and presidential scholar Marc Landy explains, "Obama is a member in good standing of the 'new class' of law and business school professors, economists, foundation executives, think tankers, congressional staffers, and media pundits who have melded with the captains of industry, finance and politics to form the patriciate of our times."

A Citizen of the World

President Obama's performance on foreign policy has been curious, ironic, and hypocritical. After fiercely criticizing most of President George W. Bush's policies and practices in the fight against terrorism, Obama has embraced nearly all of them; and in some cases he has aggressively expanded Bush policies, increasing Predator drone strikes on terrorist targets overseas. After having promised to close the Guantanamo Bay detention center for enemy combatants, Obama has reversed course and kept Gitmo open. He has also reversed course on holding civilian criminal trials for terrorist suspects, most significantly Khalid Sheikh Mohammed. And he ordered the Special Forces raid that killed Osama bin Laden inside Pakistan, without asking permission from or notifying that sovereign nation—the kind of act candidate Obama would have criticized if President Bush had been responsible for it.

Liberals who screamed from the rooftops about Bush's policies have been unsurprisingly muted in their criticism of Obama's similar policies, though a few liberal organizations such as the ACLU have protested his use of drone strikes, in particular the drone strike in Yemen that targeted and killed an American citizen, the radical Islamicist Anwar al-Awlaki. Senator Susan Collins, the moderate Republican from Maine, commented, "The administration came in determined to undo a lot of the policies of the prior administration, but in fact is finding that many of those policies were better thought-out than they realized." And Jack Goldsmith, a legal adviser for Bush's Justice Department, notes, "The new administration copied most of the Bush program, has expanded some of it, and has narrowed it only a bit. Almost all of Obama's changes have been at the level of packaging, argumentation, symbol, and rhetoric."

But still, underneath the surface, Obama gives off every indication that he has a very different conception of America's role in the world, that he wishes to diminish American influence and reduce America's capacity as a world leader. He and his leading cabinet members such as Attorney General Eric Holder and Secretary of Homeland Security Janet Napolitano refuse to refer to Islamic terrorism, or to describe our security efforts as a "war." Napolitano won't even use the term "terrorism," preferring "man-caused disasters"—as though the 9/11 attack was the functional equivalent of a natural disaster like an earthquake or a hurricane.

It is questionable whether deep down Obama's primary allegiance is to the United States, or to some version of transnational cosmopolitanism. Obama became the first presidential candidate ever to deliver a public campaign speech in a foreign nation. In his speech in Berlin in 2008, Obama declared that he was "a proud citizen of the United States and *a fellow citizen of the world*" [emphasis added]. Citizenship, of course, is an attribute of the members of sovereign nations, not of humanity as a whole. Many observers wondered whether Obama was running for President of the United States and leader of the free world, or leader of the *whole* world—a post-American world.

One of Obama's first acts after taking office was to return the bust of Winston Churchill, on loan from the British government, that George W. Bush had displayed in the Oval Office. The British had offered to let Obama keep the Churchill bust and took its return as a sign that the long-time "special relationship" between Britain and America was special no more, under

A Book You're Not Supposed to Read

The Roots of Obama's Rage by Dinesh D'Souza (Regnery, 2010).

Obama. In the first months of his presidency, Obama conducted what came to be called his "apology tour," giving speeches in the Middle East and elsewhere lamenting America's mistakes in the past. Apparently Obama even wanted to visit Hiroshima and Nagasaki in Japan to apologize for Harry Truman's decision to use the atomic bomb to end World War II. Japan's foreign minister had to issue a strong protest to our ambassador in Japan to head off this insult to Japanese and American honor alike. Obama's first eight and a half months in office culminated in his being awarded the Nobel Peace Prize (he had been nominated after serving for less than two weeks), which in recent years has only gone to America's enemies (such as Yasser Arafat) or domestic critics (such as Jimmy Carter and Al Gore). Even Obama found his Nobel Prize awkward and embarrassing.

Obama's decisions about American operations in Iraq and Afghanistan have been equivocal. After having campaigned on the charge that President Bush had ignored the "good" war in Afghanistan, Obama was hardly in a position to say "no" to our military commanders when they concluded that the Afghan campaign needed an additional 40,000 troops to have a chance of success. Obama ultimately approved 30,000 additional troops, but only after a long delay and numerous statements that conveyed that his commitment to victory was weak. Obama announced that American forces would begin withdrawal in 2011 *no matter what* the conditions on the ground were in Afghanistan.

Finally, Obama's hostility toward America's closest ally in the Middle East—Israel—is palpable. He has behaved with open rudeness toward Israel's pro-American Prime Minister Benjamin Netanyahu, and tilted toward the Palestinian position in the fruitless "peace process," clumsily setting back the already slim prospects for a serious settlement of Israeli-Palestinian claims.

Nothing more clearly displayed Obama's tentative approach to foreign and defense issues than his handling of the civil war in Libya. After giving the approval for American forces to contribute to a bombing campaign against the forces of long-time Libyan dictator Muammar Qaddafi, Obama hurriedly passed off command of the operation to Europeans, both in possible violation of the Constitution's commander-in-chief clause, and in certain violation of the War Powers Act requiring congressional notification and approval for extended military operations of this kind. Obama said the American involvement would be only in a "supporting role" and last days or weeks, but American forces ended up conducting the majority of all NATO operations in Libya, which lasted nearly six months and cost several billion dollars. Meanwhile, an Obama official described the administration's Libya policy as "leading from behind."

Obama's equivocations do not provide much confidence in what his performance would be in the event of a genuine foreign crisis, such as Iran's acquisition of a nuclear weapon, the outbreak of war between India and Pakistan, or civil war in Egypt, Turkey, or other unstable nations. American weakness always encourages the enemies of freedom to increase their mischief.

Holding the Constitution in Contempt

Obama joins Woodrow Wilson as the nation's only other president with an academic background. Obama, like Wilson, fancies himself a constitutional scholar, and though he never published a single scholarly article or book, he did teach constitutional law at the University of Chicago, one of the nation's premier law schools. Obama fully subscribes to the Progressive liberal view that the Constitution "is not a static but rather a living document, and must be read in the context of an ever-changing world." Obama did not teach, and seems to have little aptitude for or interest in, the structural aspects of the Constitution, such as the separation of powers or the nature of executive power. Instead, Obama only taught a narrow segment of constitutional law, chiefly the equal protection clause of the Fourteenth Amendment—the liberals' favorite clause and the pretext for many of the radical Supreme Court rulings of the Warren Court era. (The other constitutional law course Obama taught was "Racism and the Law.")

Obama, not surprisingly, thinks the Warren Court of the 1960s wasn't radical enough because it did not impose redistribution of wealth. Here's what Obama told a Chicago National Public Radio show in 2001: "The Supreme Court never ventured into the issues of redistribution of wealth and sort of more basic issues of political and economic justice in this society.... It didn't break free from the essential constraints that were placed by the Founding Fathers in the Constitution." Those "constraints" were the protections of property and individual liberty designed to prevent our government from becoming tyrannical and trampling individual rights. Like Wilson, Obama clearly thinks the Founders' view of the need to limit central government power is obsolete.

Nowhere is Obama's contempt for the Constitution more clear than in the centerpiece of Obamacare, the mandate that all individuals must purchase health insurance. There is no commonsense reading of the Constitution's commerce clause, which gives Congress the right to regulate interstate commerce, that can possibly be stretched into a mandate to require individuals to engage in commerce. If the Constitution can allow this, then there is nothing that Congress cannot mandate individuals to do, and the last limits on government power are essentially gone.

During the 2008 campaign Obama said, "I was a constitutional law professor, which means unlike the current president [Bush] I actually respect the Constitution." Yet Obama has continued the practice of issuing "signing statements" spelling out how the executive branch will interpret and implement new laws that Congress sends for his signature, after having bitterly criticized President Bush for this same practice. ("We're not going to use signing statements as a way of doing an end-run around Congress," candidate Obama promised in 2008.) This hypocrisy is testimony to the durability of one aspect of the Founders' constitutional design that has survived the liberal onslaught—namely, that the countervailing ambition of each branch would lead members of each branch to protect their constitutional prerogatives out of self-interest. The White House counsel's office explained that Obama did not want "to do anything that would undermine the institution of the presidency." Obama has angered some of his liberal allies with his signing statements. Even the *New York Times* noted this hypocrisy: "President Obama has issued signing statements claiming the authority to bypass dozens of provisions of bills enacted into law since he took office, provoking mounting criticism by lawmakers from both parties." Congressman Barney Frank was more direct than the *Times*: "It's outrageous. It's exactly what the Bush people did."

As senator, Obama voted against both of President Bush's nominees to the Supreme Court, John Roberts and Samuel Alito, showing that he thinks it is acceptable for senators to base their confirmation votes on ideology

★ ★ ★ ★ ★ ★ ★ ★ ★ ★ ★ ★ ★ ★

Damaging the Office?

"His political counselors do not have the slightest clue of the damage they have done to him, because they have no conception of what the office of the presidency is all about. They coach their prince to be presidential one day and populist the next, oblivious to the obvious fact that if 'presidentialism' appears as a mere pose it inevitably produces the opposite effect of what is intended."

Presidential scholar James Ceaser

rather than qualifications. So far Obama has made two appointments to the Court: Sonia Sotomayor, who made waves by saying a "wise Latina woman" would make better judgments than a white male, and Elena Kagan, former dean of Harvard Law School. Both will unquestionably be liberal votes on the Court. In his 2010 state of the union address, Obama further politicized the judiciary by singling out the Supreme Court for public criticism for a decision whose holdings Obama misstated. Judicial decorum prevents sitting Supreme Court justices from making a public response to the president (though Justice Alito, sitting in the front row right below Obama, could be seen mouthing the words, "That's not true"). It was an attack on the judiciary not seen since FDR's rhetoric during his court packing initiative of 1937.

This bullying of the justices is likely deliberate on Obama's part. Just as his reckless spending and catastrophic deficits are a bid to generate a permanent expansion of government and a higher amount of redistributive taxation, he wants to intimidate the Supreme Court into ruling that Obamacare is constitutional, and make the Court generally more favorable to other extensions of federal power that Obama would like to implement.

Because of his radical constitutional views and aggressive politicization of the judiciary, even Obama's defense of executive prerogative cannot save him from a constitutional grade of F.

Conclusion: Taking the Oath Seriously

Obama represents the nadir of the modern presidency. He is the perfect successor in many ways to Woodrow Wilson—the modern president most responsible for changing the conception and the reality of the modern president. Restoring the nation and the presidency after Obama is not simply a matter of picking a candidate with better policy views, but of reinvigorating the debate about the proper constitutional limits on the federal government. A truly constitutionally minded president will *defend* the Constitution by deliberately restoring the limits on centralized government power that the Founders intended to erect, rather than further subverting the Constitution by breaking down the few remaining limits.

Obama may have unintentionally done the nation a great favor by reviving public interest in the Constitution and its specific clauses spelling out the "few and defined" powers, as James Madison put it, of the federal government. This is what the Tea Party movement is largely about.

The election of 1912, when the parties splintered and a short-lived Progressive Party facilitated the election of Woodrow Wilson, marked the beginning of a new chapter in American political thought and practice. The election of 2012 could mark the end of this chapter and the return to an older, sounder constitutional order, if a majority of American voters take to heart the wisdom of the Founders. Might the Tea Party represent the inverse of the Progressive Party of 100 years ago? Even if the Tea Party does not become a formal political party as the Progressives did in 1912, it is clear this populist constitutional movement is having an effect on both parties—reminding us once again that the Constitution begins, "We the people ..."

SELECTED BIBLIOGRAPHY

Aitken, Jonathan. *Nixon: A Life*. Washington, DC: Regnery, 1994.

Barber, James David. *The Presidential Character: Predicting Performance in the White House*, 4th ed. Englewood, NJ: Prentice Hall, 1992.

Barnes, Fred. *Rebel-in-Chief: Inside the Bold and Controversial Presidency of George W. Bush*. New York: Crown Forum, 2006.

Berman, Larry. *Lyndon Johnson's War: The Road to Stalemate in Vietnam*. New York: Norton, 1989.

Bernstein, Irving. *Guns or Butter: The Presidency of Lyndon Johnson*. New York: Oxford University Press, 1996.

Blum, John Morton. *Woodrow Wilson and the Politics of Morality*. Boston: Little, Brown, 1956.

Burns, James MacGregor. *Roosevelt: The Lion and the Fox*. New York: Harcourt Brace, 1956.

Coolidge, Calvin. *The Autobiography of Calvin Coolidge*. Honolulu: University Press of the Pacific, 2004 (originally published 1929).

————. *Have Faith in Massachusetts*. Boston: Houghton Mifflin, 1919.

Dallek, Robert. *Flawed Giant: Lyndon Johnson and His Times, 1961–1973*. New York: Oxford University Press, 1998.

Dean, John W. *Warren G. Harding*. New York: Times Books, 2004.

D'Souza, Dinesh. *The Roots of Obama's Rage*. Washington, DC: Regnery, 2010.

Eastland, Terry. *Energy in the Executive: The Case for the Strong Presidency*. New York: Free Press, 1992.

Eden, Robert. *The New Deal and Its Legacy: Critique and Reappraisal*. New York: Greenwood Press, 1989.

Felzenberg, Alvin. *The Leaders We Deserved (and a Few We Didn't): Rethinking the Presidential Ratings Game*. New York: Basic Books, 2008.

Ferrell, Robert H. *The Presidency of Calvin Coolidge*. Lawrence, KS: University Press of Kansas, 1998.

Fisher, Louis. *Presidential War Power*. Lawrence: University Press of Kansas, 1995.

Folsom, Burton W., Jr. *New Deal or Raw Deal?* New York: Threshold, 2008.

Galbraith, John Kenneth. *The Great Crash: 1929*. Boston: Houghton Mifflin, 1954.

Goldberg, Jonah. *Liberal Fascism: The Secret History of the American Left, from Mussolini to the Politics of Meaning*. New York: Doubleday, 2007.

Greenstein, Fred I. *The Hidden-Hand Presidency: Eisenhower as Leader*. New York: Basic Books, 1982.

————. *The Presidential Difference: Leadership Style from FDR to Clinton*. New York: Free Press, 2000.

Hamby, Alonzo. *Man of the People: A Life of Harry S Truman*. New York: Oxford, 1995.

Hayward, Steven F. *The Age of Reagan: The Conservative Counter-Revolution, 1980–1989.* New York: CrownForum, 2009.

———. *The Real Jimmy Carter: How America's Worst Ex-President Undermines American Foreign Policy, Coddles Dictators, and Created the Party of Clinton and Kerry.* Washington, DC: Regnery, 2004.

Healy, Gene. *The Cult of the Presidency: America's Dangerous Devotion to Executive Power.* Washington, DC: Cato Institute, 2008.

Hoover, Herbert. *The Memoirs of Herbert Hoover: The Cabinet and the Presidency, 1920–1933.* New York: Macmillan, 1952.

Johnson, Paul. *A History of the American People.* New York: HarperCollins, 1997.

———. *Modern Times: The World from the Twenties to the Eighties.* New York: Harper & Row, 1983.

Kurtz, Stanley. *Radical in Chief: Barack Obama and the Untold Story of American Socialism.* New York: Threshold, 2010.

Landy, Marc, and Sidney M. Milkis. *Presidential Greatness.* Lawrence, KS: University Press of Kansas, 2000.

Lowry, Rich. *Legacy: Paying the Price for the Clinton Years.* Washington, DC: Regnery, 2003.

Matusow, Allen J. *Nixon's Economy: Booms, Busts, Dollars & Votes.* Lawrence: University Press of Kansas, 1998.

McCullough, David. *Truman.* New York: Simon & Schuster, 1992.

McDonald, Forrest. *The American Presidency: An Intellectual History.* Lawrence, KS: University Press of Kansas, 1994.

———. *A Constitutional History of the United States.* New York: Franklin Watts, 1982.

Milkis, Sidney M., and Michael Nelson. *The American Presidency: Origins and Development, 1776–2007.* Washington, DC: CQ Press, 2008.

Miller, Nathan. *Star-Spangled Men: America's Ten Worst Presidents.* New York: Simon & Schuster, 1998.

Moley, Raymond. *After Seven Years*. New York: Harper & Brothers, 1939.

Naftali, Timothy. *George H. W. Bush*. New York: Times Books, 2007.

Nash, George H. *The Life of Herbert Hoover: The Engineer, 1874–1914*. New York: Norton, 1983.

————. *The Life of Herbert Hoover: The Humanitarian, 1914–1917*. New York: Norton, 1988.

————. *The Life of Herbert Hoover: Master of Emergencies, 1917–1918*. New York: Norton, 1996.

Nathan, Richard P. *The Plot That Failed: Nixon and the Administrative Presidency*. New York: John Wiley & Sons, 1975.

Neustadt, Richard E. *Presidential Power and the Modern Presidents: The Politics of Leadership from Roosevelt to Reagan*. New York: Free Press, 1990.

Olson, Barbara. *The Final Days: The Last, Desperate Abuses of Power by the Clinton White House*. Washington, DC: Regnery, 2001.

Pestritto, Ronald J. *Woodrow Wilson and the Roots of Modern Liberalism*. Lanham, MD: Rowman & Littlefield, 2005.

Piereson, James. *Camelot and the Cultural Revolution: How the Assassination of John F. Kennedy Shattered American Liberalism*. New York: Encounter, 2007.

Powell, Jim. *FDR's Folly: How Roosevelt and His New Deal Prolonged the Great Depression*. New York: CrownForum, 2003.

Reeves, Richard. *President Kennedy: Profile of Power*. New York: Simon & Schuster, 1993.

Reeves, Thomas C. *A Question of Character: A Life of John F. Kennedy*. New York: Free Press, 1991.

Ross, Tara. *Enlightened Democracy: The Case for the Electoral College*. Dallas: Colonial Press, 2004.

Russell, Francis. *The Shadow of Blooming Grove: Warren G. Harding and His Times*. New York: McGraw-Hill, 1968.

Schlesinger, Arthur M., Jr. *The Imperial Presidency*. Boston: Houghton Mifflin, 1973.

Shlaes, Amity. *The Forgotten Man: A New History of the Great Depression*. New York: Harper, 2007.

Silver, Thomas B. *Coolidge and the Historians*. Durham, NC: Carolina Academic Press, 1984.

Skowronek, Stephen. *The Politics Presidents Make: Leadership from John Adams to George Bush*. Cambridge: Harvard, 1993.

Sobel, Robert. *Coolidge: An American Enigma*. Washington, DC: Regnery, 1998.

Spalding, Elizabeth Edwards. *The First Cold Warrior: Harry Truman, Containment, and the Remaking of Liberal Internationalism*. Lexington, KY: University of Kentucky Press, 2006.

Stein, Herbert. *Presidential Economics: The Making of Economic Policy from Roosevelt to Reagan and Beyond*. New York: Simon & Schuster, 1984.

Stewart, James B. *Blood Sport: The President and His Adversaries*. New York: Simon & Schuster, 1996.

Taranto, James, and Leonard Leo. *Presidential Leadership: Rating the Best and Worst in the White House*. New York; Free Press, 2004.

Tatalovich, Raymond, and Thomas S. Engeman. *The Presidency and Political Science: Two Hundred Years of Constitutional Debate*. Baltimore: Johns Hopkins, 2003.

Thach, Charles C., Jr. *The Creation of the Presidency, 1775–1789: A Study in Constitutional History*. Baltimore: Johns Hopkins University Press, 1923.

Tulis, Jeffrey K. *The Rhetorical Presidency*. Princeton University Press, 1987.

Wills, Garry. *Nixon Agonistes: The Crisis of the Self-Made Man*. Boston: Houghton Mifflin, 1969.

INDEX